17551

KU-185-864

RISK AND UNCERTAINTY IN ACCOUNTING AND FINANCE

To Christine

Risk and Uncertainty in Accounting and Finance

A book of readings

Edited by
JOHN P. DICKINSON,
University of Lancaster

SAXON **H** HOUSE | LEXINGTON BOOKS

© John P. Dickinson, 1974

All rights reserved. No part of this publication may be reproduced, stored in a retrieval system, or transmitted in any form or by any means, electronic, mechanical, photocopying, recording, or otherwise without the prior permission of D. C. Heath Ltd.

970,161

Published by

SAXON HOUSE, D. C. Heath Ltd.
Westmead, Farnborough, Hants., England.

BIRMINGHAM UNIVERSITY LIBRARY

Jointly with

LEXINGTON BOOKS, D. C. Heath & Co.
Lexington, Mass., U.S.A.

ISBN 0 347 01042 3

Library of Congress Catalog Card Number 74-3917

Printed in Great Britain
by Unwin Brothers Limited
The Gresham Press, Old Woking, Surrey
A member of the Staples Printing Group

Contents

List of figures

List of tables

Acknowledgements

I wish to express my most sincere thanks to the publishers and authors represented in this volume for their permission to reprint the various articles.

J.P.D.

Introduction

In the course of the last two or three decades a more analytical approach has been developed towards management and business decision-making. Largely this has been occasioned by the increasing size and complexity of modern business organisations, necessitating both more systematic and more objective decision-making procedures. Alongside these developments the power of modern analogue and digital computers is such that previously intractable simulations and numerical analyses can now be performed with speed and efficiency. (Of course this is not to say that all problems are now solvable — rather it means that one has at one's disposal more effective tools to attack larger problems!) It is, however, abundantly clear that the lack of familiarity with quantitative techniques and models now in evidence is likely to leave either practitioner or academic seriously disadvantaged.

The most casual glance through a random selection of recent accounting and financial literature cannot fail to reveal that particularly in this field the use of quantitative methods has increased significantly in recent years. Even though their involvement has, perhaps, been less rapid here than in other business areas, it is true to say that a collection of readings prepared under such a broad brief would run to several volumes if full justice were to be done. In the present book the aim is less ambitious, but, focusing on risk and uncertainly, the intention is to highlight the fact that the financial world — more, possibly, than many other areas — is dependent on an uncertain future. Indeed, it is perhaps one of the most difficult tasks to model in a mathematical manner, since one can rarely isolate one variable for study under the laboratory conditions enjoyed by the physical scientist, and — since one is operating in a constantly changing economic environment affected by a multitude of factors the world over — one must inevitably accept the variation of several variables. Even if one succeeds in building a valid model the exercise can be self-defeating, as in the case of shareprice behaviour. A predictive model that correctly forecasted prices would lead to a change in the market, since the behaviour of participants in the market would be affected by their ability to predict. Such a model slips out of focus on construction, and the process of refocusing is a continuous one. To continue the analogy with the physical sciences one could perhaps liken this phenomenon to the uncertainty principle of Heisenberg! Indeed as the physicist, in considering atomic phenomena, must resort to probabilistic models, so the financial modeller must look towards models involving uncertainty rather than those that are deterministic. It is with this type of model — involving for example concepts of stochastic processes as in Shank's article — that we shall largely be concerned in this book, and not with the more traditional statistical tools of data analysis. Needless to say, this approach does not always result in a practical model, since the incorporation of uncertainty at several points in the model can produce an end-product that is virtually worthless in terms of predictive power. The property of compounding of errors is not an unfamiliar one, and can be simply illustrated by considering the evaluation of the Net Present Valve (NPV) of a future stream of cash flows in capital budgeting. Here one has to estimate not only future yearly flows, but also an appropriate discount factor each year, with a final figure for NPV that is subject to a typically high degree of uncertainty.

The objective in providing the present collection, the readership to which it is directed, and the policy used in making the final selection of papers are closely interrelated. In the first place it should be clear — if not before reading the book, then hopefully afterwards — that there exists a very forceful argument for closer liaison between the statistical and the accounting and financial professions. There is little doubt that the majority of statisticians are unfamiliar with the concepts and problems involved in financial work, and that a high proportion of their counterparts in accounting and finance are unaware of the powerful techniques in the statistician's toolkit. It is hoped that this book will be of interest and benefit to both professions, and that it will assist in stimulating a greater cross-fertilisation of ideas between them. Accordingly, the book is directed towards the professional man, to the researcher, and to the academic, in both disciplines.

In compiling the collection a detailed search has been made through many statistical, accounting, and financial journals and periodicals over a number of years. The underlying policy in making the selection is divisible into two parts. Firstly, examples have been provided of recent work in already well-established areas of study, such as capital budgeting. In these instances fairly extensive additional lists of references have been provided to enable the reader to place the work firmly in perspective, and to pursue ancillary lines of work if he so wishes. Secondly, the book includes examples of more recent work which are considered to be in areas of great potential importance and development. The subject of probabilistic depreciation is perhaps the most obvious of these.

Inevitably any book of readings must suffer to some extent from subjectivity. However careful the editor, his own prejudices and biases are likely to conflict with those of some of his readers. No apology is offered for this, but a simple request is made for an understanding of the dilemma facing an editor making a personal choice from literally hundreds of articles! One omission however — that of a section devoted to portfolio analysis and share-price behaviour — does require some explanation. To treat this subject in anything approaching a comprehensive way requires a separate collection of articles. Such a collection is now in preparation in this series.

Depreciation

Current practice in accounting for depreciation is to choose one from a number of deterministic methods exemplified by straight-line and sum-of-the-years digits. However, from a severely practical viewpoint this approach is suspect, since on acquisition neither the lifetime of an asset, nor its ultimate salvage value, is known with certainty.

The authors of the first paper in this section have earlier proposed a probabilistic method of depreciation based on an assumed probability distribution for the life of an asset. Such a distribution can be derived most satisfactorily by considering historical data on the behaviour of similar assets in the past. The purpose of their present paper, however, is to extend the previous simple model to take into account the fact that as the asset ages, the probability distribution of its lifetime alters. Bayesian analysis is used to update these distributions in the light of the asset's having already survived a known number of years.

The second paper in this section takes this model one stage further by abandoning the unrealistic assumption that on acquisition the eventual salvage value has a uniquely determined value. Instead, a probability distribution is assigned to the salvage values as well as to the service life.

Although probabilistic depreciation is not known to have been used in practice, the method does have considerable advantages. In particular it avoids the tendency of conventional deterministic methods to underdepreciate in the first few years' life — a tendency which is even more apparent in the case of group depreciation. Undoubtedly there is scope for further work in the derivation of the most appropriate probability distributions. On exactly this point some recent work[1] has shown that asset lives may often be well described by a Weibull distribution, and the incorporation of this modification into the model described here might well produce some interesting results.

[1] Henderson, J. A., and Cowles, H. A., 'The Weibull distribution and the life of physical plant' *The Engineering Economist* vol. 15, 1970, pp. 159–73.

Sequential Models in Probabilistic Depreciation[1]

Introduction

Conventional depreciation methods treat the service life of an asset as a given constant.[2] When there is some uncertainty as to the actual service life, an average (expected) value is used. The depreciation rates are then calculated based on this given service life. Contrary to this deterministic approach, we proposed in an earlier paper [2] a probabilistic approach to depreciation where the service life is treated as a random variable which has a given probability distribution. In probabilistic depreciation, the depreciation rates are calculated for each possible service life of the asset and then the weighted average is computed using the service life probabilities as weights. Thus, if the asset's life is equally likely to be one, two, or three years, the depreciation rate for the first year under the probabilistic straight-line method is the average of 100 per cent, 50 per cent, and $33\frac{1}{3}$ per cent or $61\frac{1}{9}$ per cent. This is in contrast to the conventional straight-line method which first computes an average service life, two years in this case, and then calculates the depreciation rate as 50 per cent for the first and second year.

We demonstrated that for single asset depreciation, conventional depreciation methods result in underdepreciation in the earlier years of an asset's service life.[3] In the case of group depreciation, conventional methods will typically result in underdepreciation throughout the service life of the items in the group. The analysis computed the depreciation rate for each year based only on a single estimate of the probability distribution of the service life, namely, the one known when the asset was first put into service. As the asset's service life expires, we obtain more information about the actual probability distribution governing the particular asset under study. It becomes reasonable, then, to modify the probability distribution to include this increased knowledge.

In the numerical example above, if the asset survives the first year, we know that the one-year service life situation did not occur. Therefore, we need only consider the case of two and three years of the service life. The conditional probability distribution of the service life, given that the asset

3

has survived the first year, is 0·5 for the two year life and 0·5 for the three year life. Hence, the first year depreciation rate for the asset after it has survived the first year in service is $(\frac{1}{2})(\frac{1}{2}+\frac{1}{3}) = 5/12 = 0·42$ under the straight-line method.

In this paper, we analyse the effect on the depreciation patterns for a single asset and for assets depreciated as a group when such a 'sequential probabilistic depreciation' approach is used as compared with the 'static probabilistic' approach.[4] These results are then extended, using Bayesian analysis for estimating the service life distribution when the parameters of this distribution are not precisely known.

Sequential probabilistic depreciation: single asset case

Before proceeding, we shall define our criteria in selecting depreciation methods. In this paper, we want to set aside the issue of whether depreciation rates should be based on the consumption of service potentials, or on the decline of the market values, or on any other factors. We assume that these economic considerations have been included in the depreciation vector $h_j = (j_{1j}, h_{2j}, \dots, h_{jj})$ where h_{ij} is the proportion of the depreciable cost (acquisition cost less estimated salvage value) to be depreciated in the ith year if the service life of the asset is j years. We shall assume that $h_{ij} \geqslant 0$ for all $i = 1, 2, \dots, j$ and $j = 1, 2, \dots$, and that $\Sigma_{i=1}^{j} h_{ij} = 1$, so that the asset is fully depreciated by the end of its service life. For the straight-line method, $h_{ij} = 1/j$; for the sum-of-years'-digits method, $h_{ij} = 2(j - i + 1)/[j\ (j + 1)]$; and for the double-declining-balance method, $h_{ij} = (1 - 2/j)^{i-1} (2/j)$.

With these assumptions, we consider the situation in which the service life j is not given with certainty but is a random variable with a given probability distribution. The criterion used in selecting a depreciation vector is that the depreciation rate under the selected depreciation vector be, year for year, equal to the expected value of the depreciation rate under the given probability distribution. We refer to this property as the *unbiasedness* of the depreciation rates. The method for deriving unbiased probabilistic depreciation vectors when the asset is first placed in service was discussed in our earlier paper.[5] This same criterion of unbiasedness will be used in this paper. However, additional information will be used as it becomes available to minimise the discrepancies between the *ex ante* depreciation rates based on the prior service life distribution and the *ex post* depreciation rates based on the actual experience with the asset.

Consider an asset with a service life distribution given by $(p_1, p_2, \dots,)$

where p_j is the probability that the asset is retired at the end of the jth year in service. We assume that retirement occurs only at the end of a year.

In order to compute the unbiased estimate of the depreciation rate for the ith year, we must consider three cases. First, if the asset is retired in the $i-1$st year or earlier, we have $d_i^- = 0$ where d_i^- is the depreciation rate for the ith year when the asset has been retired in an earlier year. If the asset is retired in the ith year, then $d_i^{\,0} = h_{ii}$ where $d_i^{\,0}$ is the depreciation rate for the ith year when the asset has been retired at the end of the ith year. Note that in both of these cases the service life is known with certainty so that there is no averaging required to compute the proper depreciation rate.

The third case occurs if the asset survives through the ith year so that the service life is known to be greater than i. In this situation the probability that the service life is $j(> i)$ years is, by the definition of conditional probability,

$$p_j \Big/ \sum_{k=i+1}^{\infty} p_k = p_j / S_i \qquad j = 1+1,\, 1+2, \dots ,$$

where $S_i \equiv \sum_{k=i+1}^{\infty} p_k$ is the *a priori* probability that the asset is not retired in the first i years.

If, in fact, the asset is retired in the jth year, the depreciation rate in the ith year should be h_{ij}. Since we do not, at this stage, know what the actual service life will be, we compute the expected depreciation rate by averaging over all possible service lives. Thus,

$$d_i^+ = \sum_{j=i+1}^{\infty} h_{ij}\,(p_j/S_i) = (1/S_i) \sum_{j=i+1}^{\infty} h_{ij} p_j$$

where d_i^+ is the depreciation rate for the ith year when the asset has survived through the ith year.

The actual depreciation rate for the ith year is a random variable since we do not know at the time the asset is first put into service whether it will be retired before, at the end of, or after the ith year. The expected value of the actual ith year depreciation rate is given by

$$\sum_{j=1}^{i-1} p_j d_i^- + p_i d_i^{\,0} + \sum_{j=i+1}^{\infty} p_j d_i^+ = p_i h_{ii} + \sum_{j=i+1}^{\infty} p_j h_{ij} = \sum_{j=i}^{\infty} p_j h_{ij} .$$

This is equal to the static probabilistic depreciation rate for the ith year as derived in our earlier paper. Note that the sum of these expected depreciation rates for $i = 1, 2, \dots,$ is unity since

5

$$\sum_{i=1}^{\infty} \sum_{j=i}^{\infty} p_j h_{ij} = \sum_{j=1}^{\infty} \sum_{i=1}^{\infty} p_j h_{ij} = \sum_{j=1}^{\infty} p_j \sum_{i=1}^{j} h_{ij} = 1.$$

Suppose that the depreciation rate for the ith year when the asset has survived the ith year was chosen to be d_i^* ($\neq d_i^+$). Then the mean squared deviation between the actual depreciation rate and the proper depreciation rate is given by

$$(1/S_i) \sum_{j=i+1}^{\infty} p_j (h_{ij} - d_i^*)^2 .$$

Then,

$$(1/S_i) \sum_{j=i+1}^{\infty} p_j [h_{ij} - d_i^*]^2 = (1/S_i) \sum_{j=i+1}^{\infty} p_j [(h_{ij} - d_i^+) + (d_i^+ - d_i^*)]^2$$

$$= (1/S_i) \left\{ \sum_{j=i+1}^{\infty} p_j (h_{ij} - d_i^+)^2 + (d_i^+ - d_i^*)^2 \sum_{j=i+1}^{\infty} p_j \right.$$

$$\left. + 2(d_i^+ - d_i^-) \sum_{j=i+1}^{\infty} p_j (h_{ij} - d_i^+) \right\}$$

$$= (1/S_i) \left\{ \sum_{j=i+1}^{\infty} p_j (h_{ij} - d_i^+)^2 + (d_i^+ - d_i^*)^2 S_i \right\}$$

since $\sum_{j=i+1}^{\infty} p_j (h_{ij} - d_i^+) = 0$ by the choice of d_i^+.

Thus, the mean squared deviation between the actual depreciation rate and the proper depreciation rate is minimised when we choose $d_i^* = d_i^+$.

So far we have concentrated on computing the actual depreciation rate for the ith year ($i = 1, 2, \ldots$,) to give as accurate a figure as possible for use in the income statement. We now consider what the accumulated depreciation rate should be at the end of the ith year after charging depreciation at the ith year rate.

Let a_i be the proportion of the depreciable cost that has already been depreciated by the end of the ith year. Clearly, if the asset has been retired by the end of the ith year, a_i should equal one. If the asset is still in service at the end of the ith year, a_i should equal one minus the sum of the expected depreciation rates in each of the remaining years. This is necessary for a_i to be an unbiased estimate of the proper accumulated depreciation rate when the asset is still in service at the end of the ith year.

The expected value of the depreciation rate in the kth year given that the asset is in service at the end of the ith year is

$$(1/S_i) \left(\sum_{j=i+1}^{k-1} p_j \cdot 0 + p_k h_{kk} + \sum_{j=k+1}^{\infty} p_j d_k^+ \right) = (1/S_i) \sum_{j=k}^{\infty} p_j h_{kj} .$$

Therefore, the sum of the expected depreciation rates in all years after the ith year is

$$(1/S_i) \sum_{k=i+1}^{\infty} \sum_{j=k}^{\infty} p_j h_{kj} = (1/S_i) \sum_{j=i+1}^{\infty} p_j \sum_{k=i+1}^{\infty} h_{kj} .$$

Thus,

$$a_i^+ = 1 - (1/S_i) \sum_{j=i+1}^{\infty} p_j \sum_{k=i+1}^{j} h_{kj} = (1/S_i) \sum_{j=i+1}^{\infty} p_j \sum_{k=1}^{i} h_{kj}$$

since

$$\sum_{k=1}^{j} h_{kj} = \sum_{k=1}^{i} h_{kj} + \sum_{k=i+1}^{j} h_{kj} = 1 .$$

Note that a_i^+ equals the sum of the expected depreciation rates that should have been taken in years 1 to i if it had been known that the asset would still be in service at the end of the ith year.

Knowing a_i^+, we can compute the expected accumulated depreciation rate after i years to be

$$\sum_{j=1}^{i} p_j \cdot 1 + \left(\sum_{j=i+1}^{\infty} p_j \right) a_i^+ = \sum_{j=1}^{i} p_j + S_i (1/S_i) \sum_{j=i+1}^{\infty} p_j \sum_{k=1}^{i} h_{kj}$$

$$= \sum_{j=1}^{i} p_j \sum_{k=1}^{j} h_{kj} + \sum_{j=i+1}^{\infty} p_j \sum_{k=1}^{i} h_{kj}$$

$$= \sum_{k=1}^{i} \sum_{j=k}^{i} p_j h_{kj} + \sum_{k=1}^{i} \sum_{j=i+1}^{\infty} p_j h_{kj}$$

$$= \sum_{k=1}^{i} \sum_{j=k}^{\infty} p_j h_{kj}$$

which is exactly equal to the accumulated depreciation rate under the static probabilistic method as derived in our earlier paper. However, since this quantity, which is less than unity, is a convex combination of 1 and a_i^+, we know that the accumulated depreciation for nonretired assets is always less using sequential probabilistic depreciation (a_i^+) than when using static probabilistic depreciation.

In general, the accumulated depreciation rate will not be the sum of the depreciation rates in each year. This is because the two rates are derived separately. If the asset is still in service at the end of year $i - 1$, its accumulated depreciation rate is given by a_{i-1}^+. If it survives the ith year, the depreciation rate is given by d_i^+. The difference, $a_i^+ - (a_{i-1}^+ + d_i^+)$, may be considered as an entry to an account for adjusting prior income, and is attributable to the uncertainty in the service life of the asset. Similarly, if the asset is retired in the ith year[6], the depreciation rate is $d_i{}^\circ$ and the adjustment is given by $1 - (a_{i-1}^+ + d_i{}^\circ)$.

7

An interesting feature of this method is that a_i^+ does not necessarily increase as i increases. For example, if $p_2 = p_{10} = 0{\cdot}5$ (all other $p_i = 0$), and if straight-line depreciation is used, the accumulated depreciation rate after one year, a_i^+, is $\cdot5(\frac{1}{2}) + \cdot5(\frac{1}{10}) = \frac{3}{10}$. If the asset is still in service at the end of the second year, its accumulated depreciation rate a_2^+ should be $1(\frac{2}{10})$, or $\frac{1}{10}$ less than a_1^+. Since the asset is still in service at the end of the second year, its service life is now known to be ten years with certainty; therefore the first year's depreciation rate should have been $\frac{1}{10}$. This plus the depreciation rate in the second year of $\frac{1}{10}$ equals a_2^+. The difference between $a_1^+ = \frac{3}{10}$ and what it should have been, $\frac{1}{10}$, is attributable to the uncertainty in the service life. A proper accounting treatment would be to debit depreciation by $\frac{1}{10}$ for the second year, debit $\frac{1}{10}$ to the accumulated depreciation rate, and credit $\frac{2}{10}$ to an account for adjusting prior income.

In general, the expected value of the adjustment required in the ith year is

$$[a_i^+ - (a_{i-1}^+ + d_i^+)]\, S_i + [1 - (a_{i-1}^+ + d_i^{\,0})]\, p_i$$

$$= \sum_{j=i+1}^{\infty} p_j \sum_{k=1}^{i} h_{kj} - \sum_{j=1}^{\infty} h_{ij}p_j + p_i - \sum_{j=i}^{\infty} p_j \sum_{k=1}^{i-1} h_{kj}$$

$$= \sum_{j=i+1}^{\infty} p_j \sum_{k=1}^{i} h_{kj} - \sum_{j=1}^{\infty} p_j \sum_{k=i}^{i} h_{kj} + p_i$$

$$= 0\,,$$

so that the adjustment is due solely to the inherent fluctuations caused by the variability in the service life of the asset.

Sequential group depreciation

The sequential probabilistic depreciation method developed in the preceding section can be easily applied to group depreciation in which assets of a similar nature are grouped together and depreciated in a single account. At the end of any year, the original group of assets can be partitioned into three groups: those that were retired in year $i - 1$ or earlier, those that have just been retired in year i, and those that are still in service. The items in the first group have already been fully depreciated and no further charges are required. Those items which have just been retired are charged at a rate equal to $d_i^{\,0} = h_{ii}$ while those items still in service are charged at a rate equal to

$$d_i^+ = (1/S_i) \sum_{j=i+1}^{\infty} h_{ij}p_j \; .$$

Let N be the number of items originally placed in service at the start of the first year. Let n_i be the number of items that have been retired at the end of the ith year and let m_i be the number of items that were retired just at the end of the ith year. Thus,

$$n_i = n_{i-1} + m_i \; .$$

The ith year depreciation rate, based on the total depreciable cost for the N items, is given by

$$\frac{n_{i-1}}{N} d_i^- + \frac{m_i}{N} d_i^{\,0} + \frac{(N - n_i)}{N} d_i^+ = \frac{m_i}{N} h_{ii} + \frac{(N - n_i)}{NS_i} \sum_{j=i+1}^{\infty} h_{ij}p_j \; ,$$

where d_i^-, $d_i^{\,0}$, and d_i^+ are as defined in the preceding section. In order to compute the expected depreciation rate in the ith year, we need to compute only $E(m_i/N)$ and $E[(N - n_i)/N]$ since $d_i^{\,0}$ and d_i^+ are fixed positive numbers and $d_i^- = 0$. The probability mass functions for the random variables m_i and $N - n_i$ are given by a binomial distribution with parameters $n = N$ (for both variables) and $p = p_i$ and S_i respectively. Since the expected value of a binomial distribution with parameters n and p is np, we have

$$E\,(m_i/N) = p_i \; ,$$

and

$$E\,(N - n_i)/N = S_i \; .$$

Therefore the expected ith year sequential group depreciation charge is given by

$$[p_i h_{ii}] + S_i\,(1/S_i) \sum_{j=i+1}^{\infty} h_{ij}p_j = \sum_{j=i}^{\infty} h_{ij}p_j \; ,$$

the static group probabilistic rate computed in our previous paper.

A similar analysis shows that the accumulated depreciation rate after i years is

$$\frac{n_i}{N} \cdot 1 + \frac{(N - n_i)}{N} a_i^+ = \frac{n_i}{N} + \frac{(N - n_i)}{NS_i} \sum_{j=i+1}^{\infty} p_j \sum_{k=1}^{i} h_{kj} \; .$$

Using this result, the expected accumulated depreciation rate after i years is

9

$$(1 - S_i) + S_i\,(1/S_i)\sum_{j=i+1}^{\infty} p_j \sum_{k=1}^{i} h_{kj} \;=\; \sum_{j=1}^{i} p_j + \sum_{j=i+1}^{\infty} p_j \sum_{k=1}^{i} h_{kj}$$

$$= \sum_{k=1}^{i} \sum_{j=k}^{\infty} p_j h_{kj}$$

which is the accumulated depreciation rate after i years under the static probabilistic method.

Note that for straight-line depreciation ($h_{kj} = 1/j$), the conventional (deterministic) method computes the average lifetime L ($L = \Sigma_j j p_j$) and applies the rate $1/L$ to those assets still in service at the start of the year. If the actual pattern of asset retirement follows the expected pattern (i.e. a fraction p_j of the original group is retired during year j), then the deterministic depreciation rate in year k is given by $\Sigma_{j=k}^{\infty}\,p_j/L$ and the accumulated depreciation rate after i years is given by $\Sigma_{k=1}^{i}\,\Sigma_{j=k}^{\infty}\,p_j/L$. Therefore, the difference, D_i, between the expected probabilistic accumulated depreciation rate after i years and the deterministic rate, is given by

$$D_i = \sum_{k=1}^{i} \sum_{j=k}^{\infty} p_j \left(\frac{1}{j} - \frac{1}{L}\right).$$

This may be rewritten as

$$D_i = \sum_{j=i+1}^{\infty} p_j\,(j - i) \left(\frac{1}{L} - \frac{1}{j}\right)$$

or

$$\frac{D_i}{S_i} = \sum_{j=i+1}^{\infty} (p_j/S_i)\,(j - i) \left(\frac{1}{L} - \frac{1}{j}\right).$$

Now $D_i \geq 0$ if $(j - i)[(1/L) - (1/j)]$ is a convex function of j (by Jensen's Inequality; see Lemma 1 of our previous paper). But $(j - i)[(1/L) - (1/j)]$ is easily seen to be a convex function of j since it consists of some constants ($- i/L - 1$), a linear term (j/L) and a term (i/j) convex in j. Therefore, sequential probabilistic depreciation will, in general, result in accumulated group depreciation that is greater than or equal to the deterministic method throughout the lifetime of the assets. (The proof of Theorem 4 in our previous paper is to be superseded by this proof which obtains the desired result directly.)

As in the single asset case, an adjustment is generally needed each year to keep the accounts balanced. The amount of this adjustment is

10

$$(1 - h_{ii}) \frac{[m_i - p_i (N - n_{i-1})]}{NS_{i-1}} + \sum_{j=i+1}^{\infty} p_j \sum_{k=1}^{i-1} h_{kj} \left[\frac{N - n_i}{NS_i} - \frac{N - n_{i-1}}{NS_{i-1}} \right]$$

and one can readily check that the expected value of this adjustment is zero.

Bayesian analysis

For the calculations described in the previous sections, we have implicitly assumed that the service life distribution, $\{ p_j : j = 1, 2, \dots , \}$, was precisely known. In our previous paper we discussed the use of parametric distributions such as the normal, rectangular, Poisson, and geometric to provide convenient representations for the service life distributions. The use of these distributions implies that the probabilities of asset retirement follow the pattern indicated by the distribution so that only one or two parameters need to be specified in order to completely characterise the distribution.

In practice, we may be willing to accept the assumption that a particular distribution is appropriate and yet still be unsure about the parameters that characterise the distribution. In this case, Bayesian analysis might prove useful (see [3]).

Assume we have a group of N identical assets each having an independent and identically distributed service life distribution given by $\{ p_j ; j = 1, 2, \dots , \}$. Then the probability that exactly n_1 are retired in the first year (assuming $p_1 > 0$) is given by

$$\binom{N}{n_1} p_1^{n_1} (1 - p_1)^{N - n_1} .$$

Assume also that p_1 is not known for certain. Our objective is to use our prior information on p_1 with the actual retirement number, say n_1, in the first year to get a new estimate on p_1 and indirectly on $p_2, p_3, \dots$. We could then use the same procedure to update our estimate of the parameter(s) of the distribution under study at the end of subsequent years by noting the actual retirement patterns.

Let $f_0 (p_1)$ be our prior density function on p_1 where

$$f_0 (p_1) \geqslant 0 \quad \text{for} \quad 0 \leqslant p_1 \leqslant 1$$

and

$$\int_0^1 f_0 (p_1) \, dp = 1 .$$

11

After observing n_1, retirements in the first year, our new (posterior) density function on p_1 (denoted by $f_1 (p_1)$) is given by

$$f_1 (p_1) = \frac{p_1^{n_1} (1 - p_1)^{N - n_1} f_0 (p_1)}{\int_0^1 p_1^{n_1} (1 - p_1)^{N - n_1} f_0 (p_1) \, dp} \qquad 0 \leqslant p_1 \leqslant 1.$$

In general, however, we would not be solely interested in p_1 but rather in what the information on p_1 implies about the parameter(s) that are specifying the complete service life distribution.

For example, suppose we believe that the geometric distribution is a reasonable approximation to the service life distribution so that

$$p_j = (1 - p)^{j - 1} p, \qquad j = 1, 2, \dots .^7$$

One way of estimating p is by noting that the expected lifetime is given by $\Sigma_{j=1}^{\infty} j p_j = 1/p$. However, we may not have had sufficient experience with items similar to the assets currently being used to place complete faith in a point estimate of p. Therefore, we might wish to select a prior density on p and let the experience with the actual items now in service also influence our estimate of p.

For exposition purposes, it is convenient in this situation to choose a beta-distribution as the prior density for p,[8] i.e.,

$$f_0 (p) = A_0 p^{r - 1} (1 - p^{t - r - 1}); \qquad 0 \leqslant p \leqslant 1; \qquad 0 < r < t,$$

where

$$A_0 = \frac{(t - 1)!}{(r - 1)! \, (t - r - 1)!}.$$

The parameters r and t may be estimated by using the relations

$$E(p) = r/t$$

and

$$\text{Var}(p) = r/t^2.$$

Another interpretation of how r and t may be estimated will become clearer as we proceed.

If n_1 out of N items are retired in the first year in service,

$$f_1(p) = \frac{A_0 p^{n_1}(1-p)^{N-n_1} p^{r-1}(1-p)^{t-r-1}}{A_0 \int_p^{n_1}(1-p)^{N-n_1} p^{r-1}(1-p)^{t-r-1}\, dp}$$

$$= \frac{(N+t-1)!}{(r+n_1-1)!\,(N+t-r-n_1-1)!} p^{r+n_1-1}(1-p)^{N+t-(r+n_1)-1}$$

which is a β-distribution with parameters $r+n_1$, $N+t$.

At the start of the second period, we have $N-n_1$ items still in service. Suppose that $n_2 - n_1 (\geq 0)$ items fail in the second period. The probability of this event, given p, is

$$\binom{N-n_1}{n_2-n_1} p^{n_2-n_1}(1-p)^{N-n_2}.$$

Therefore, if our prior on p is given by $f_1(p)$ above, the posterior (after the second period) density of p is

$$f_2(p) = A_2 p^{n_2-n_1}(1-p)^{N-n_2} p^{r+n_1-1}(1-p)^{N+t-(r+n_1)-1}$$

$$= A_2 p^{r+n_2-1}(1-p)^{N+(N-n_1)+t-(n_2+r)-1},$$

where

$$A_2 = \frac{(N+N-n_1+t-1)!}{(r+n_2-1)!\,(2N+t-n_1-r-n_2-1)!}$$

Proceeding in this manner, it can be readily shown by induction that if $n_j - n_{j-1}$ items have been retired in the jth period ($j = 1, 2, \dots, k; n_0 = 0$), the posterior density of p after the kth period is given by

$$f_k(p) = A_k p^{r+n_k-1}(1-p)^{t+\sum_{i=0}^{k-1}(N-n_i)-(n_k+r)-1}$$

where

$$A_k = \frac{\left(t+\sum_{i=0}^{k-1}(n-n_i)-1\right)!}{(r+n_k-1)!\,\left(t+\sum_{i=0}^{k-1}(N-n_i)-(r+n_k)-1\right)!}$$

13

Note that $f_k(p)$ depends on the entire history of retirements (as represented by $n_1, \dots, n_k$) and not just on n_k, the cumulative number of retirements at the end of the kth year.

The initial parameters r and t can be interpreted as if we had a prior experience of observing t of these identical items in use at the start of a period with r of them having been retired by the end of the period. Thus the greater t is, the larger the influence of the prior density on the posterior densities of later periods. In the limit, where we know p with certainty so that a Bayesian analysis is not useful, r and t both go to infinity with the ratio r/t remaining equal to p.

Finally, to compute the probabilistic depreciation rate and accumulated depreciation rate after the kth period, we need to determine p_j for $j = k + 1, k + 2, \dots$. We know that for a given value of p, $p_j \,/\, p = (1 - p)^{j-k-1} p$. Therefore, to find the unconditional value of p_j, we multiply by the density function for p, $f_k(p)$, and integrate over 0 to 1; i.e.,

$$
p_j = \int_0^1 (p_j | p) f_k(p)\, dp
$$

$$
= A_k \cdot \int_0^1 p^{r+n_k} (1-p)^{[t + \sum_{i=0}^{k-1}(N-n_i) - (r+n_k) + (j-k-1) - 1]}\, dp
$$

$$
= (r + n_k)\, \frac{\left[t + \sum_{i=0}^{k-1}(N-n_i) - 1 \right]!}{\left[t + \sum_{i=0}^{k-1}(N-n_i) + (j-k) - 1 \right]!}
$$

$$
\cdot\, \frac{\left[t + \sum_{i=0}^{k-1}(N-n_i) - (n_k + r) + (j-k-1) - 1 \right]!}{\left[t + \sum_{i=0}^{k-1}(N-n_i) - (n_k + r) - 1 \right]!}
$$

$$
j = k + 1, k + 2, \dots .
$$

For example,

$$
p_{k+1} = \frac{r + n_k}{t + \sum_{i=0}^{k-1}(N - n_i)}
$$

and

$$
p_{k+2} = \frac{r + n_k}{t + \sum_{i=0}^{k-1}(N - n_i)} \cdot \frac{t + \sum_{i=0}^{k-1}(N - n_i) - (n_k + r)}{t + \sum_{i=0}^{k-1}(N - n_i) + 1}
$$

14

so that if $k = 1$ (have observed one period with n_1 failures), our revised estimates of p_2 and p_3 are given by[9]

$$p_2 = \frac{r + n_1}{t + N} \quad \text{and} \quad p_3 = \frac{r + n_1}{t + N} \, \frac{t + N - (n_1 + r)}{t + N + 1}.$$

The values of p_j for $j = k + 1, k + 2, \ldots$, are then inserted into the formulae developed in the previous section to compute the kth year depreciation rate and accumulated depreciation rate under the sequential probabilistic method.

In the above example, the posterior was always a β-distribution with the two parameters a simple linear function of the prior estimates of r and t and the observed retirement history. The ease with which we obtained the posterior density of p given $n_1, \ldots , n_k$ was due to the special structure that was assumed: the geometric distribution of the service lives and the β-distribution as the prior density on p. Departures from either one of these assumptions will result in considerably more complexity in the computation of the posterior density function.

For example, in our previous paper we postulated the use of a Poisson distribution as a good approximation to actual mortality curves of equipment. With the Poisson distribution, we define $p_i = [\lambda^{i-1} /(i - 1)!] e^{-\lambda}$ for $i = 1, 2, \ldots$. We would like to be able to treat the case in which λ is a random variable specified initially by a prior density function $f(\lambda)$. We are unaware of any prior density for λ that after observing a sequence of retirements will yield a posterior density for λ of the same general form. However, if a prior density on λ is chosen, it is still possible to carry out the required computations to determine, numerically, the posterior density of λ.

Let λ be specified by a prior density, $f(\lambda)$. Then with N identical items, the probability that n_1 are retired in the first period is given by

$$Pr\,[n_1 \mid N, \lambda] = \binom{N}{n_1} (e^{-\lambda})^{n_1} (1 - e^{-\lambda})^{N - n_1}.$$

Therefore, after observing n_1 retirements, the posterior density of λ is

$$f_1 (\lambda) = A_1 (e^{-\lambda})^{n_1} (1 - e^{-\lambda})^{N - n_1} f(\lambda)$$

where A_1 is chosen so that

$$\int_0^\infty f_1 (\lambda) \, d\lambda = 1.$$

In general, let $p_k(\lambda)$ be the probability, given λ, that an item is retired in the kth period given that it is still in service at the end of the k-1st period. Therefore,

$$p_k(\lambda) = [\lambda^{k-1}/(k-1)!] \Big/ \Big[\sum_{j=k}^{\infty} \lambda^{j-1}/(j-1)!\Big].$$

Also, let $f_{k-1}(\lambda)$ be the posterior density of λ based on the actual retirement experience up through the k-1st period. Then if $N - n_{k-1}$ items are still in service at the start of the kth period and $n_k - n_{k-1}$ retirements are observed in the kth period, the new posterior density of λ is given by

$$f_k(\lambda) = A_k [p_k(\lambda)]^{n_k - n_{k-1}} [1 - p_k(\lambda)]^{N - n_k} f_{k-1}(\lambda) \quad \text{for } \lambda > 0;$$
$$k = 1, 2, \dots,$$

with A_k chosen so that

$$\int_0^{\infty} f_k(\lambda)\, d\lambda = 1.$$

Thus to compute the sequential depreciation rate for the kth period, we need to determine the unconditional value of p_j for $j = k+1, k+2, \dots$, as given by

$$p_j = \int_0^{\infty} \frac{[\lambda^{j-1}/(j-1)!]}{\sum_{i=k+1}^{\infty} [\lambda^{i-1}/(i-1)!]} f_k(\lambda)\, d\lambda \quad \text{for } j = k+1, k+2, \dots,$$

The above recursive computations are straightfoward, albeit tedious, and can be programmed for solution on a digital computer.

Summary

In this paper, we have explored the nature of sequential probabilistic depreciation. In practice, it is important to adjust the lifetime probability distribution sequentially since actual experience may differ from that expected at the time the initial probability estimates are made. In making these adjustments, it is desirable to avoid any bias toward over- or under-depreciation and methods for deriving unbiased depreciation rates sequentially have been introduced. It was pointed out that in trying to keep the book value of the asset and the accumulated depreciation unbiased at all times, a net depreciation charge may occur in special situations.

The idea of sequential probabilistic depreciation was then extended to group depreciation, and Bayesian analysis was used to develop practical methods for updating the probability estimates based on a prior distribution and actual failure experiences with the assets.

Notes

[1] Reprinted by kind permission from *Journal of Accounting Research* vol. 8, 1970, pp. 34–44.
[2] For a comprehensive treatment of conventional depreciation methods, see [1].
[3] See [2].
[4] The sequential probabilistic depreciation approach is discussed in [2].
[5] See [2].
[6] If the asset is retired in one of the first few years of its possible service life, this adjustment might be quite substantial. However, to offset this effect, the salvage value may be larger than expected because of the few years in service and hence may reduce the amount of this writeoff.
[7] A more general form of the geometric distribution might allow for a minimum lifetime of m years so that $p_j = 0$ for $j = 1, 2, \ldots, m$, and $p_j = (1 - p)^{j - m - 1} p$ for $j = m + 1, m + 2, \ldots$.
[8] The β-distribution is the conjugate prior for the Bernoulli process being described here where the probability of retirement in each year is a constant, p, for those items which are still in service.
[9] It is easy to verify that the prior estimates p_2 and p_3 are given by $p_2 = r/t$ and $p_3 = (r/t)[(t - r)/(r + 1)]$.

References

1 Grant, E., and Norton, P., *Depreciation*, The Ronald Press, New York 1949.
2 Ijiri, Y., and Kaplan, R., 'Probabilistic depreciation and its implications for group depreciation' *The Accounting Review* vol. 44, October 1969, pp. 743–56.
3 Raiffa, H., and Schlaifer, R., *Applied Statistical Decision Theory*, Harvard University Press 1961.

Probabilistic Depreciation with a Varying Salvage Value[1]

Introduction

All depreciation methods, including the new probabilistic method, assume salvage value to be a single, known quantity. That is, the depreciation calculator uses acquisition cost and *one* estimated salvage value for the asset to get a total depreciable base (Acquisition cost–Salvage value) to be used for depreciation calculations. The purpose of this paper is to examine the implications of allowing salvage value to vary over the life of the asset. Varying salvage value will be incorporated into a probabilistic depreciation framework and implementation problems will be examined.

Probabilistic depreciation

Theoretically, probabilistic depreciation is vastly superior to deterministic depreciation. This has been shown by both Ijiri and Kaplan [2] and Jen and Huefner [4]. The basic difference between the two methods is in *when* averaging takes place. In deterministic depreciation the probability distribution of asset service life is used to obtain the mean of that distribution *immediately*. Once this mean life is determined, it is used, along with estimated depreciable base (Acquisition cost–Estimated salvage value), to calculate depreciation expense over the life of the asset. However, in probabilistic depreciation, depreciation is calculated for each possible service life, and then the average is taken, using the probability distribution of service life to weight the depreciations calculated.

In their second paper Ijiri and Kaplan [3] outline a sequential model to modify the probability distribution of service life. As the asset service life expires, more information is obtained about the probability distribution – information that may be incorporated into the model. This model is essentially the one to be used in this paper, so an example will be given to demonstrate it. Assume

(a) Straight line depreciation (any method possible)
(b) Acquisition cost = $1,200
(c) Estimated salvage value = $200
(d) Probability distribution of possible service life:

$$P (L = 1) = P (L = 2) = P (L = 3) = \tfrac{1}{3} .$$

Then the probabilistic depreciation calculations proceed over time as in Table 1.1.

The $I - K$ method shown in Table 1.1 has certain implications. At time t_0, probabilistic depreciation is calculated for all three years. One year later, at time t_1, the depreciation calculator pauses to view the asset. If it failed at the end of year one, he knows the $611·11 calculated at t_0 should have been $1000.[2] Consequently, he would correct year one's income to increase expense by $388·99. On the other hand, if the asset survives year one, he knows the event $L = 1$ did not occur, and he would recalculate depreciation for all three years. A correction of year one income is again needed. In this case, expense would be reduced $194·44 ($611·11−$416·67). At t_2 the calculator again stops to view the asset. If

Table 1.1

Sequential depreciation calculations over time

Point in time	Life (i)	$P(L = i)$	Expense distribution with L = 1, 2, 3			
			Year 1	Year 2	Year 3	
t_0	1	$\frac{1}{3}$	1000	0	0	
	2	$\frac{1}{3}$	500	500	0	
	3	$\frac{1}{3}$	333·33	333·33	333·33	
	Calculated depreciation:		611·11	277·77	111·11	Total 1000
t_1	1	0	1000	0	0	
	2	$\frac{1}{2}$	500	500	0	
	3	$\frac{1}{2}$	333·33	333·33	333·33	
	Calculated depreciation:		416·67	416·67	166·67	Total 1000
t_2	1	0	1000	0	0	
	2	0 ·	500	500	0	
	3	1	333·33	333·33	333·33	
	Calculated depreciation:		333·33	333·33	333·33	Total 1000

the asset failed at the end of year two, he knows years one and two expense should have been $500, $500, instead of $416·67, $416·67. If the asset did not fail, he would know the event $L = 3$ has to occur, and depreciations would be recalculated accordingly. In either case corrections of years one and two income would be necessary.

The $I-K$ model requires corrections of prior years' incomes because of the uncertainty about the service life of the asset. Such corrections are not acceptable in current practice. By disallowing prior-period corrections for depreciation the Accounting Principles Board (APB) obviously wants to avoid 'manipulations'. However, throughout this paper the goal of depreciation calculations is assumed to be 'truth', and although misestimates would occur, 'manipulations' would not. Ijiri and Kaplan make the point in their paper of proving their estimates are unbiased. That is, the expected value of corrections is zero. Thus, corrections are not manipulative, but are caused by uncertainty only. If a world of no corrections prevails, the $I-K$ model could certainly be adjusted to correct only present and future years' depreciation expenses on the basis of *remaining* depreciable cost.

Probabilistic depreciation with probabilistic salvage value

Whereas acquisition cost is essentially an objectively determined dollar amount, future salvage value is not. Salvage values are really only subjective guesses or estimates. It is my contention that salvage value is not necessarily constant; a varying salvage value can be incorporated into the probabilistic depreciation model. It takes little imagination to realise salvage value could vary over an asset's life. In most situations salvage value would vary inversely with asset service life. If asset service life happened to be short, salvage value would probably be higher than if service life happened to be long. Of course, this will not be the case for all assets. There will be cases where salvage value does not fall over time. It is even conceivable that an asset could have a salvage value higher than acquisition cost.

In any event, a varying salvage value assumption is more realistic and introduces increased flexibility into the model. Just as we assumed probability distributions for asset service life, we can assume probability distributions for salvage value *conditional* on asset service life. That is, for each possible service life we can assess a conditional salvage value probability distribution. For example, expanding our initial example, assume that we assess the conditional salvage value probability distributions shown in Table 1.2. Probabilistic depreciation calculations thus proceed over time as in

Table 1.3. Naturally, at each point in time (t_0, t_1, t_2) the same implications for corrections of prior years' incomes would prevail that prevailed for probabilistic depreciation with constant salvage value (Table 1.1).

Notice in Table 1.3 we did *not* calculate depreciation for all possible salvage values, at each service life possibility, and then multiply by those salvage values' probabilities. This was unnecessary since the mean of the depreciation expenses of the varying salvage values is exactly equal to the depreciation expense calculated using the mean salvage value. For salvage value it does not matter *when* averaging takes place (See Appendix I for proof). Notice also the differences between depreciation calculated with constant salvage value (Table 1.1) and depreciation calculated with varying salvage value (Table 1.3). The timing and amounts of expense recognition are different.

At t_0 the range of depreciation expenses for the three years is not as wide for varying salvage value (s.v.) as for constant s.v. The range seems to have been dampened by a varying s.v. The cause of this is the equal probability weighting of less cost spread over fewer periods with more cost spread over more periods. However, total depreciation calculated under both methods is the same, $1000. The reason is that the grand mean of the varying s.v.s equals the constant s.v. assumed in the first case.[3] At t_1 the ranges are the same width for both methods, but total depreciation is more for varying s.v. ($1100 vs $1000). Here the average of the varying s.v.s is 100,[4] which implies a depreciable cost of $1100. At

Table 1.2

Conditional probability distributions of salvage value

Asset life (i)	Salvage value	P (Salvage value | $L = i$)	Mean
1	500	$\frac{1}{3}$	400
	400	$\frac{1}{3}$	
	300	$\frac{1}{3}$	
2	300	$\frac{1}{3}$	200
	200	$\frac{1}{3}$	
	100	$\frac{1}{3}$	
3	100	$\frac{1}{3}$	0
	0	$\frac{1}{3}$	
	−100	$\frac{1}{3}$	

t_2 the range is zero for both methods since it is known with certainty the asset life is three years. The difference in total depreciation is caused by the average varying s.v. (zero) differing from the constant s.v. ($200). Finally, notice how under both methods the pattern of depreciation expense approaches a complete straight line charge through time. Although different for the two methods, at t_1 the calculated expense is the same for both year one and year two, and at t_2 complete straight line is reached. This characteristic is inherent in the sequential probabilistic method, given the straight line assumption. The effect would be even more dramatic for an example considering longer lives.

Assessing probability distributions

In the discussion above we have assumed all probability distributions, both service life and salvage value, were given. In practice they will not be given. They will have to be assessed somehow. When assessing these distributions all objective information at hand should be used.

Table 1.3

Sequential depreciation calculations over time
with a varying salvage value

Point in time	Life (i)	$P(L=i)$	Expense distribution with $L = 1, 2, 3$		
			Year 1	Year 2	Year 3
t_0	1	$\frac{1}{3}$	800	0	0
	2	$\frac{1}{3}$	500	500	0
	3	$\frac{1}{3}$	400	400	400
	Calculated depreciation:		566·67	300	133·33	Total 1000
t_1	1	0	800	0	0
	2	$\frac{1}{2}$	500	500	0
	3	$\frac{1}{2}$	400	400	400
	Calculated depreciation:		450	450	200	Total 1100
t_2	1	0	800	0	0
	2	0	500	500	0
	3	1	400	400	400
	Calculated depreciation:		400	400	400	Total 1200

23

Service life distributions

If mortality statistics are available for many similar assets in the company, strong indications are given for the form of the service life distribution. The larger the sample of information, the stronger the indication. If the sample is very large (size = N), then perhaps the best estimate of service life probability distribution is:

$$P(L = i)$$
$$= \frac{\text{Number in sample that lived exactly } i \text{ years}}{N}$$

If the sample is smaller, it may be desirable to plot Number living i years vs i and fit a curve to the sample points as in Figure 1.1. The dashed line in Figure 1.1 is management's guess for what the distribution would look like if the sample were large. Discrete probabilities would be assigned accordingly. Of course, the most convenient and desirable forms for the distribution to take are the objective distributions – such as Poisson, geometric, normal etc.[5] If it is obvious that such a distribution approximates fairly well the actual mortality rates, it probably should be adopted for the inherent ease of calculation. This is convenient, but not a must. If the asset will survive, they will have feelings or judgements about the asset's distribution estimation. Even if management has no evidence on how long the asset will survive, they will have feelings or judgements about the asset's life. Moreover, there are methods available to construct subjective probability distributions (Schlaifer [5] and Winkler [6]). The Schlaifer process consists of asking the estimator a series of questions:

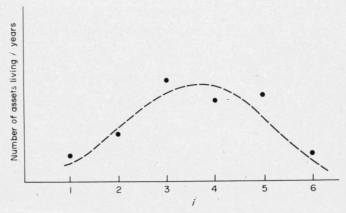

Fig. 1.1   Small sample distribution plot

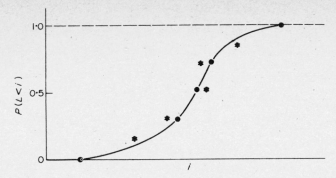

Fig. 1.2 Assessing a cumulative probability distribution

1 For what life do you think the asset has an equal chance of living longer or shorter?
2 For what life do you think the probability of the asset living longer than that is negligible?
3 For what life do you think the probability of the asset living shorter than that is negligible? Etc.

As each question is answered a point is plotted to form a cumulative probability distribution (Figure 1.2). An unavoidable problem in constructing a cumulative probability distribution is in getting consistent answers so that a smooth curve may be drawn. Aberrant points will arise (shown as stars in Figure 1.2). Schlaifer claims if the process is repeated over and over with the questions posed from different points of view, consistency will arise. Aberrant points will become obvious. Examples of different points of view are: 'What is the probability the asset will survive *at least* five years?' and 'What is the probability the asset will survive *less than* three years?', etc. Once all consistent points are identified, the cumulative distribution can be sketched in. As an alternative, computer programmes are available to obtain best fits.[6]These programmes eliminate the need for complete consistency in the points.

The resulting cumulative distribution is *continuous*. But a *discrete* distribution simplifies probabilistic depreciation calculations. An approximation may be obtained by dividing the horizontal axis of the cumulative distribution into segments one year long. Figure 1.3 illustrates this approach. From Figure 1.3 we get:

$$P_1 = P(L \leqslant 1)$$
$$P_2 = P(L \leqslant 2) - P(L \leqslant 1)$$
$$P_3 = P(L \leqslant 3) - P(L \leqslant 2)$$
etc.

25

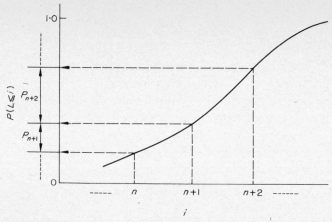

Fig. 1.3   Assessing an approximate discrete distribution from a continuous cumulative distribution

There are other ways to obtain subjective probability distributions. One is direct estimation of the distribution, assigning probabilities to each possible year directly.[7] Winkler claims this method results in a bias toward normal distributions because people think this is what probability distributions 'should' look like.[8] Winkler mentions two other indirect methods that involve working backward from a posterior distribution to a prior distribution after posing hypothetical sample information to the estimator to get the posterior. An interesting, but not surprising, conclusion of Winkler's study was that the four methods of assessing prior distributions could result in widely different distributions for an individual estimator. In addition, Winkler found a relationship between an individual's understanding of probability concepts and consistency of his prior distributions.[9] This emphasises the importance of a clear understanding by the estimator of exactly what he is trying to do.The cumulative distribution method is best for assets with anything but a very short life, but the estimator must understand the question he is being asked.

Perhaps the easiest way to avoid the difficulties in creating a subjective distribution is to use the beta distribution. The beta has the formula:

$$B\,(i) \;=\; (\text{constant}) \cdot (i - a)^{\alpha}\;\;(b - i)^{\gamma}, \quad \alpha \geqslant 0,\; \gamma \geqslant 0\,.$$

It is a single-mounded distribution continuous over its finite range, $a \leq i \leq b$. It can be skewed in either direction by altering α and γ, and the constant may be adjusted to make $\int_{a}^{b} B(i)\,di = 1$. This is exactly what is needed in a distribution. What is nice about the beta is that if we assume the standard deviation of the distribution is one-sixth the range (as in PERT), we can completely specify the distribution by making only three estimates: Earliest possible life = a, Latest possible life = b, and Most likely life = M. M can be specified anywhere between a and b. This is how skewness is determined since α and γ are functions of M.

Greer [1] provides a method of going 'from raw subjective time estimates to finished probability numbers in a matter of minutes while using nothing more complex than arithmetic'. Greer first standardises the beta distribution. That is, he makes the range of the distribution from 0 to 1 instead of from a to b; thus:

$$B(x) = (\text{constant}) \cdot (x - a)^{\alpha} (b - x)^{\gamma}$$

where $x = (i - a)/(b - a)$. Then M' becomes $(M - a)/(b - a)$, which Greer calls r. The resulting beta is plotted in Figure 1.4.

Utilising the inherent relationships between the variables. Greer creates a 'Beta Curve Area Chart'.[10] The chart yields the area under the standardised beta from 0 to x, for any desired x between 0 and 1, given only the appropriate r value. Thus we can calculate the area between any two x's (or i's) by finding the respective area for each and performing a simple subtraction. The result is a discrete probability distribution for service life if we merely find the areas between each adjacent possible life. Greer has worked out a numerical example in his paper and his area chart is reproduced in Appendix II.

Thus, management does not have to create an entire subjective probability distribution. By making three service life estimates (minimum, maximum, and most likely), and using Greer's approach they can quickly implement probabilistic depreciation calculations. The entire process is

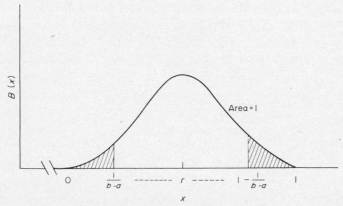

Fig. 1.4   Standardised beta distribution

simple once the three estimates are made, and it could easily be programmed for calculation on a digital computer. Another advantage of such an approach is that PERT has already made this kind of estimation and analysis using the beta an accepted method.

Salvage value distributions

Just as a cumulative probability distribution was assessed for asset service life, cumulative conditional probability distributions could be assessed for salvage value for *each* possible service life. This would be extremely arduous. For example, if an asset could survive from one to twenty years, twenty cumulative distributions would have to be determined, one for each year! This would clearly be an unacceptable and impossible approach. Short-cuts are possible, however, since we need only estimate the means of these twenty distributions for calculating depreciation. (Remember depreciation calculated with mean salvage value equals the mean of depreciations using all salvage values.) There are three possible short-cuts.

First, management could just estimate the mean salvage value for each possible life without trying to define the whole probability distribution. This would be simple, but probably not very accurate.

Second, management could get an approximate distribution by assuming some well-defined distribution − like the beta. With the beta distribution a close approximation of the mean is easily calculated. Management merely estimates minimum, maximum, and most likely values for salvage value, and assuming again the standard deviation is one-sixth the range, then:

$$\text{Mean} \approx \frac{\text{Min} + 4 \text{ (most likely)} + \text{Max}}{6}$$

A mean salvage value must be calculated for each possible life.

Third, management could assume mean salvage value varies over time according to some well-defined function, as in Figure 1.5. What would be the form of $F(i)$ in Figure 1.5? This is an open question, and empirical research would be needed to verify any function suggested. But it seems reasonable to suppose salvage value would fall from acquisition cost over time. That it would fall rapidly at first (for $i \leq i'$ in Figure 1.5). It would fall less rapidly in intermediate years ($i' \leq i \leq i''$). And it would level off in later years ($i \geq i''$). This would seem reasonable, for example, to anyone who has owned an automobile. A fairly new car that 'wears out' is not worth anywhere near what was paid for it. Yet there is a floor to how low a car's salvage value could go in the distant future − scrap metal value. Hence the hypothesis suggested is:

28

Min Scrap Value $\leq F(i) \leq$ Cost

$dF/di < 0$, slope is negative

$d^2 F/di^2 > 0$, negative slope is decreasing

$d^3 F/di^3 < 0$, slope decreasing at decreasing rate

One possible functional form for $F(i)$ that satisfies the functional requirements is:

$$F_{u,v}(i) = \frac{C - MSV}{ui^v + 1} + MSV$$

$$= \frac{C + ui^v \cdot MSV}{ui^v + 1}$$

where u and $v > 0$ and $C \geqslant MSV$. If $i = 0$, $F_{u,v}(i) = C =$ Acquisition cost. As i gets larger, $F_{u,v}(i)$ gets smaller. And as i approaches infinity, $F_{u,v}(i)$ approaches MSV asymptotically. How fast $F_{u,v}(i)$ falls towards MSV can be regulated by varying v, the power of i, and/or u, the i-term coefficient. If a very slow fall in $F_{u,v}(i)$ is desired, v should be made small. On the other hand, a very rapid fall in $F_{u,v}(i)$ can be obtained by making v large. More refined adjustments can be made by raising or lowering u. Altering a coefficient has less effect than altering a power. General effects may be observed by viewing the families of curves shown in Figure 1.6.

$F_{u,v}(i)$ is flexible enough to allow a reasonable fit for whatever variation over time is found empirically to apply to a certain 'type' of asset.

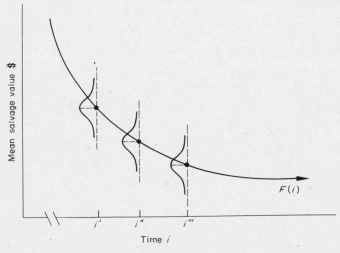

Fig. 1.5   Salvage value as a function of time

For example, in applying the beta distribution to calculate probabilistic depreciation, one would undoubtedly want $F_{u,v}(i)$ to approach MSV at the maximum possible life. An $F_{u,v}(i)$ could be fitted to accomplish this. Using $F_{u,v}(i)$ simplifies probabilistic depreciation calculations with a varying salvage value. The estimator does not have to worry about the conditional probability distribution of salvage value anymore. Direct calculations are possible. A substantial saving in time and effort would be possible, especially for a very long-lived asset. For a possible twenty-year asset direct calculation of salvage value would save twenty estimations and twenty plugs into the depreciation formula.

Any of these three approaches can provide management with the mean salvage value needed for each possible service life. Which approach is chosen will be determined by how much effort management wants to put

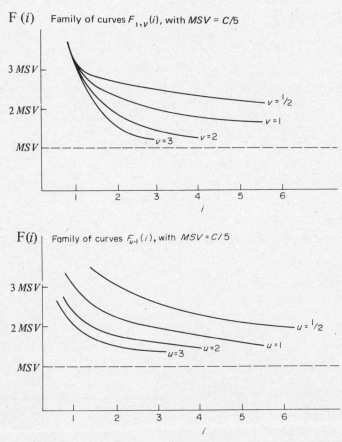

Fig. 1.6   Families of curves $F_{u,v}(i)$

30

into finding the means, how much experience they have with estimating mean salvage values, and how much data they have to make the third approach feasible.

Updating probability distributions

In the discussion above we have assumed the probability distributions of service life and salvage values, once determined, are known with certainty. That is, the distributions do not change over time. This static assumption is not necessarily valid. Over the life of the asset we may realise our initial probability distributions were wrong and we may want to alter them. Ijiri and Kaplan provide a way of updating probability distributions of service life using Bayesian analysis.[11] Their scheme is set in a group depreciation framework wherein the actual mortality rates in a group of similar assets are used to update the prior distribution to get a posterior distribution. They claim this method will work and, although tedious, can be programmed for solution on a digital computer.

The only problem with their method is that it is designed for use in a group depreciation framework.[12] It is not easily applied in certain situations:

1 In a smaller company that might not have enough assets to form 'similar groups' of assets.
2 In updating the distributions of a dissimilar asset, one that is unlike any groups of similar assets.

Updating should occur in these situations also.

In calculating probabilistic depreciation, suppose we assess an initial distribution of service life, possibly through cumulative distribution building:

$$P(L = 1) = p_1$$
$$P(L = 2) = p_2$$
$$\cdot$$
$$\cdot$$
$$\cdot$$
$$P(L = n) = p_n .$$

Suppose further that this distribution is used (sequentially updating) for five years to calculate depreciation. And, at the end of five years, the asset shows negligible wear and obsolescence. After examining the asset we now reassess the probability distribution of service life to:

31

$$P(L = 1) \quad = \dots = P(L = 5) = 0$$
$$P(L = 6) \quad = p'_6$$

$$\cdot$$
$$\cdot$$
$$\cdot$$

$$P(L = n + 5) = p'_{n+5}$$

Or suppose at the end of five years the asset shows substantially more wear than expected, or perhaps obsolescence becomes imminent, and we reassess the distribution of service life to

$$P(L = 1) = \dots = P(L = 5) = 0$$
$$P(L = 6) = p'_6$$
$$P(L = 7) = p'_7$$
$$P(L = 8) = \dots = P(L = n) = 0 .$$

In either of these situations are we helpless to change to the new distribution because we do not have objective evidence, like a sample of mortality rates on similar assets? Not so. We can switch to the new applicable distribution, whichever one, since this is analogous to altering service life estimates in a simple deterministic model without probabilities.

In a deterministic model, if over the life of the asset it becomes obvious service life or salvage value has been misestimated, it will be changed to the new estimate. Depreciation expense would be changed to take account of the new information. In the real world if corrections of prior years' incomes were allowed, depreciation for *all* years would be recalculated, and a complete parallel would exist with the method proposed. Just as the service life estimates were updated in the two situations above, so would be the salvage value distributions conditional on service life. If $F_{u,v}(i)$ had been incorporated into the model, the parameters of $F_{u,v}(i)$ would be updated.

Conclusion

If probabilistic depreciation is to be implemented, allowance for varying salvage value should be incorporated. Salvage value can vary over time. An attempt to include this variation will be theoretically superior to an assumption of a static salvage value. We have seen how this variation could be incorporated and how some inevitable problems could be 'solved'. But the real problem with new mathematical models in general, and probabilistic depreciation with varying salvage value in particular, is not model formulation but widespread acceptance. There is a reluctance to change from accepted methods, but change is inevitable. More mathematical models are inevitable. More computer applications are inevitable. More logic in seemingly pure judgement situations is inevitable. Judgements will be made, but they will be more rational.

Probabilistic depreciation with varying salvage value is a foretelling of things to come. Depreciation is really only an allocation problem. Perhaps all allocation problems should be, and will be in the future, approached from a probabilistic standpoint. The big question is: 'Why use gross averages when one can be more specific?' This question has widespread implications throughout accounting. The idea is to come up with more meaningful numbers. Probabilistic depreciation with a varying salvage value may yield more meaningful numbers.

Appendix I

Incorporation of the entire conditional probability distribution of salvage value for each possible service life is unnecessary. Only the calculation of mean salvage value is necessary for each possible life. Depreciation calculated from mean salvage value = Mean of depreciations calculated from all salvage values.

Proof: Let d_{ij} be the proportion of acquisition cost less salvage value that is to be depreciated in period j if i is the service life of the asset. Let C be the acquisition cost and x_i be a random variable for the salvage value of an asset with service life of i. Then, depreciation in period j is d_{ij} times $(C - x_i)$ and its mean is:

$$
\begin{aligned}
E\left[d_{ij}\left(C - x_i\right)\right] &= d_{ij}C - d_{ij}E\left(x_i\right) \\
&= d_{ij}C - d_{ij}\overline{x} \\
&= d_{ij}\left(C - \overline{x}\right),
\end{aligned} \tag{1}
$$

which is depreciation with the mean salvage value $\overline{x} = E\left(x_i\right)$. In particular, for a discrete case, the expression (1) becomes

$$
\begin{aligned}
\Sigma p_k \cdot d_{ij}\left(C - x_{ik}\right) &= d_{ij}C\, \Sigma P_k - d_{ij}\, \Sigma p_k x_{ik} \\
&= d_{ij}C - d_{ij}\overline{x} \\
&= d_{ij}\left(C - \overline{x}\right)
\end{aligned} \tag{2}
$$

since $\Sigma p_k = 1$. \hfill QED

Appendix II

The chart[12] is read from the left-hand edge (*r*-value) to the right until the appropriate *x*-value is reached. Then by dropping straight down to the bottom axis, the appropriate area may be read off. The dotted line presents an exercise to find the area between $x = 0.375$ and $x = 0.500$, with $r = 0.375$. The chart yields

Area between 0 and 0·500
$$= P\,(0 \leqslant x \leqslant 0.500) \;=\; 0.707$$
Area between 0 and 0·375
$$= P\,(0 \leqslant x \leqslant 0.375) \;=\; 0.448.$$

Thus,

$$P\,(0.375 \leqslant x \leqslant 0.500) \;=\; 0.707 - 0.448 \;=\; 0.259\,.$$

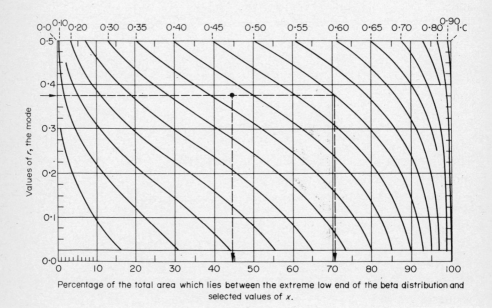

Fig. 1.7   Beta curve area chart. Values of *x*, points within the range

34

Notes

1   Reprinted by kind permission from *The Accounting Review*, vol. 48, 1973, pp. 50–60.

2   A standard assumption in probabilistic depreciation calculations is asset failures at year-ends only.

3   See Table 1.2.

$$\sum_{i}^{3} = 1\, P\,(L = i) \cdot (\text{Average s.v.} \mid L = i)$$
$$= \tfrac{1}{3}\,(400) + \tfrac{1}{3}\,(200) + \tfrac{1}{3}\,(0) = 200$$
$$= \text{constant s.v. assumed.}$$

4   $0(400) + \tfrac{1}{2}(200) + \tfrac{1}{2}(0) = 100$.

5   In their first paper (pp. 746–8) Ijiri and Kaplan discuss the use of these distributions, although they specifically use the Poisson distribution because it approximates Kurtz's mortality curves so well.

6   Schlaifer describes one such programme, SMOOTH, pp. 268–71.

7   Direct probability assignment is the only acceptable method of obtaining distributions for short-life assets. A cumulative distribution built over *few* years is not worth the effort. Direct assignment is done by successive pairwise comparisons. For example, for an asset with a three-year maximum life, the estimator may judge $L = 1$ twice as likely as $L = 2$, and $L = 2$ twice as likely as $L = 3$, and $L = 1$ four times as likely as $L = 3$. Then

$$p_1 = 2p_2$$
$$p_2 = 2p_3$$
$$p_3 = \tfrac{1}{4} \cdot p_1$$

and

$$p_1 + p_2 + p_3 = 1$$
$$\Rightarrow p_1 = \tfrac{4}{7}, \quad p_2 = \tfrac{2}{7}, \quad p_3 = \tfrac{1}{7}$$

The only real problem for the estimator is to get all the pairwise comparisons to be consistent with one another.

8   See [6], p. 785.

9   Ibid., p. 789.

10   [1], p. 112.

11   See [3], pp. 41–6.

12   Note that it is mathematically possible to substitute group size $N = 1$ in Ijiri and Kaplan's group updating framework, but the value of doing so is questionable.

13   From [1]. Used with permission.

References

1   Greer, W. R., Jr, 'Capital budgeting analysis with the timing of events uncertain' *The Accounting Review* vol. 45, January 1970, pp.111–118.
2   Ijiri, Y., and Kaplan, R. S., 'Probabilistic depreciation and its implications for group depreciation' *The Accounting Review* vol. 44, October 1969, pp. 743–56.
3   Ijiri, Y., and Kaplan, R. S., 'Sequential models in probabilistic depreciation' *Journal of Accounting Research* vol. 8, 1970, pp. 34–46 (reprinted in this volume).
4   Jen, F. C., and Huefner, R. J., 'Depreciation by probability life' *The Accounting Review* vol. 45, April 1970, pp. 290–8.
5   Schlaifer, R., *Analysis of Decisions Under Uncertainty*, McGraw-Hill, 1969, Chapters 7 and 8.
6   Winkler, R. L., 'The assessment of prior distributions in Bayesian analysis' *Journal of the American Statistical Association* vol. 62, 1967, pp. 777–800.

SECTION 2

Auditing

?

The use of sampling methods in auditing is perhaps one of the more obvious applications of statistical theory, and it has certainly found a very significant place in accounting literature. Indeed it is now well known that in practice a sample audit may not only save a great deal of time — and therefore expense — but may also lead to more accurate results than a complete audit.

In much of the earlier work in this area, attention was devoted to examining and implementing sampling schemes with only the audit objectives of estimation and hypothesis testing in mind. The initial paper represents one of the most important advances, since the authors are the first to recognise that the auditor has objectives in addition to those of an inferential nature.

In view of these further objectives — which are clearly identified — methods are developed for evaluating sampling procedures. The paper should provide the stimulus for a more realistic and rational approach to sample auditing. In contrast, the contribution by Aly and Duboff provides one of the few empirical investigations into the use of sampling in auditing, and in so doing provides a valuable comparison between alternative techniques.

A Model for Integrating Sampling Objectives in Auditing[1]

Introduction

This paper is concerned with integrating the diverse objectives that the auditor attempts to achieve with a given sampling plan. In a previous paper [7] we noted that sampling objectives in auditing have been traditionally aimed at estimation and hypothesis testing. We called these applications, which include estimation, acceptance, and discovery sampling,[2] *representative sampling*. Each has the objective of obtaining a sample which satisfactorily represents the population so that estimates may be made of a population parameter. For example, if we are trying to estimate the error rate of a population of invoices, and if, in fact, 2 per cent of the invoices are in error, the ideal sample for representative sampling would be one in which 2 per cent of the items sampled turned out to be in error.

However, the auditors' objectives in sampling seem to be much broader than those aimed at in representative sampling. Specifically, we believe that the auditors' behaviour implies at least three other objectives when they sample a population. We refer to these additional objectives as corrective sampling, protective sampling, and preventive sampling.

In *corrective sampling*, the auditor wishes to select a sample which contains the maximum number of errors so that these may be corrected. In this case, the auditor wishes to minimise the number of errors remaining in the population. An ideal sample in corrective sampling would be one which contained the maximum number of those items in the population which were in error.

In *protective sampling*, the auditor's objective is to maximise the dollar value of those items which have been included in the sample. Contrary to corrective sampling, which is an offensive approach against errors and fraud, protective sampling is a defensive approach. The auditor recognises the difficulty of detecting errors and frauds which may occur in only a small fraction of the population and tries to protect himself by verifying that at least a relatively significant portion of the population is free from errors and fraud. An ideal sample for protective sampling is one which

41

maximises the dollar value of those items which are included in the sample.

The goal of *preventive sampling* is to reduce the probability that the auditor's sampling plan will be predictable. It is a control mechanism that aims at creating the impression that no area is audit-free in order to prevent the occurrence of irregular items in the future in areas thought to be relatively immune from intensive audits. Thus, an ideal sample for this objective is one which creates the maximum degree of uncertainty in the minds of auditees as to which items are likely to be audited in the future.

There are examples in practice which illustrate these four objectives. If an auditor finds a specific area where the internal control system is particularly weak or where there is a high probability of irregular items (which may lead to a material misrepresentation in financial statements), he will certainly sample heavily from such an area. This behaviour of auditors cannot be explained from the viewpoint of representative sampling. It is an instance where the objective of corrective sampling is dominant. Similarly, the objective of protective sampling is evident from the auditors' inclination to select higher valued items for his samples. The objective of preventive sampling is reflected in the auditors' tendency to vary the areas of intensive audits (branches visited, months or accounts selected for a complete check, etc.) from year to year. This strategy is partly an effort to obtain an unbiased sample, but it can be more directly explained by introducing the notion of preventive sampling.

While we believe these four objectives exist in auditors' minds when they take a sample, we do not suggest that auditors are legally responsible for them. Nevertheless, they seem to consider these objectives, perhaps as a part of 'due professional care'. Instead of arguing whether auditors should be held responsible for these objectives, we propose a method for formulating a sampling plan when the four objectives are present.

These four objectives do not require four separate samples, one for each objective. Rather a single sampling plan can be developed to satisfy all of them. Each item included in a sample has a potential contribution to each of the four objectives. Therefore, an item should be evaluated for inclusion in the sample from all of these four viewpoints rather than just from the traditional viewpoint of representative sampling.

We begin with a verbal description of a process that may be used by the auditor when little prior information is available. We then assume that the auditor can provide some initial estimates of the population which enables us to develop a mathematical model of the sampling process. In the final section, we present some ideas as to how the various objectives may be integrated into a single sampling plan.

Limited information case

Consider a simple situation in which the auditor has no information at all about the items to be sampled. Such a situation is rather unusual since the auditor usually has at least the recorded values of items which provide some guidance as to which should be selected. However, it is instructive to start our analysis by working with this simple situation.

In the no-information case, the auditor starts by taking a random sample. The sample size need not be fixed ahead of time. It will typically be determined after observing the results from a check of the items that have already been selected. After a number of items have been selected and checked, the auditor evaluates the results relative to the four objectives described above. For representative sampling, the auditor may be concerned with the width of the confidence intervals about the estimates of the proportion of items in error and the dollar value of items in the population. If the confidence interval is too wide, a meaningful inference of the population characteristics is not possible. Hence the auditor will require additional items to be sampled in order to reduce the variance of his estimate. For the corrective sampling objective, the auditor reviews the results of his first sample to see whether further sampling is likely to be productive in finding errors. Obviously, the more error items in the sample taken, the more interested the auditor is in checking further. For protective sampling, the auditor checks the ratio of the total dollar value of items sampled to the total dollar value of items in the entire population. If the dollar-value proportion covered by the sample is less than the minimum that he wishes to cover in order to protect himself, he will continue to sample items. Of course, this evaluation may not be possible if the auditor does not know the actual total dollar value of the population. In such instances, this quantity will have to be estimated from the sample (for example, by representative sampling). Finally, from the preventive sampling viewpoint, the auditor evaluates the items that have already been checked to see whether they are spread over the various control areas of the organisation. If the sample already taken leaves a large number of areas unsampled, the auditor will require a further sample.

This qualitative characterisation of the auditor's objectives in sampling can be made clearer by introducing a measure for each of the objectives. There are many ways of measuring the degree of achievement in each of the objectives, so the following measures are merely illustrative.

1   Representative sampling: the width w of a confidence interval at a given level of significance.

2 Corrective sampling: the estimated number r of unchecked items in error,i.e., the product of the number of items *not* in the sample and the proportion of items in error in the sample.

3 Protective sampling: the ratio u of the total dollar value of items not in the sample to the (estimated) total dollar value of the population. If necessary, u may be estimated by 1–(dollar value of items already checked/estimated dollar value of the population)

4 Preventive sampling: the ratio v of the number of areas in which a specified minimum number of items (say, one or two) have *not* been selected in the sample to the total number of areas.

It is not hard to see why, on the average, each of these four variables decreases as the sample size s is increased. In representative sampling, the central limit theorem assures us that on the average, w decreases as s increases. For corrective sampling, the number of unchecked items decreases linearly with sample size while the estimated proportion of items in error may fluctuate but converges (using the central limit theorem again) to the population error rate as the sample size increases. Hence, r will generally decrease as s increases. The ratio u also decreases as s increases since the dollar value of items not included in the sample must decrease, by definition, as the sample size increases. Even if the total dollar value of the population is not known but is estimated from the sample, this estimate will converge to the population value as more samples are taken. For preventive sampling, v must decrease as s is increased since each additional item cannot increase the proportion of areas still unsampled. Because of the finite population in each area, v must decrease eventually even in the most biased sampling plan which initially concentrates on only a small number of areas.

Thus the auditor may set lower cutoff limits for each of his four objectives, say w_c, r_c, u_c, v_c, and continue to sample until each of the four variables – w, r, u and v – falls below its respective cutoff point. For example, in corrective sampling, r_c is the maximum number of error items remaining unchecked in the population that the auditor feels he can tolerate.[3]

A good sampling design is one which is likely to yield a sample in which the four cutoff levels are reached with the smallest possible sample size. We may define the effectiveness of a sampling design to be the ratio of the average number of items *not* in the sample when all four cutoff levels are first reached to the total number of items in the population. Such a measure takes on values between zero and one, with higher values corresponding to greater effectiveness of design.

Note that schemes such as stratified sampling or use of ratio estimates are ways of improving the effectiveness when only representative sampling is considered. Clearly it is possible to develop sampling theories aimed at more effective techniques for corrective, protective, and preventive sampling. To develop such theories, we must assume that an auditor has some prior knowledge about the items in the population before the sampling process begins.

Model incorporating auditor's prior knowledge

The first type of prior knowledge we introduce is the recorded dollar value of each item in the population. As mentioned earlier, the auditor normally has the recorded values of the items from which samples are to be taken. With such a list, it is obvious that the maximum effectiveness for protective sampling is achieved by selecting those items with the highest recorded dollar values. This list may also be helpful in improving the effectiveness of representative sampling since there is usually a high correlation between the recorded dollar value and the verified dollar value so that ratio estimates may be used.

We next assume that an auditor can, on the basis of preliminary screening, classify items as to how likely they are to be in error. It is in this classification that the auditor's prior experience and judgement become fully utilised. Experienced auditors may be distinguished from novices by their greater ability to determine where errors are likely to be found. For example, items which have been newly added or dropped, transactions at the end or beginning of a month or year, or accounts with unusually high or low (possibly negative) balances may be considered as error-prone. In contrast, items which are consistent with the auditor's prior expectations or which are known to have experienced extensive internal checks may be considered to have a low probability of error. With such an error-rate classification, the maximum effectiveness for corrective sampling is achieved by sampling those items which are most likely to be in error. The auditor may, of course, sample items which he judged unlikely to be in error in order to confirm his initial classification.

Finally, for preventive sampling, we assume that the auditor knows the particular control area in the organisation that generated each item in the population. With this knowledge, the maximum effectiveness in preventive sampling is obviously achieved by allocating only the minimum number of items required in each control area until the cutoff level, v_c, is reached. If such knowledge is not available to the auditor, he must then hope that the sample generated by the other three criteria includes items from a large number of different control areas.

A procedure for integrating the four objectives

Assuming that all three types of prior information are available,we wish to choose a sampling design that maximises overall effectiveness, not just effectiveness for a given criterion. We shall briefly state a procedure which will guarantee that the cutoff levels of the four objectives are all satisfied and then proceed to a more rigorous mathematical analysis of the sampling design.

1   First develop a sampling design as if representative sampling were the only objective. The variance, the correlation coefficient, etc., may be estimated from the results of previous audits in order to draw a random sample which meets the specification in the sampling design. Before checking the items included in the sample, however, evaluate them from the viewpoints of other sampling objectives as elaborated in (2) to (4) below.

2   Evaluate the items selected in (1) to see whether enough items have been included from the corrective sampling viewpoint. For this evaluation a prior estimate of error rate for each stratum is necessary. This may be supplied based on the results in previous audits or based on other factors. If there is a deficiency in any stratum, take an additional random sample for the stratum which, together with the ones that were selected in (1), will be sufficient for the given cutoff criterion (assuming that the estimate of the error rate is correct).

3   Evaluate the items selected in (1) and (2) to see whether the proportion of unsampled areas (the areas in which the minimum number of items have not been allocated) exceeds the cutoff level. If not, select an unsampled area in which the largest number of items (but below the minimum level) have been allocated and take additional samples randomly until the minimum level is reached. Repeat the procedure until the cutoff level is reached.

4   Evaluate the items selected in (1), (2) and (3) to determine whether their total dollar value is large enough to meet the cutoff level for protective sampling. If not, select an item not in the sample with the largest dollar value. Repeat the selection until the cutoff level is satisfied.

The procedures described above will insure that the four objectives in the auditor's sampling are satisfied *a priori*. However, when the items

46

selected are examined, the auditor may discover his prior estimates of the factors used in determining the sample size were in error. In such cases, he must recalculate the necessary sample size using revised estimates of these factors.

We started with representative and corrective sampling since the results of a random sampling can be used for other non-statistical purposes, but a non-random sample selected for other purposes cannot be used for making statistical statements. Similarly, the preventive sampling objective should be satisfied before the protective sampling objective, because each item has some contribution to the latter objective but may not have any contribution at all in terms of the former (more restrictive) objective. The random sampling for the preventive sampling described in (3) is for the purpose of creating the maximum degree of uncertainty on the part of the auditees, and not for statistical sampling reasons.

The fact that the criterion variables w, r, u, and v become equal to zero when (at worst) the entire population is sampled insures that the above procedure yields a sample which will satisfy all four objectives no matter what their cutoff level may be.

A mathematical analysis

Let us now proceed to a more rigorous mathematical analysis of the various factors involved in sampling designs.

We initially ignore preventive sampling and assume that the auditor stratifies the population of all items along two dimensions. One dimension is the reported dollar value. Thus if we wish to have three strata in this dimension, each item would be classified as either a high, moderate or low dollar value item. In general, if there are b strata in the dollar value dimension, we let D_j denote the average dollar value of an item in the jth stratum ($j = 1, \dots , b$).

The other dimension for stratification is the estimated error rate. If there are three strata in the error-rate dimension, we assume that the auditor can classify each item as being (1) more likely than the average to be in error, (2) having about an average probability of error, and (3) having a lower than average probability of error. In general, if there are a strata along the estimated error rate dimension, we let p_i denote the average probability that an item in the ith stratum ($i = 1, \dots , a$) is in error.

Each item in the population is therefore classified into a particular cell according to its estimated probability of being in error and its reported

47

dollar value. We introduce the following notation for the development in the remaining sections. Let N be the total number of items in the population and let n_{ij} be the number of items in cell ij (ith error rate stratum, jth dollar value stratum; $i = 1, \ldots, a, j = 1, \ldots, b$). Then,

$$\sum_{i=1}^{a} \sum_{j=1}^{b} n_{ij} = N \; .$$

Define $w_{ij} = n_{ij}/N$ to be the proportion of all items in cell ij. We assume that the stratification along the two dimensions is independent so that an item classified into cell ij_1 has the same probability of being in error as an item in cell ij_2 ($j_2 \neq j_1$) even though the dollar value of the two items is different.

We also assume that there is a fixed number of samples to allocate among the various strata and that the marginal cost of a sample in each stratum is constant. Thus if s is the total number of samples to be allocated, we let x_{ij} be the number of samples allocated to cell ij with

$$\sum_{i=1}^{a} \sum_{j=1}^{b} x_{ij} = s \; .$$

Extensions of the present work would allow for sequential and adaptive sampling as well as varying cost structures in each stratum.

With this structure of the population from which a sample is to be taken, we now review in turn each of the four objectives of the auditor's sampling process.

Representative sampling

The objective in representative sampling is to estimate a parameter of the population with a specified level of confidence and degree of precision. If this estimate indicates a lack of satisfactory internal control, the auditor may then decide to inspect the entire population. Typically, estimates of two parameters of the population are made: the error rate and the true dollar value of items in error (or equivalently, the true dollar value of the entire population).[4] With our stratified model, we have more information than is typically available for estimation or acceptance sampling.[5] If we wish to estimate the overall error rate in the population, it is more efficient (in the sense of minimising the variance of our unbiased estimate) to use our prior estimates of the different error rates when allocating our fixed sample size to each stratum. With a stratified population in which w_i is the proportion of items, S_i is the standard deviation, and $x_i = (\Sigma_j x_{ij})$ is the number of samples allocated in the ith stratum ($i = 1, \ldots, a$), the variance of the overall population parameter estimate will be:

$$\sum_{i=1}^{a} \frac{w_i^2 S_i^2}{x_i} .$$

For our first case, where the estimated error rate in stratum i is p_i, the standard deviation of the estimated error in the ith stratum is $[p_i (1 - p_i)]^{1/2}$. Therefore, the variance of our overall estimate of the error rate is:

$$\sum_{i=1}^{a} \frac{(w_i^2 p_i (1 - p_i))}{x_i} .$$

Since the width of the confidence interval varies directly with the square root of the variance of our estimate, reducing the variance below some specified level is equivalent to reducing the width of the confidence interval. Without any other sampling objectives, it is a simple exercise to choose the x_i's that minimise the above objective subject to the requirement that the total number of samples is equal to s (or alternatively, to choose s so that the variance of our estimate is below some prespecified limit).

Another objective in representative sampling is to estimate the dollar value of items in error.[6] For this objective we need to make a prior estimate of the error variance expected in each dollar value stratum. For cell ij, there will be a large number of items with no errors, The remaining items will have errors of varying amounts about the reported dollar value. For illustration, we will make the following specific assumptions about the error distribution. We assume that the error distribution has a mean of zero. In the case of a symmetrical distribution, this assumption implies that an error is equally likely to be positive or negative. We further assume that the standard deviation of the error distribution is proportional to the average dollar value, D_j, of the cell. Thus if the constant of proportionality, which we will denote by f, is equal to, say, 0·05 and the average dollar value is $1,000, the standard deviation of errors is $50. Thus we might expect errors such as $38·23, $-65·76, and $25·16. For a cell in which the average dollar value is $100, the standard deviation of errors would be $5 and we might expect errors like $6·10, $-3·80, and $4·35.

We now need to compute the standard deviation of the error dollar value for an item chosen at random from cell ij. With probability $(1 - p_i)$ the error will be identically zero, while with probability p_i there will be an error which has an expected value of zero. Therefore, the expected value of an error is zero. To compute the variance of the error, therefore, we

49

need only to find the expected value of the squared value of the error. Again, with probability $(1 - p_i)$, the error will be zero. With probability p_i, an error will occur and the expected value of the squared error equals the variance of the error distribution which is $(fD_j)^2$. Therefore, the variance (or standard deviation squared) of error dollar value in cell $i - j$ is $p_i (fD_j)^2$.

If we allocate x_{ij} samples to cell $i - j$ $(i = 1, ..., a, j = 1, ... , b)$, the variance of our overall estimate will be:

$$\sum_{i=1}^{a} \sum_{j=1}^{b} \frac{w_{ij}^2 p_i (fD_j)^2}{x_{ij}} .$$

Notice that this expression differs from that given for estimating the overall error rate so that allocations to given cells would differ depending upon which objective were deemed more important.

Corrective and protective sampling

Corrective sampling incorporates the auditor's desire to find and correct as many errors as possible during the course of an audit. If x_i $(= \sum_{j=1}^{b} x_{ij})$ samples are allocated to the ith error rate stratum (which has an average error rate of p_i), the expected number of errors that will be found is $\sum_{i=1}^{a} p_i \sum_{j=1}^{b} x_{ij}$. Therefore, the expected number of errors remaining in the population is $\sum_{i=1}^{a} \sum_{j=1}^{b} p_i (n_{ij} - x_{ij}) = r$.

In the absence of other objectives, this expression is minimised by sampling all items in the high error rate categories before moving on to lower error rate categories.

In protective sampling, the auditor wishes to verify as many of the high dollar-valued items as possible. Just as corrective sampling is based only on the estimated error in each cell, protective sampling is based only on the dollar value of items in each cell. With a sample of 100 items out of a population of 10,000 items, the auditor will feel more secure if he has checked 50 per cent of the total dollar value in an account than if he has checked only one per cent (as may occur if only a random sample is taken).

Thus if D_j is the average dollar amount in cell ij for $i = 1, ... , a$ (note that the estimated error rate is not required for this sampling design), and x_{ij} samples are to be taken in cell ij, the auditor will wish to maximise

$$\sum_{i=1}^{a} \sum_{j=1}^{b} x_{ij} D_j$$

or equivalently to minimise

$$\frac{\sum\limits_{i=1}^{a} \sum\limits_{j=1}^{b} D_j (n_{ij} - x_{ij})}{\sum\limits_{i=1}^{a} \sum\limits_{j=1}^{b} n_{ij}D_j} = u \, .$$

In a manner similar to that of corrective sampling, the auditor for whom protective sampling is the sole objective would completely sample the high dollar value categories, before allocating any remaining samples to lower dollar value items.

It is possible to combine the corrective and protective objectives into an additional sampling objective. With such a hybrid objective, the auditor would wish to minimise the expected dollar value of those unsampled items which remain in error in the population. Operating under this criterion, the auditor recognises that the first cell he wishes to sample is the one which jointly has the highest estimated error rate and the highest average dollar value. Some high dollar value items may not be sampled since they have a very low (or zero) probability of error (e.g., extensive internal checks exist for such items). Other items which have a relatively high probability of error may not be sampled because they involve dollar amounts which are insignificant compared to other items.[7]

If x_{ij} samples are allocated to cell ij and there are n_{ij} items in this cell, then $n_{ij} - x_{ij}$ items will remain unchecked. With an average dollar value of D_j and average error rate of p_i in this cell, the expected reported dollar value in error is $(n_{ij} - x_{ij})p_iD_j$. Therefore, under this last criterion, the auditor would minimise $\sum_{i=1}^{a} \sum_{j=1}^{b} (n_{ij} - x_{ij})p_iD_j$. Variations of this criterion are possible which would make use of other assumptions, such as those made for representative sampling, and those concerning the amount of error, given that an error has occurred. However, the above formulation suffices for illustrative purposes.

Preventive sampling

Preventive sampling is used as a control mechanism to reduce the probability that the auditor's pattern of sampling will be predictable. In the previous two sections, various sampling objectives were formulated which might lead the auditor to consistently check the same type of transactions year after year. This strategy can be modified by having the auditor place those transaction types that were not sampled the year before into a high error rate category the following year. Otherwise there will be areas which

BIRMINGHAM UNIVERSITY LIBRARY

are unlikely to be checked, or at most checked very lightly. This may lead to the possibility of fraud in these areas. The object of preventive sampling is to maximise the uncertainty the auditee has about the auditor's pattern, or, equivalently, to minimise the predictability of those areas to be checked in an audit.[8]

For preventive sampling, the two dimensions of error-rate and reported dollar value are no longer the most important. Instead, the auditor will try to achieve a finer classification so that each possible control area in the company has a unique cell. For example, a transaction may be classified by the originating branch office or department, by the level of personnel who processed or authorised the transaction, by the supplier or outside agency at the other end of the transaction, by the month and period within a month of its occurrence, etc.

There are two methods that an auditor may use to investigate frauds that may have arisen in any of a number of different areas. One is to allocate the fixed sample size each year over all areas so that at least a few samples are randomly taken with each area. This increases the probability of detecting fraud in any area in which it may arise. Another technique is to choose a small number of areas (possibly one) at random each year and concentrate a large number of 'preventive' samples in these chosen areas. Under this second plan, the sample size in an area is made large enough so that any fraud that exists will be detected with probability close to one. The method to be preferred depends upon the auditor's judgement as to how deep an investigation needs to be made to uncover fraud. If only a very thorough examination would reveal discrepancies in recorded transactions, sampling lightly in every control area is unlikely to be much of a deterrent. However, if frauds are difficult to hide from even a fairly cursory examination, the knowledge that every area is likely to be examined each year should suffice to inhibit the occurrence of fraud. In practice, a combination of the two approaches might yield the greatest benefits for preventive sampling.

While a mathematical model for preventive sampling can be developed by adjoining a third subscript to our decision variables (i.e., x_{ijk} for the number of samples to be taken in the ith error rate stratum, jth dollar value stratum, and kth control area), we will treat this objective more simply than the prior three objectives. We will assume that a sampling plan is developed that satisfies the other objectives. Then after the sample is taken, the auditor reviews the control areas that have been included in the sample. Those areas which are not adequately represented in the sample area are then singled out and further sampling is done in these areas until the auditor is satisfied that every control area has been adequately covered.

Sampling allocation model

In previous sections, a number of expressions were developed, each of which is minimised for a different objective. Given a large enough sample size, s, any prespecified goal such as the cutoff limits introduced earlier can be satisfied. However, there is still a question of how a total sample size should be allocated to the strata since this will affect the actual size needed to meet each of the goals.

One possibility is to set goals for each of the functions to be minimised (variance of estimates, expected number of uncorrected errors, etc.) and determine the smallest total sample size along with its allocation that simultaneously meets each of these goals. Such a problem can be solved by use of mathematical programming techniques. To illustrate, consider the five functions we developed for minimisation:

(1) $\displaystyle\sum_{i=1}^{a} \frac{w_i^2 p_i (1 - p_i)}{\displaystyle\sum_{j=1}^{b} x_{ij}}$ (variance of error rate estimate)

(2) $\displaystyle\sum_{i=1}^{a} \sum_{j=1}^{b} \frac{w_{ij}^2 p_i (f D_j)^2}{x_{ij}}$ (variance of estimate of dollar value recorded in error)

(3) $\displaystyle\sum_{i=1}^{a} \sum_{j=1}^{b} p_i (n_{ij} - x_{ij})$ (expected number of errors remaining in the population)

(4) $\displaystyle\sum_{i=1}^{a} \sum_{j=1}^{b} D_j (n_{ij} - x_{ij})$ (dollar value remaining unchecked in the population)

(5) $\displaystyle\sum_{i=1}^{a} \sum_{j=1}^{b} p_i D_j (n_{ij} - x_{ij})$ (expected dollar value of unsampled items which remain in error in the population.

Let us set goals g_1, g_2, ..., g_5 which represent maximum allowable limits for each of the five functions. For example, g_1 and g_2 can be determined from w_c, the maximum allowable width of the confidence interval for each estimate at a given level of significance (say, 95 per cent); g_3 is exactly r_c, and g_4 is u_c multiplied by the total dollar value of the population. If a function is not considered important in a particular application, its corresponding goal can be made arbitrarily large so that it will not affect the computations.

Having set these goals, we can state our sample size minimisation and allocation problem as:

Minimise

$$\sum_{i=1}^{a} \sum_{j=1}^{b} x_{ij}$$

subject to

$$\sum_{i=1}^{a} \frac{w_i^2 p_i (1 - p_i)}{\sum_{j=1}^{b} x_{ij}} \leqslant g_1$$

$$\sum_{i=1}^{a} \sum_{j=1}^{b} \frac{w_{ij}^2 p_i (fD_j)^2}{x_{ij}} \leqslant g_2$$

$$\sum_{i=1}^{a} \sum_{j=1}^{b} p_i (n_{ij} - x_{ij}) \leqslant g_3$$

$$\sum_{i=1}^{a} \sum_{j=1}^{b} D_j (n_{ij} - x_{ij}) \leqslant g_4$$

$$\sum_{i=1}^{a} \sum_{j=1}^{b} p_i D_j (n_{ij} - x_{ij}) \leqslant g_5$$

$$x_{ij} \leqslant n_{ij}$$

and

$$x_{ij} \geqslant 0 \quad i = 1, \ldots, a$$
$$j = 1, \ldots, b \ .$$

The last two sets of constraints state the obvious restrictions that we cannot take more samples from a stratum than there are items in the stratum and that we cannot take a negative number of samples. These constraints define a convex set of feasible solutions. Note, however, that the first two constraints are non-linear so that standard linear programming codes cannot be used. However, there are procedures available[9] for minimising linear functions over convex sets even with non-linear constraints so that, in general, the minimisation problem can be solved. Recall from the previous section that even after an optimal allocation has been determined, additional samples may be required for preventive sampling. Also, since the sample size is determined on an *ex ante* basis, if the auditor's prior parameter estimates turn out to be far from the true values, additional samples may be required to meet the stated goals, *ex post*.

A complementary approach for integrating the sampling objectives

54

would be to choose a sample size, s, in advance (as may actually happen because of cost and/or time restrictions) and try to meet each of the goals to the extent possible with this upper limit on the sample size. The technique of goal programming is especially useful here in determining the allocation of samples to the strata. [10]

A goal programming approach to this problem is:
Minimise

$$\sum_{l=1}^{5} (h_l^+ y_l^+ + h_l^- y_l^-)$$

subject to

$$\sum_{i=1}^{a} \frac{w_i^2 p_i (1 - p_i)}{\sum_{j=1}^{b} x_{ij}} - y_1^+ + y_1^- \quad = g_1$$

$$\sum_{i=1}^{a} \sum_{j=1}^{b} \frac{w^2_{ij} p_i (fD_j)^2}{x_{ij}} - y_2^+ + y_2^- \quad = g_2$$

$$\sum_{i=1}^{a} \sum_{j=1}^{b} p_i (n_{ij} - x_{ij}) - y_3^+ + y_3^- \quad = g_3$$

$$\sum_{i=1}^{a} \sum_{j=1}^{b} D_j (n_{ij} - x_{ij}) - y_4^+ + y_4^- \quad = g_4$$

$$\sum_{i=1}^{a} \sum_{j=1}^{b} p_i D_j (n_{ij} - x_{ij}) - y_5^+ + y_5^- \quad = g_5$$

$$\sum_{i=1}^{a} \sum_{j=1}^{b} x_{ij} \leqslant s$$

$$0 \leqslant x_{ij} \leqslant n_{ij} \qquad i = 1, 2, \dots, a$$
$$j = 1, 2, \dots, b$$

$$y_l^+, y_l^- = 0 \qquad l = 1, 2, \dots, 5$$
$$y_l^+, y_l^- \geqslant 0$$

A variety of goal analyses may be made by changing the coefficients h_i^+ and h_i^-, e.g., by incorporating some preemptive priority factors (non-Archimedian numbers) for ordering goals as well as ordinary numbers for weighting of goals. [11] Preventive sampling may be incorporated in the above formulation by assuming that the necessary minimum numbers of items have been allocated to each control area and solving the above problem for additional items to be sampled.

Summary

In this paper, we considered four objectives that we believe an auditor has in mind when he samples a population. We indicated how measures for each of these objectives can be formulated so that a proposed sampling plan can be evaluated in terms of satisfying each of these diverse objectives. A simple procedure for developing a comprehensive plan was described that incorporated an auditor's prior knowledge about both the estimated dollar value of an item and its probability of being in error. In order to achieve a more efficient sampling plan, detailed mathematical models were developed to describe how each sampling objective is affected by sample allocations. With these models, it was shown how nonlinear programming algorithms could be used to minimise total sample size while satisfying prespecified goals for each sampling objective. Alternatively, goal programming was proposed when a fixed total sample size had to be used to satisfy each sampling objective as well as possible.

We hope that the analytical presentation of these multiple sampling objectives will stimulate further discussion and research on this unique statistical requirement for auditing. We have tried to show why traditional statistical methods are not adequate in this application, and we feel that this may explain some of the reluctance of auditors to give up their judgemental sampling approach in favour of the random sampling plan required for representative sampling.

Notes

[1] Reprinted by kind permission from *Journal of Accounting Research* vol. 9, 1971, pp. 73-87.

[2] See [8] for a review and discussion of these applications.

[3] An alternative measure in corrective sampling is the maximum tolerable error rate in the population. In this case, the auditor may compute a cutoff rate based on a cost-benefit analysis. He would then start sampling in an area where the error rate is likely to be high and continue sampling until he estimates that the error rate is low enough so that further checking is not worthwhile. If the error rate is too high, the auditor may decide he is better off by checking the entire population. For future illustration, we assume that the cutoff limit, r_c, defined first, will be used for corrective sampling.

[4] Of course, these parameters are never known exactly unless the entire population is inspected.

⁵ See [3] for a discussion of stratified sampling theory.

⁶ For simplicity we assume that a simple weighted estimate based on a random sample from each stratum is used. Extentions would allow for the use of a ratio estimate in this situation. See [3].

⁷ Of course if there is the possibility of fraud in these low-valued items, so that the actual dollar amount may be significant, these should also be checked. We are here assuming that the reported dollar value will be reasonably close to the true dollar value. Corrective sampling and preventive sampling (see the next section) will be more value in the case of fraud or major errors in low dollar-valued items.

⁸ For evidence on the psychological function of audits, see [2].

⁹ For a review of non-linear programmingtechniques, see [9]. A particular technique for which computer codes already exist is described in [4] and [5].

¹⁰ For a discussion of goal programming and an interpretation of the coefficients that appear in the objective function, see [1] and [6].

¹¹ See [6].

References

1 Charnes, A., and Cooper, W.W., *Mangament Models and Industrial Applications of Linear Programming*, John Wiley and Sons, Inc., New York 1961.

2 Churchill, N.C., and Cooper, W.W., 'Effects of auditing records: individual task accomplishment and organisation objectives'. Chapter IV in W.W. Cooper, H.J. Leavitt, M.W. Shelby II (eds), *New Perspective in Organisational Research*, John Wiley and Sons, Inc., New York 1964.

3 Cochran, W.G., *Sampling Techniques*, 2nd ed., John Wiley and Sons, Inc., New York 1963.

4 Fiacco, A.V., and McCormick, G.P., 'Computational algorithm for the sequential unconstrained minimisation technique for nonlinear programming' *Management Science* vol. 10, no. 2, 1964, pp. 601-17.

5 Fiacco, A.V., and McCormick, G.P., 'The sequential unconstrained minimisation technique for nonlinear programming, a primal-dual method' *Management Science* vol. 10, no. 2, 1964, pp. 360-6.

6 Ijiri, Y., *Management goals and accounting for control* North Holland Publishing Co. and Rand McNally and Co., Amsterdam and Chicago, 1965.

7 Ijiri, Y., and Kaplan, R.S., 'The four roles of sampling in auditing:

representative, corrective, protective and preventive' *Management Accounting* vol. 52, December 1970.

8 Vance, L.L., 'A review of developments in statistical sampling for accountants' *The Accounting Review*, vol. 35, January 1960, pp. 19-28.

9 Zangwill, W., *Nonlinear Programming: A Unified Approach*, Prentice Hall, Inc., Englewood Cliffs, NJ, 1969.

Statistical vs Judgement Sampling: An Empirical Study of Auditing the Accounts Receivable of a Small Retail Store[1]

Introduction

Almost four decades ago, the application of statistical techniques to auditing problems was advocated in accounting literature. Despite the fact that theoretical arguments and debates on statistical sampling, as opposed to judgement sampling, have frequently appeared in professional journals, empirical research on the subject is, indeed, meagre. It is the purpose of this paper to report and discuss the results of an empirical investigation in the alternative sampling techniques (statistical vs judgement) in auditing the accounts receivable of a small industrial-supply-retail store. In so doing, it is organised around four sections: statement of the problem, research design and procedure, discussion of the results and findings, and finally implications for future research on the subject.

Statement of the problem

Applying the concept of statistical sampling was first advocated by Corman [3]. Thereafter, a number of articles have appeared arguing the pros and cons of adopting the techniques in auditing problems. Statistical sampling, it has been stated, aids the auditor in defining the extent of his test through permitting specifications of the audit objectives in terms of precision and degree of risk; minimises personal bias; provides more assurance that the chosen sample is representative of the universe from which it is drawn; and permits drawing scientific conclusions from the sample findings and results. Furthermore, statistical sampling plans not only would allow more accurate planning, budgeting, and control of the actual field work, but also would result in cost reduction in most areas of auditing through smaller samples. Yet, the approach was assaulted on the basis of auditors' lack of training in mathematical statistics, and the fact that judgement must be used anyway in evaluating the internal control systems, precision, and determining the acceptable degrees of risk.

Findings of empirical research

A review of accounting literature reveals three empirical studies on the subject. Brown [2] provided an actual case study of a corporation (designated as 'P') in illustrating the correct application of statistical sampling. The structure of the accounts receivable of the P Corporation was defined as follows:

Number of accounts	Average balance	Total amount
3,782	$ 200·81	$ 759,475·62
809	$1,502·51	$1,215,531·06
4,591	$ 430·19	$1,975,006·68

Both judgement and statistical samples were determined for auditing the accounts receivable of the firm, and the results were reported as follows:

	Non-statistical	Statistical
Total number of items examined	2,273	474
Total number of errors	46	10
Error percentage disclosed	2·02	2·11

Thus, it was concluded that statistical sampling has the double advantage of reducing the sample size and ability to measure the precision and risk of the results. Yet, 'extensive tests of a statistical nature in auditing are needed before arriving at conclusions as to the validity of estimation sampling' (p. 52). Smurthwaite [5] reported a case of an accounting firm which assigned a team to investigate the use of statistical sampling in audit practice. The paper described the steps followed to investigate and apply the technique to the audit of a large client account after 'certain work having already been done in connection with the audits of medium-sized clients'. The author argued that statistical sampling allowed measuring the

60

risk and precision of audit information and more speed in obtaining essential facts on which to base an audit opinion.

Kolb [4] tested the confirmation of the accounts receivable for a consumer finance company. The firm has approximately 19,600 accounts at confirmation date and the total amount of the accounts receivable was approximately $75,000,000·00. A precision level equal to one quarter of 1 per cent was specified in the sample design and 392 accounts were selected for confirmation. It was found that the use of statistical sampling did not have a significant effect on the extent of the overall audit test. While sample sizes and related audit time were increased for certain audit tests, comparable decreases were observed for others. However, by being able to specify the audit objectives in terms of monetary precision, auditors were able to direct their efforts to the areas of greater significance.

Purpose and hypothesis

This study is an empirical comparison of statistical and judgement sampling as applied to a small retail store (referred to as the Peoria firm). For that purpose, the following hypotheses were developed for auditing the accounts receivable of the Peoria firm (to be tested at the 95 per cent confidence level):

(a) There is no significant difference in the sizes of the personal judgement sample and the statistically determined sample chosen for estimating the total accounts receivable.
(b) Given the same precision, there is no significant difference in the estimated total of accounts receivable as ascertained by either a personal judgement or a statistically determined sample.

The choice of a small store was based on the fact that previous research had been concerned with medium and large concerns coupled with the doubts raised concerning the efficiency of statistical sampling in small firms. It has been thought that statistical sampling has better chances of adoption, because of efficiency and reduction in sample size, in medium and large firms. Larger populations usually have more chances for a normal distribution representation which, in turn, might result in more economical sampling plans as compared with judgement sampling. In the Peoria firm, the total number of accounts was less than four hundred, and the balances ranged from CR $500·00 to DR $32,000·00. Thus, the Peoria firm, may be described as a small-sized firm with a wide range of accounts receivable balances.

A significant variation of this research from previous empirical work on

61

the subject is seen in the way the personal judgement sample was obtained. In contrast with previous research in which the judgement sample was made by one auditor, the present study utilised a questionnaire sent to a randomly selected sample of Illinois CPAs. It was felt that such an approach is more appropriate and representative of personal judgement sampling. It also allowed, for the first time, to test the statistical significance of the restulting differences, if any, in sample sizes (statistical vs judgement).

Research design and methodology

The accounts receivable of an actual firm, disguised as the Peoria firm, were utilised in testing the hypotheses. The balances provided were for the fiscal period ending 30 June 1969. At this date, the firm had a total of 373 accounts, sixteen of them had credit balances (instead of debit balances). Both personal judgement and statistical samples were obtained, analysed, and compared with each other. In order to encourage a greater

Table 2.1

Dollar ranges and number of accounts receivable in the Peoria firm

Stratum	Range	Number of accounts
I	$ 0·00 – 9·99	52
II	10·00 – 49·99	104
III	50·00 – 99·99	58
IV	100·00 – 499·99	98
V	500·00 – 999·99	18
VI	1,000·00 – 1,999·99	17
VII	2,000·00 – 4,999·99	7
VIII	5,000·00 – 9,999·99	1
IX	10,000·00 – 32,000·00	2
X	CR 0·00 – 9·99	9
XI	CR 10·00 – 49·99	5
XII	CR 50·00 – 99·99	0
XIII	CR 100·00 – 499·99	2
Total		373

number of responses and to facilitate and minimise the estimation sampling, the balances of the accounts receivable were presented in thirteen frequency ranges as shown in Table 2.1.

Personal judgement sample

The personal judgement sample was obtained through a questionnaire sent to a randomly selected sample of 666 practising CPAs belonging to the Illinois Society. The accountants contacted were selected by a systematic random sample, i.e. random selection of the first name and every Nth name thereafter until the total sample was selected. The size of our sample was based on a feasibility study of time and cost limitations.

The questionnaire, accompanied by a self-addressed envelope, consisted of three parts. The first part was the cover letter which explained the purpose and the significance of the study, and the addressee's role in co-operating to fulfil the goals of our research. The second part consisted of a brief description of the firm, the dollar size and frequency of sales, the complete internal control system, and process of handling credit sales and accounts receivable. It also included information from the auditor's report of the preceding year on the balance, the extent and type of confirmation, and the degree of precision accepted by management and the auditor.

The third part was the questionnaire itself. The auditors were given the ranges of accounts receivable and the number of accounts in each of these ranges. They were asked to indicate the number of accounts to be confirmed, the type of confirmation (positive or negative), how many positive returns they were willing to accept for the audit, and the variation (percentage error or dollar amount) in the total amount of accounts receivable they would accept under the case conditions.

Subjects were also asked to state the method of selecting the number of accounts confirmed; whether personal judgement sample, statistical random sample, or any other method (in which case they were asked to describe the method and basis of selection). The responses which indicated the use of statistical sampling were not used in the study since the purpose of the questionnaire was to determine the size and estimation of a personal judgement sample. A few respondents indicated they would use some form of statistical sample and yet the responses specified the size of their sample by personal judgement. These responses were considered judgement sampling since the sample size was determined by the personal judgement of the respondents.

The average sample sizes were calculated from the usable returns for each of the ranges, and these were considered as the sizes of the average judgement sample. The sample items were selected through the use of a table of random numbers. The random selection of the sample items did not change the nature of the sample to a statistical sample since the sample sizes, the core of the study, were based on personal judgement. The estimated total of accounts receivable in each range was obtained by multiplying the sample mean by the number of elements in the population. The estimated balance of the total accounts receivable was found by adding the estimated total for all ranges, and then it was compared with the actual total balance of accounts receivable in the light of the overall average precision specified by the respondents.

Determining the statistical sample

The stratification of the accounts receivable balances, which is shown previously, was modified for estimating the statistical sample. First, the credit balances were included in the corresponding debit ranges to which they belonged by virtue of absolute value. In other words, stratum X was integrated in stratum I, stratum XI was integrated in Stratum II, etc. These credit balances might have been tested separately, but it was felt that the use of statistical sampling was aimed at reducing the number of items verified, and in the meantime maintaining an equal chance of selection for population elements. Second, stratum VIII and IX were eliminated from the determination of sample sizes and fully tested due to the small number of accounts as well as the high value of balances in these strata. This, in turn, would have required eliminating the two strata and recalculating the sample sizes for the remaining strata. It was also desired that the sampling procedure provide an estimate of the total accounts receivable with an accuracy of ± 1 per cent ($\pm$ \$1,437·10).

The standard deviation for each of the seven strata was estimated by means of a preliminary random sample drawn from the stratum. The sizes of samples were found by applying the Arkin formula (1963) for the optimum sample size allocation, which is given as:

$$ n_i = \frac{N_i S_i \sum\limits_{i=1}^{M} (N_i S_i)}{N^2 (\cdot 51\ SE)^2 + \sum\limits_{i=1}^{M} (N_i S_i^2)} $$

where,

n_i = Number of sample items for each stratum (at a 95 per cent confidence level)

SE = Desired sample precision for an average ($) precision of the estimated total population divided by number of items in the total population

N_i = Total number of items in stratum i

S_i = Standard deviation of the stratum i

M = Number of strata.

Applying the above formula for each stratum resulted in the sample sizes shown in Table 2.2.

By using the random number tables, the samples were selected for all the strata. By multiplying the average balance of the sample by the number of accounts in its range, the estimated value of accounts receivable balance was determined for each stratum. The estimated total for the firm's accounts receivable was found by adding the estimated total for all the strata, and the outcome was compared with the firm's actual total balance to determine the degree of error.

Table 2.2

Size of statistical samples
in auditing the accounts receivable of the Peoria firm

Stratum	n_i	N_i	n_i/N_i (per cent)
I	1	61	1·6
II	5	109	4·6
III	4	58	6·9
IV	46	100	46·0
V	11	18	61·0
VI	17	17	100·0*
VII	7	7	100·0*
VIII	1	1	100·0*
IX	2	2	100·0*

* These strata were tested 100 per cent since the statistical sample was, or would have been, greater than the population size.

Findings of the Study

Out of the 666 questionnaires sent out, 177 CPAs responded representing a 25 per cent return.[2] Of the total received, twelve could not be used; they were either incomplete or explainable by the fact that the respondents were engaged mainly in taxation. Seven other respondents indicated that they would use statistical sampling, and thus their returns were discarded. Therefore, the actual usable returns, for the purpose of judgement sampling, were 158 or 24 per cent of the questionnaires sent out. The results and findings of comparing judgement and estimation sampling are stated in terms of the sample size and estimating the total balance of accounts receivable.

The sample size

The size of the *judgement sample* varied widely among respondents; the minimum was less than 10 per cent and the maximum was a full investigation and testing of the accounts receivable in the Peoria firm. Table 2.3. presents the per cent frequency of the sample size (compared to the population) chosen by the respondents for each stratum of the accounts receivable. It may be observed that as the dollar range increased, the

Table 2.3

A summary of respondents' judgement sample selection
of accounts to be confirmed (total responses = 158)
Number of accounts to be confirmed in per cent frequency ranges

Account receivable range in dollars	Number of accounts	0–10	11–25	26–50	51–75	76–100
0 – 9·99	52	94	27	10	3	24
10·00 – 49·99	104	78	33	16	4	27
50·00 – 99·99	58	71	38	10	6	33
100·00 – 499·99	98	57	26	25	10	40
500·00 – 999·99	18	38	26	15	7	72
1,000·00 – 1,999·99	17	17	12	17	4	108
2,000·00 – 4,999·99	7	3	2	4		149
5,000·00 – 9,999·99	1	1				157
10,000·00 – 32,000·00	2	2				156
CR 0 – 9·99	9	106	9	10		33
CR 10·00 – 49·99	5	70	25	12	6	45
CR100·00 – 499·99	2	43		15		100

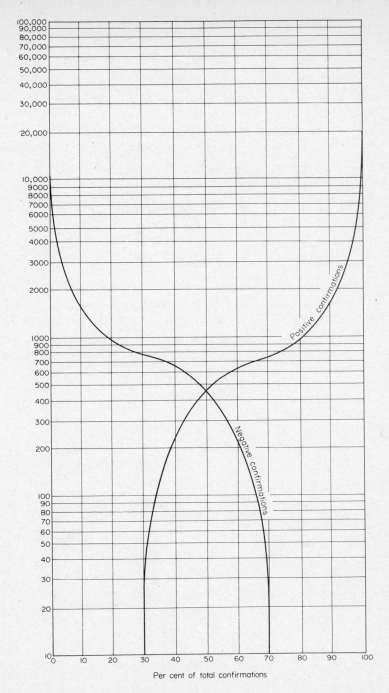

Per cent of total confirmations

Fig. 2.1   Positive and negative confirmations as a percentage of the total

67

accountant's desired sample sizes increased also. In other words, they were less willing to take chances with the account balances which individually formed larger portions of the total balance.

As to the type of confirmation, the questionnaire was broken down into positive and negative choices to conform with the accepted practices of the professional respondents. Figure 2.1 shows both the positive and negative confirmations, chosen by the respondents, and plotted as a percentage of the total confirmation in each range. From the chart, one may note that as the dollar range becomes larger, the CPAs want more assurance of the accounts' balances, and thus higher percentages of positive confirmations are required.

The *statistical sample* was estimated according to the procedure described in the previous section of this paper. Table 2.4 shows the average judgement sample and the estimated statistical sample for each stratum as a percentage of the total number of accounts in each stratum. The tests of the statistical significances of the differences between the judgement sam-

Table 2.4

Testing the statistical significance of the size differences
between judgement and statistical sampling
in confirming the accounts receivable of the Peoria firm
(number of respondents = 158)

Stratum	Per cent average judgement sample	Per cent statistical sample	·05 test of statistical significance
I	24·6	1·6	Significant*
II	30·3	4·6	Significant*
III	32·3	6·9	Significant*
IV	41·0	46·0	Not significant
V	55·6	61·0	Not significant
VI	76·5	100·0	Significant*
VII	100·0	100·0	Not significant
VIII	100·0	100·0	Not significant
IX	100·0	100·0	Not significant
Total	37·8	·25·2	Significant*

* These tests were also significant at the ·01 level.

ples and the statistical samples were made at the 5 per cent significance level. Based on the results the following conclusions are made.

1 The larger sizes of the average judgement samples compared to the statistical samples in the first three strata are found statistically significant at both the ·05 and ·01 level. In other words, there are more than ninety-nine chances in 100 that the average CPA's samples are larger than statistical samples in these strata.

2 Both judgement and statistical samples have been chosen to test the total population in strata VII, VIII, and IX. This was due to the larger size of the balances and the fewer number of accounts in these ranges.

3 The statistical samples were less than the average judgement samples in strata IV, V, and VI. Yet, only stratum VI had a statistically significant difference between the two sample sizes (at both the ·05 and ·01 levels).

4 The average total judgement sample was significantly larger than the total statistical sample chosen to audit the accounts receivable of the Peoria firm. This difference was statistically significant at both the ·05 and ·01 test levels. Thus, there are more than ninety-nine chances in 100 that the total statistical sample is less than the average judgement sample chosen by Illinois CPAs.

From the above results, one may conclude that even in a small firm, such as the Peoria firm, statistical sampling results in smaller sample items compared to the average personal judgement sample as determined by the CPAs. Thus, the first hypothesis of the study is rejected.

Estimating the accounts receivable

The second objective of the research was to test the estimation of accounts receivable balance by judgement and statistical samples. The average variation, specified as ±2·02 per cent, by 121 respondents was adopted and considered acceptable for both judgement and statistical sampling. Thus, the estimation of accounts receivable was allowed to vary between $140,807·40 and $146,613·30. In other words, the choices of all respondents were pooled and presented as a single choice through their average (in each section and in the total).

Table 2.5 shows the estimated total of the accounts receivable for the Peoria firm as determined from the respondents' judgement sample. As it has been stated previously, elements of the judgement samples were randomly drawn from their respective strata, the mean was computed, and the estimated balance for each stratum was found by multiplying the sample's mean by the number of accounts reported in the stratum. From

69

Table 2.5

Total estimated accounts receivable by respondents' judgement samples

Accounts receivable range in dollars	Population size	Judgement sample	Sample mean	Accounts receivable estimated	Accounts receivable actual	Variation
0 — 9·99	52	13	6·04	314·08	287·48	+ 26·60
10·00 — 49·99	104	31	22·16	2,304·64	2,627·58	− 322·94
50·00 — 99·99	58	19	71·18	4,127·28	4,179·52	− 52·24
100·00 — 499·99	98	39	217·97	21,361·06	22,998·75	− 1,637·69
500·00 — 999·99	18	10	688·66	12,395·88	12,354·71	+ 41·17
1,000·00 — 1,999·99	17	13	1,321·24	22,461·08	22,633·22	− 172·14
2,000·00 — 4,999·99	7	7	2,725·55	19,078·88	19,078·88	0
5,000·00 — 9,999·99	1	1	5,213·51	5,213·51	5,213·51	0
10,000·00 — 32,000·00	2	2	27,575·22	55,150·44	55,150·44	0
CR 0 — 9·99	9	2	2·89	26·01	51·10	− 25·09
CR 10·00 — 49·99	5	2	11·67	58·35	71·67	− 13·32
CR100·00 — 499·99	2	2	345·48	690·97	690·97	0
Total	378	141	38,201·57	141,631·52	143,710·35	−2,078·83

Per cent error by judgement = 2,078·83/143,710·35 = 1·44 per cent.

70

Table 2.6

Statistical sampling by stratum. Total estimated accounts receivable

Accounts receivable range in dollars	Stratum size	Average account balance	Estimated accounts receivable	Actual accounts receivable	Variation	Sample size
0 – 9.99	61	3·05	186·05	236·38	– 50·33	1
10·00 – 49·99	109	22·51	2,453·59	2,555·91	– 102·32	5
50·00 – 99·99	58	70·64	4,097·12	4,179·52	– 82·40	4
100·00 – 499·99	100	237·85	23,785·00	22,307·78	+1,477·22	46
500·00 – 999·99	18	716·28	12,893·04	12,354·71	+ 538·33	11
1,000·00 – 1,999·99	17	1,331·37	22,633·22	22,633·22	0	17
2,000·00 – 4,999·99	7	2,725·55	19,078·88	19,078·88	0	7
5,000·00 – 9,999·99	1	5,213·51	5,213·51	5,213·51	0	1
10,000·00 – 32,000·00	2	27,575·22	55,150·44	55,150·44	0	2
Total	373	37,895·98	145,490·85	143,710·35	–1,780·50	94

Per cent error = 1,780·50/143,710·35 = 1·23 per cent.

the table, the estimated total balance of the accounts receivable in the Peoria firm was $141,631·52. The net variation, or estimation error, was figured as $−2,078·83, i.e. 1·44 per cent ($2,078·83/ $143,710·35). The per cent error of estimating the accounts receivable balances by judgement sampling was, therefore, within the 2·02 per cent precision range acceptable by the CPAs.[3]

Table 2.6 shows the estimated total of accounts receivable for the Peoria firm through the use of the statistical sampling plan. After the sample was randomly selected from each stratum, the sample mean was figured, and the estimated balance for the said stratum was determined by multiplying the population size (of the stratum) by the sample's mean. The

Table 2.7

Test of the significance of the differences
between sample means of judgement and statistical samples for five strata*

Stratum	t-value[†]	t·025 (statistical table)[†]
II	− ·42	±2·02
III	·06	±2·08
IV	1·64	±1·98
V	·52	±2·09
VI	− ·09	±2·05

* Strata VII, VIII, and IX were tested 100 per cent in both cases, and thus they are excluded in the t-test. Stratum I was not tested since there was no variance in the statistical sample.

[†]

$$t = \frac{\overline{X}_j - \overline{X}_s}{\sqrt{\dfrac{S_j^2 + S_s^2}{(n_j + n_s - 2)}\left[\dfrac{1}{n_j} + \dfrac{1}{n_s}\right]}}$$

where

$\overline{X}_j$ = Mean of the judgement sample from the stratum
$\overline{X}_s$ = Mean of the statistical sample from the stratum
n_j = Sample size of the stratum judgement sample
n_s = Sample size of the stratum statistical sample
S_j^2 = Variance of the judgement sample from the stratum, and
S_s^2 = Variance of the statistical sample from the stratum.

table shows that the estimated total of accounts receivable balance was $145,490·85, with a per cent estimation error amounting to 1·23 per cent ($1,780·50/$143,710·35). Thus, the statistical sampling estimate of the total accounts receivable was within the 2·02 per cent precision range acceptable in the study. In sum, both judgement and statistical sampling estimated the total accounts receivable balance within the predetermined precision range (2·02 per cent).

To determine if there were significant differences in the sample means of each stratum as ascertained by the two sampling methods, the t-test was applied at the 95 per cent confidence level.

Table 2.7 shows the t-values computed from the different sample means of both judgement and statistical samples, compared with the t-values found in a standard t-table at the required confidence level. As may be seen from the table, the computed t-values are within the ranges specified by the t-table for all strata, and thus, in all strata there is no significant difference between the means of the accounts receivable determined by the statistical and judgement sampling plans.

Summary and conclusions

This research is an empirical comparison of judgement and statistical sampling in the estimation of the accounts receivable balance of an actual small industrial supply firm. The number of accounts receivable of the Peoria firm was less than 400 and the ranges of their balances were wide. The personal judgement sample was obtained through a questionnaire filled and returned by a total of 158 Illinois CPAs, while the statistical samples were computed by means of a statistical formula [1]. The study resulted in the two following conclusions:

1 The size of the statistically determined sample was smaller than the personal judgement samples obtained from Illinois CPAs. Yet, one may not conclude that a statistically determined sample would be less costly for the auditor than the personal judgement sample. In auditing the accounts receivable, statistical sampling might require more set-up work such as numbering the accounts, estimating the variance for each stratum by a preliminary sample, and applying the sampling formulae. It is possible that the increase in set-up work would cost more than the savings realised from decreasing the size of the auditor's sample.

2 Both estimation and judgement samples estimated the total balance of the accounts receivable within the prescribed precision range of 2·02 per cent. It is noteworthy, however, that statistical sampling followed a more

selective strategy than judgement sampling; the size of the statistical sample was significantly smaller in the lower ranges and larger in the upper ones. This selective approach resulted in an overall smaller statistical sample despite the fact that the precision limits were similar for both plans.

In terms of implications for further research, this study is only a first step toward more complete empirical tests and verifications on the subject. Replicating the research not only to different size firms but also to different industries is essential for drawing generalisations on personal vs statistical sampling. Research concerning the cost analysis in relation to sample size and reliability of data should be undertaken. Finally, questionnaires to CPAs and field studies inquiring about statistical sampling, its applicability, difficulties and strength may be useful for complete information on the practical matters concerning the technique.

Notes

[1] Reprinted by kind permission from *The Accounting Review* vol. 46, January 1971, pp. 119-28.
[2] The reader may be informed that the following presentation of findings and statistical tests are based on the responses only. No test of non-responses was made. A 25 percentage return is usually considered normal in mailed questionnaires.
[3] Although the precision specified in the design of the statistical sample was ±1 per cent, this level was changed, after analysing the questionnaire, to ±2·02 per cent in order to conform with the mean precision prescribed by the respondents.

References

1 Arkin, H., *Handbook of Sampling for Auditing and Accounting*, McGraw-Hill, New York 1963.
2 Brown, R.G., 'Statistical sampling tables for auditors' *Journal of Accountancy* vol. 3, 1961, pp. 46-54.
3 Corman, L.A., 'The efficacy tests' *American Accountant*, December 1933, pp. 360-6.
4 Kolb, J.W., 'Statistical sampling in auditing' *Illinois CPA*, Autumn 1967, pp. 24-8.
5 Smurthwaite, J., 'Statistical sampling techniques as an audit tool' *Accountancy* vol. 26, March 1965, pp. 201-9.

Additional references

The importance of sampling in auditing and related areas of accounting is such that a large amount of work has appeared on the subject. The following list is not intended to be exhaustive, but it should enable the reader to place the preceding paper firmly in context, and to pursue other aspects of the topic which might be of interest.

AICPA, 'Relationship of statistical sampling to generally accepted auditing standards (Committee on Statistical Sampling)' *Journal of Accountancy* vol. 118, 1964, p. 56.

AICPA, *An Introduction to Statistical Concepts and Estimation of Dollar Values*, 1968.

AICPA, *Sampling for Attributes*, 1968.

Arkin, H., *Handbook of Sampling for Auditing and Accounting*, McGraw-Hill, 1963.

Birnberg, J.G., 'Bayesian statistics: a review' *Journal of Accounting Research* vol. 2, 1964, pp. 108-16.

Corless, J.C., 'Assessing prior distributions for applying Bayesian statistics in auditing' *The Accounting Review* vol. 47, 1972, pp. 556-66.

Cyert, R.M., and Davidson, H.J., *Statistical Sampling for Accounting Information*, Prentice-Hall, New York 1962.

Dalleck, W.C., 'Inductive accounting – an application of Statistical sampling techniques' *OR Applied Special Report* no. 17, AMA, New York 1965.

Hall, W.D., 'Inventory determination by statistical sample' *Journal of Accountancy (New York)* vol. 123, 1967, pp. 65-71.

Haworth, T.G., 'Statistical sampling: a practical approach' *Accountancy* vol. 80, 1969, pp. 101-9.

Howard, L.R., *Principles of Auditing*, Macdonald and Evans, London 1972.

Kraft, W.H., 'Statistical sampling for auditors: a new look' *Journal of Accountancy* vol. 126, August 1968, pp. 49-56.

McComb, D., 'Valuation of stock in trade by statistical sample' *The Accountant* vol. 159, 1969, pp. 312-17.

McRae, T.W., 'Statistical cost allocation' *Accountancy* vol. 81, 1970, pp. 101-5.

Neter, J., 'The applicability of statistical sampling techniques to the confirmation of accounts receivable' *The Accounting Review* vol. 31, 1956, pp. 82-94.

Ridilla, R.A., 'A simplified statistical technique for use in verifying accounts receivable' *Accounting Review* vol. 34, 1959, pp. 547-54.

Rudell, A.L., 'Applied sampling doubles inventory accuracy, halves costs' *NAA Bulletin*, October 1957.

Sauls, E., 'Nonsampling errors in accounts receivable confirmation' *The Accounting Review* vol. 47, 1972, pp. 109-15.

Sherwood, K.A., 'An auditor's approach to sampling' *The Accountant* vol. 60, 1964, pp. 554-8.

Smith, K.A., 'The relationship of internal control evaluation and audit sample size' *The Accounting Review* vol. 47, 1972, pp. 260-9.

Smurthwaite, J., 'Statistical sampling techniques as an audit tool' *Accountancy* vol. 76, 1965, pp. 201-9.

Sorensen, J.E., 'Bayesian analysis in auditing' *The Accounting Review* vol. 44, 1969, pp. 555-61.

Stephan, F.F., 'Faulty advice about statistical sampling' *The Accounting Review* vol. 35, 1960, pp. 29-32 (see also Ridilla, R.A.)

Stettler, H.F., 'Some observations on statistical sampling in auditing' *Journal of Accountancy* vol. 122, April 1966, pp. 55-60.

Stettler, H.F., *Auditing Principles*, Prentice-Hall, New Jersey 1970.

Tracy, J.A., 'Bayesian statistical methods in auditing' *The Accounting Review* vol. 44, 1969, pp. 90-8.

Vance, L.L., and Neter, J., *Statistical Sampling for Auditors and Accountants*, John Wiley and Sons, New York 1956.

Willingham, J.J., and Carmichael, D.R., *Auditing concepts and Methods*, McGraw-Hill, 1971.

Winkler, R.L., 'The assessment of prior distributions in Bayesian analysis' *Journal of the American Statistical Association* vol. 62, 1967, pp. 777-800.

Corporate Income

The first half of this section is devoted to the extremely difficult task of determining periodic income. It is generally agreed that such a measurement rests on the concept of a change in value, and that value is defined in terms of the NPV of a flow of future receipts. Shank however emphasises that this definition is dependent upon the manner in which one handles the uncertainty involved in evaluating such a flow, and provides a model in which this uncertainty is treated more thoroughly than hitherto.

In the second half of the section the authors investigate, in the case of US corporations, the behaviour over time of conventionally calculated corporate incomes. Although the sample of firms used is small the evidence is sufficient to suggest that successive changes in periodic incomes are independent of each other.

Income Determination Under Uncertainty: An Application of Markov Chains[1]

Introduction

One of the most important and troublesome aspects of periodic income determination in a business enterprise is the underlying uncertainty of business events. All models of periodic income determination represent attempts to assess immediately past accomplishments in an environment in which the measure of that accomplishment is heavily dependent upon inherently uncertain future events. The way such models treat this uncertainty is thus of fundamental importance in evaluating their effectiveness. The purpose of this paper is to illustrate for a test firm an operational earnings determination model based on a more systematic treatment of business uncertainty than that found in the conventional accounting and economic approaches.

Uncertainty in conventional approaches to earnings determination

Accounting and economic approaches to income determination have tended to diverge significantly with respect to their treatment of business uncertainty. In fact, many have argued that this divergence represents the major difference between the two approaches.[2] Both views are based fundamentally on the idea that income is what Bierman and Davidson have called a 'value increment' measure.[3] The two approaches also share a common view of what is meant by 'value' in the context of an ongoing business enterprise. Value in use is defined, conceptually, in terms of the discounted sum of future net receipt streams. Among economists, Irving Fisher [15] and Erik Lindahl [26] are perhaps most closely associated, historically, with this view although it is widely held today.[4] Among accountants, Sprouse and Moonitz have recently espoused the view.[5] An earlier reference is the 1957 statement by the Committee on Concepts and Standards Underlying Corporate Financial Statements of the American

81

Accounting Association which expressed the idea in these terms: 'The value of an asset is the money-equivalent of its service potentials. Conceptually, this is the sum of the future market prices of all streams of service to be derived, discounted by probability and interest factors to their present worth'.[6]

Where the two approaches diverge is in the way they implement this concept of value in models of income determination. Many economic models incorporate directly this discounted cash flow concept of value, measuring periodic income or earnings in terms of change in the value or wealth aggregate of the firm.[7] As Karl Borch has pointed out, calculational schemata based on this approach have tended to treat the uncertainty associated with future flows by assuming it away.[8] Typically, point estimates of future flows are built into the models in a manner which gives little formal regard to the fact that it is stochastic variables and not known constants which are being manipulated.[9] In those cases where the stochastic nature of the future flows is acknowledged, it is usually treated by reducing the individual flows to separate 'certainty equivalents' in terms of some measure of central tendency adjusted by a utility measure.[10] The stochastic interdependence of the flows is thus still ignored.

Accountants, on the other hand, have generally rejected the discounted cash flow concept of value when considering periodic earnings determination models because of its inherently conjectural nature. As Hendriksen has pointed out, such an approach requires knowledge or estimates of future flow amounts, the timing of the flows, and of an appropriate discount rate. None of these elements, he argues, can be verified to the satisfaction of the accountant.[11] The conventional accounting schema for earnings determination instead emphasises the transactions approach based on the matching of revenue and expense flows which are realised during the period. Where valuations of stock quantities such as property or inventory are required in adjusting the stream of transactions to properly reflect the flows assignable to each period, an indirect approach is taken based on acquisition cost or the lower of cost or market. Its emphasis on verifiable evidence causes the accounting model to stress past events and thus to treat business uncertainty by yielding to it.

In summary, although both the economic and accounting approaches to earnings determination have attracted large numbers of adherents, neither of them represents a totally satisfactory treatment of business uncertainty. The economic model, in attempting to reflect as closely as possible the conceptually sound view of value and of earnings as the periodic increment to value, treats the uncertainty associated with the elements of the conceptual view by assuming it away. In emphasising factual information

82

and the verifiability of an earnings measure the accounting model yields to the uncertainty by waiting until results are known before reporting them.

A stochastic approach to earnings determination

Assuming that earnings models which incorporate prospective data in an operational way would be relevant for some business purposes,[12] and that future events are subject to significant variability, it would seem desirable to explore the possibilities of a more formal and systematic treatment of business uncertainty in such models. Considering the widespread efforts of the past ten years to develop more comprehensive ways of handling uncertainty in many varied business decision-making contexts,[13] it is even more appropriate for accountants to consider the relevance of such efforts to our own discipline.

In general, in applying this idea to a business firm, one would evaluate the environment in which it operates and the characteristics of its operating process from the standpoint of determining the nature of the uncertainty which underlies its activities. If this uncertainty is regular and if one could specify the form of the stochastic process of which it is a manifestation, then one might be able to develop an operational income determination model for the firm which incorporates this probabilistic process. It is argued here that such an approach would be superior to the traditional accounting and economic ones for purposes of evaluating firm performance because it would allow systematically for the uncertainty upon which such evaluations rest. It would be preferable to accounting income models because it would openly acknowledge the predictive nature of any income measurement, even accountants' 'realised' income.[14] It would be preferable to traditional economic income models because it would incorporate the necessary predictions in a manner consistent with the actual stochastic character of the business process being monitored. If one interprets 'objectivity' in the Ijiri/Jaedicke[15] sense, such a model could also exhibit this desired property of all accounting measurements.

As noted above, the purpose of this paper is to illustrate such a model.

The test firm: a Markov representation

Because the stochastic process known as a Markov Chain seems to be very well suited to the kind of analysis envisioned here, and because of the desire to demonstrate a successful application of a stochastic earnings model in a pilot study such as this, a test firm was selected on the basis of its anticipated amenability to Markov Chain analysis. Specifically, a small West Virginia Christmas tree nursery comprising about 25,000 trees on twenty acres was chosen for the research. Although it has been observed that conventional accounting methods are of less help in evaluating nursery performance than they are for almost any other segment of American industry,[16] this consideration was not important in the choice of a firm. What was important was a regular form of operating uncertainty which is amenable to systematic analysis, a small enough size to allow comprehensive manipulation of sample variables without excessive complications, and the availability of sufficient information to make possible the necessary measurements and calculations.

As strange as it may seem to the discriminating consumer, the development of a white pine Christmas tree is reckoned by the grower almost exclusively in terms of height. Since shape and thickness can be controlled by pruning, and colour is determined by spray dyes, these characteristics are not even relevant to the pricing mechanism at the wholesale level. Because of their uniformity, they can be ignored in considering the 'production' process. The stage of 'production' or development is simply the height of the tree measured to the nearest foot. When planted, seedlings are about one foot tall and no tree in the test nursery is ever allowed to grow beyond ten feet tall. These sizes thus span the range we must consider in representing the development process. For purposes of this research the process will be characterised in terms of the following discrete stages:

A — tree is 0—1 foot tall
B — tree is 1—2 feet tall
C — tree is 2—3 feet tall
D — tree is 3—4 feet tall
E — tree is 4—5 feet tall
F — tree is 5—6 feet tall
G — tree is 6—7 feet tall
H — tree is 7—8 feet tall
I — tree is 8—9 feet tall
J — tree is 9—10 feet tall

A discrete representation such as this based on height to the nearest foot is considered appropriate because it corresponds to the observed industry pricing mechanism at the retail level. Once a tree has entered the process (has been planted) its growth can be terminated in only one of two ways, through sale or scrap. For nurseries such as the one being used here which sell trees in areal blocks rather than allowing a buyer to cut selectively, the pricing structure is very simple. Trees less than six feet tall are sold for $1·50 and trees over six feet tall are sold for $2·00 unless they are saleable but clearly defective in some manner in which case they revert to the lesser price. These prices are also fairly stable from year to year. A 1965 news release by the West Virginia Rural Development Council, for example, quoted $2·00 as a fair wholesale price at that time as well. Considering these two ways for terminating the growth of a tree, we can add three additional stages to complete our description of the development process:

K — tree is sold for $1·50
L — tree is sold for $2·00
M — tree dies or is destroyed because of blight, disease, or deformity.

Let us assume that there is a number, p_{ij}, which represents the probability that a tree now in stage i will switch to stage j in the next time period.[17] Since the elements, p_{ij}, are probabilities, we must have $0 \leqslant p_{ij} \leqslant 1$, for all i and j. Also, since a tree cannot leave the system, we must have $\Sigma_j p_{ii} = 1$. Let us further assume that switches in any time period depend only on the stage the tree was in during the immediately preceding time period [18] (single stage assumption), and that the transition probabilities do not themselves change over time [19] (stationary assumption). If we define a stochastic process to be any sequence of events which follows probabilistic laws, the development cycle we have just described would be such a process. More precisely, it would be called a finite, absorbing Markov Chain with stationary transition probabilities. It is finite because it has a finite number of stages. It is a Markov process because it has the single-stage property. It is called a chain because the stages are discrete. It is an absorbing process because it contains at least one absorbing stage or state. An absorbing stage is one which can be reached from other stages but which, once reached, can never be left. More precisely, stage i is an absorbing stage just when $p_{ii} = 1$. For the test firm, stages K, L, and M are all absorbing. In considering a Markov Chain such as this, it is customary to array the transition probabilities in matrix form. Based on a random sample of actual observed transitions at the test nursery in 1966, 1967 and 1968, the estimated transition matrix shown as Table 3.1 was constructed. Letting x_{ij} represent the number of observed transitions from state i to state j over a one year period, the estimate of p_{ij}, $\hat{p}_{ij}$, is given by: $\hat{p}_{ij} = x_{ij}/\Sigma_j x_{ij}$.

A transition matrix arranged like this with the absorbing states listed first, followed by the non-absorbing or 'transient' states, is said to be in standard or 'canonical' form. The importance of this arrangement stems from

Table 3.1

Estimated transition matrix

	$1·50	$2·00	Scrap	0–1	1–2	2–3	3–4	4–5	5–6	6–7	7–8	8–9	9–10
$1·50	1	0	0	0	0	0	0	0	0	0	0	0	0
$2·00	0	1	0	0	0	0	0	0	0	0	0	0	0
Scrap	0	0	1	0	0	0	0	0	0	0	0	0	0
0–1	0	0	·156	·098	·746	0	0	0	0	0	0	0	0
1–2	0	0	·099	0	·101	·800	0	0	0	0	0	0	0
2–3	0	0	·045	0	0	·098	·857	0	0	0	0	0	0
3–4	0	0	·010	0	0	0	·102	·888	0	0	0	0	0
4–5	·047	0	·011	0	0	0	0	·103	·839	0	0	0	0
5–6	·151	0	·008	0	0	0	0	0	·092	·749	0	0	0
6–7	0	·138	·021	0	0	0	0	0	0	·095	·746	0	0
7–8	0	·201	·011	0	0	0	0	0	0	0	·097	·691	0
8–9	0	·354	·009	0	0	0	0	0	0	0	0	·101	·536
9–10	0	·929	·022	0	0	0	0	0	0	0	0	0	·049

the fact that it facilitates the analysis of many interesting properties of a Markov process. For future reference, we will denote the sub-sections (partitions) of the canonical matrix in the following customary manner:

$$\begin{bmatrix} I & O \\ \hline R & Q \end{bmatrix}$$

In this notation, since there are three absorbing stages and ten transient ones, I is a 3×3 identity matrix, 0 is a 3×10 zero matrix, R is a matrix of dimension 10×3 and Q is a matrix of dimension 10×10.

Although there have been many applications of Markov models to business problems, [20] the approach has generally been received with only limited enthusiasm. This cautious acceptance is due to two main shortcomings of such models. First, they are based on the single stage and stationary assumptions which have often seemed unrealistic in the context of the intended applications. Second, they have very high and specific data requirements which are often not fulfillable. For the test firm in this study, however, data availability was not a problem and it was thus possible to construct the model in a manner which facilitated statistical testing of the crucial assumptions. The appropriate tests, taken from Anderson and Goodman [3], are parametric in character and are based on the multinomial properties of Markov variables. They make use of specially constructed X^2 statistics which measure the 'goodness-of-fit' between observed transition results and the expected results from a true Markov process. Based on these tests for the sample firm, the null hypothesis of stationary transition probabilities could not be rejected even if a 25 per cent chance of rejecting a true null was considered tolerable. Similarly, the single-stage null hypothesis could not be rejected at even the 20 per cent alpha error level. Based on these results, it was concluded that there is sufficient empirical justification for accepting the Markov model as a fair representation of the uncertainty facing the nursery.

Earnings models: a conceptual view

Before discussing how one might incorporate this Markov representation of the firm into a specific calculational schema for periodic earnings, it is necessary to outline a conceptual framework to shape such efforts. The purpose is not to propose a particular theoretical structure as the only one appropriate for periodic earnings determination. Rather, the intent is only to pick one structure from the set of ones accorded some general theoretical acceptance and then to construct a stochastic earnings model for the test firm which incorporates that structure in a consistent manner. As mentioned earlier, we will focus upon developing a model which would be useful externally in evaluating overall firm performance. The distinction between management performance and firm performance, although important in many contexts, is considered to be beyond the scope of this research. Hicks' classic definition of income will be taken as a guide. Namely, the income of an individual for a period is the maximum value he can consume during the period and still be as well-off at the end of the period as he was at the beginning. [21] Switching to the context of a firm, we will adopt a somewhat proprietary view and substitute the phrase 'distribute to owners' for the word 'consume'. Such a concept clearly requires a criterion of 'well-offness' against which to measure relative change. Although at the most fundamental level the 'well-offness' of an individual refers to the level of his psychic well-being or subjective satisfactions, it is customary to adopt a less abstract and more operational view in the context of a firm. As a surrogate for psychic well-being there is economic well-being which is defined in terms of command over economic goods and services. Hicks noted two alternative interpretations of this view of well-offness: [22]

1   The discounted present value of expected future money receipts.
2   The discounted present value of expected future money receipts adjusted for expected price level changes.

Although other criteria could be proposed,[23] periodic earnings would in all cases be defined in terms of the increment to the particular measure of well-offness from the beginning of the period to the end, adjusted for withdrawals and additional capital contributions. As Carl Nelson has pointed out, no one of such criteria really measures 'true' earnings because different ones might be preferred for different uses of the earnings measure.[24] Ignoring changes in price levels, Hicks' first one represents the concept adopted by Fisher and Lindahl and thus the one incorporated in the theoretical accounting and economic models mentioned in the first section of the paper. Since this research is based upon Fisher's valuation model as a goal and assumes that price levels are constant,[25] concept number one will also be adopted here.

Since, in a world of uncertainty, one's expectation of future receipts as of any point in time will change depending on the time at which the expectation is reckoned, one must also consider the differences between *ex ante* and *ex post* measures in any earnings model based on expectations. More specifically, if one's estimate of a value aggregate at time T measured as of time $T + 1$ is greater than the estimate for time T measured as of time T is the increment part of earnings (change in well-offness) for the period from T to $T + 1$, or it is just a revision of our earlier estimate of wealth at time T? As Alexander has noted, there is no clear-cut answer to this question. [26] In his classic paper on income measurement he discussed one model (mixed economic income) which includes the increment or capital gain in period income and one (variable income) which does not. His advocacy of the latter model was based on the idea that one can obtain a better measure of managerial performance by excluding all unanticipated gains than by including them all when there is no objective way of determining which are the result of management actions and which are windfalls. [27] Since we are concerned here with the broader context of firm performance rather than management performance *per se* we will argue that including such gains is more in keeping with the change in well-offness models where well-offness is taken to be a best present expectation of future realisations,

Alexander argued that the main differences among income concepts centre around three issues: real versus monetary measures, treatment of capital gains, and accrual versus realisation as the criterion for recognition.[28] Although this paper is not intended as a definitive position statement on these issues, any effort to build an earnings model must deal with them in one way or another. Failure to confront the issues explicitly results in an implicit treatment which may not be consistent with the basic framework intended. In summary, the framework for this research involves treating capital gains as earnings of the period in which they are discovered. It assumes a constant price level and thus equates real and monetary measures. Finally, it adopts the accrual approach to earnings recognition by focusing upon changes in expectations rather than past realisations.

As noted above our purpose is only to demonstrate that it is possible to build an earnings model, consistent with an acceptable theoretical structure, which is operational and objective and also systematically incorporates the underlying Markovian operating uncertainty. Varying the elements of what constitutes an 'acceptable' theoretical structure thus would in no way detract from the research. If a different structure were preferred, an alternate model could be developed incorporating it. With these comments in mind, we will now turn to the main purpose of the paper — developing a specific stochastic earnings model for the test firm.

Earlier research: a Markov approach to expected net rewards

One cannot really undertake a serious consideration of the relevance of Markov Chains to the problem of uncertainty in earnings determination without relating the effort to the almost classic work in this area by Ronald Howard in his book, *Dynamic Programming and Markov Processes*.[29] Although Howard's work is more helpful conceptually than operationally as we will show in a moment, it is worth reviewing here because the operational weaknesses in it yield insights into the characteristics required of an acceptable alternative model.

Howard introduces a matrix, G, whose i, jth entry, g_{ij}, represents the 'net reward' to the firm associated with the transition of a unit of product from the ith stage of production to the jth stage. Using this matrix, he suggests an approach based on Markov methods for measuring expected earnings (net rewards) over specified future time spans. Specifically, using generating function techniques applied to a non-absorbing 2×2 transition matrix, he develops a closed form expression for the vector $V(n)$ whose ith element, $v_i(n)$, represents the expected rewards over n periods for a unit now in transient state i. The expression is in terms only of the transition matrix, P, and the net rewards matrix G. By adopting the 'going concern' convention we can consider the asymptotic behaviour of $V(n)$, denoted by

V, to be an expected rewards vector over the whole future life of the firm. [30] Howard's methodology also facilitates calculation of the limiting behaviour of $V(n)$.

If we denote by w_i the number of trees currently in transient state i, we have W as the ten-component row vector representing the size distribution of the tree inventory. Combining this vector with the expected value vector, V, we note that the dot product, $W.V$, represents a stochastic measure of the expected net realisable value of the tree inventory at any point in time. Assuming that the tree inventory is the wealth stock in terms of which well-offness is measured, earnings for a period are defined in terms of realized flows during the period ± the change in $W.V$ from the beginning of the period to the end. Before discussing how we would amend Howard's model for an absorbing chain or how such an approach would be booked, let us consider more fully some of the conceptual problems associated with it.

Although Howard does not discuss the theoretical justification for the 'net rewards' matrix, it appears to be based upon the economic concept of 'value added'. It should be noted that Howard presented this approach as one way of evaluating the results from a given policy or set of decisions. This evaluative scheme is only a small preliminary part of his book, the main thrust of which was the development of a new iterative algorithm for choosing optimal policies. His orientation was internal decision making. Ours is to evaluate results after a policy has been adopted by the firm. The fact that the broad economic or accounting implications of his evaluation model were not discussed at any length is attributable to the fact that they were peripheral to his main interests and not to any weakness in his analysis.

To the extent that the matrix, G, is based on the concept of 'value added', it draws heavily from the literature on factor pricing for its theoretical support. In static micro-economic theory the value to the firm of an incremental unit of an input factor is defined to be the marginal revenue product for the factor less its marginal cost. [31] We will argue that Howard had a similar concept in mind. The value or 'net reward' to the firm of any particular transition is defined in terms of the effect of the transition on expected marginal revenue less the cost of the transition. What is envisioned is an attempt to assign, in a theoretically sound manner, the total profit from any unit (selling price less unit cost) to the various stages through which the unit must pass before the profit is realised. In effect, this is an attempt to measure the net value added by each transition. Considering the nature of the factor pricing literature, the operationality of the net rewards matrix is questionable. Even if one grants

90

the operationality of a concept such as marginal revenue product of a factor of production, there is serious question as to its transferability to transitions instead of factors. Can the unit of product really be viewed as a sum of transitions in the same sense that it is a sum of factor inputs?

Even if the net reward matrix could be made operational, a model such as this contains a conceptual flaw which largely negates its usefulness. It does not consider the time value of future flows. Flows to be realised far in the future are deemed just as significant as those to be realised in the next period. One could easily enough introduce a discounting factor into the model, but there is serious question as to what is accomplished by discounting net rewards which do not correspond directly to cash flows. In what sense can one discount future 'accrued' flows? There is not really a 'time value' of accrued flows. Thus, the problem is not so much that discounting cannot be incorporated into our interpretation of Howard's method of measuring the net value of inventories, but rather that the model's emphasis on accrued flows represents a conceptual flaw with respect to evaluating current wealth aggregates in terms of a time sequence of future flows.

Because of this conceptual weakness, we will not devote any further attention to the development of an operational net rewards or value added matrix. Instead, we will turn to a model emphasising cash flows which is much more operational and is also amenable to discounting.

A Markovian earnings model for the test firm

Specifically, the model we will propose is based on a stochastic view of the long run expected net realisable value of the tree inventory in a framework emphasising cash flow differentials. It makes use of a matrix, C, whose i, jth entry, c_{ij}, represents the out-of-pocket costs (or into-pocket receipts) associated with the transition of a Christmas tree from stage i to stage j. Such cash differentials are directly measurable in principle, even though the matrix entries themselves have to be estimated from past history. We will again restrict our attention to inventories as the wealth stock in terms of which well-offness will be measured for the test firm. Well-offness is thus conceived in terms of future expected sales receipts less the expected costs to be incurred in achieving them. This is clearly not the same thing as the Hicksian concept of an overall wealth stock. However, to the extent that receipts by the firm are the result of inventory transactions, and expenses are directly relatable to the inventory, this restriction should not distort the measurement of period performance in terms of change in the well-offness stock. We will deal more fully with the problem of evaluating this restriction in a later section of the paper.

The cash flow approach lends itself to an expected value measure of future flows which is fully amenable to discounting. Thus, the differential timing of the flows can be formally acknowledged. In one sense, the matrix represents a retreat from Howard's goal of recognising value as it accrues, just as periodic cash flows are not as good an indicator of period performance as accrued flows in the conventional accounting framework. However, we will argue, as has Reed Storey,[32] that over the life of the firm there is no difference between net cash flows and net accrued flows anyway. Distinctions between cash movements and 'accrued value' flows are just a problem in short term allocation. Thus, when dealing with long-term expectations, it is just as theoretically valid to deal with cash differentials as with accrued value.

The model will make a distinction between those costs which are directly relatable to tree transitions, varying according to the development process (variable costs), and those costs which are directly relatable only to the time period of incurrence (non-variable costs). In this context, a cost is variable or not depending on how it relates to tree transitions, rather than on its susceptibility to control over some fixed time horizon which is the more general usage of the term. Avoiding arbitrary allocations, only the variable costs will be considered in developing the C matrix which will

Table 3.2

Cost differential matrix

	0–1	1–2	2–3	3–4	4–5	5–6	6–7	7–8	8–9	9–10	$1·50	$2·00	Scrap
0–1	·045	·045	0	0	0	0	0	0	0	0	0	0	·095
1–2	0	·045	·045	0	0	0	0	0	0	0	0	0	·095
2–3	0	0	·068	·068	0	0	0	0	0	0	0	0	·1175
3–4	0	0	0	·08	·08	0	0	0	0	0	0	0	·13
4–5	0	0	0	0	·088	·088	0	0	0	0	(1·413)	0	·1375
5–6	0	0	0	0	0	·10	·10	0	0	0	(1·40)	0	·15
6–7	0	0	0	0	0	0	·1755	·1755	0	0	0	(1·823)	·2275
7–8	0	0	0	0	0	0	0	·19	·19	0	0	(1·81)	·24
8–9	0	0	0	0	0	0	0	0	·2025	·2025	0	(1·798)	·2525
9–10	0	0	0	0	0	0	0	0	0	·215	0	(1·79)	·265

Note: The costs of $0·115 associated with a tree entering the process (births) are not included in the matrix.

be used in assessing the net realisable value of the tree inventory. Non-variable costs will be expensed as incurred. It is not fair, however, to classify the model as a variable costing one because that term only has meaning in cost-based inventory systems whereas we are emphasising net realisable value. It is true, though, that under this approach future non-variable cash outflows are not considered in the 'well-offness stock'.

Since the labour and material costs associated with the development process can and do vary wthin certain limits, the entries in the C matrix, reproduced as Table 3.2, are based on informally estimated attainable standards for the various operations involved. These standards were developed by the author in conjunction with the owners of the nursery. [33] To eliminate any possible confusion about algebraic signs in the following discussion, we will break the C matrix down into three partitions as follows:

$$[O \mid S \mid G]$$

In this notation, O refers to the cash outflows for transient-to-transient transitions, S refers to net cash receipts for absorptions into revenue states, and G refers to cash outflows for absorptions into the scrap state.

Ignoring discounting for the moment, the model will define the net realisable value of a unit now in transient state i, v_i, by the following recursion relation:

$$v_i = \Sigma_j r_{ij} s_{ij} - r_{i3} g_i + \Sigma_j q_{ij} (v_j - o_{ij}).$$

The elements r_{ij} and q_{ij} refer to the respective partitions of the canonical transition matrix. The first summation, over the revenue absorbing states, represents the contribution to expected value due to sale in the next period. The following term represents the expected cost due to scrapping in the next period. The second summation, over the transient states, represents the contribution to expected value for a unit which switches to another transient state in the next period, allowing for the costs incurred in making that transition. If we denote $\Sigma_j r_{ij} s_{ij}$ by $\bar{s}_i$, $r_{i3} g_i$, by $\bar{g}_i$, and $\Sigma_j q_{ij} o_{ij}$ by $\bar{o}_i$, the recursion relation becomes:

$$v_i = \bar{s}_i - \bar{g}_i + \Sigma_j (q_{ij} v_j) - \bar{o}_i.$$

Letting $h_i = (\bar{s}_i - \bar{g}_i - \bar{o}_i)$ and switching to vector notation, we have:

$$V = H + QV.$$

Solving for V we have:

$$V - QV = H,$$
$$(I - Q) V = H,$$
$$V = (I - Q)^{-1} H.$$

Using more advanced methods, it can be shown that $(I-Q)^{-1}$ does exist and is unique.[34] Using the above approach in measuring the expected net realisable value of individual trees and remembering our earlier definition of the vector W, we observe that the dot product $W.V$ is, again, a measure of the inventory wealth stock at any point in time. Earnings for a period can then still be computed as realised flows during the period ± the change in $W.V$ over the period.

A refinement of the model to reflect discounting

The first problem raised by discounting is that of selecting an appropriate discount rate. Several alternative views have been presented as to what such a rate should represent. In the capital budgeting literature it is generally acknowledged that if future cash flows are reduced to 'certainty equivalents' the appropriate discount rate to use is a 'risk-free' one.[35] Although no known interest paying investment is totally risk free, the rate on a long-term government bond is often suggested as reflecting the least risk of any actual debt instrument. In a recent article in *The Accounting Review*, Snavely also proposed using a risk-free rate. He equated this with the return on a perpetual government bond or consol.[36] Shwayder has proposed using a rate which reflects the firm's 'time preference for cash'.[37] Although he includes himself among the proponents of a riskless rate, his concept really seems to be based on what Keynes called 'liquidity preference' which has no necessary relation to any existing market rate. In the case at hand, since we are not suppressing the uncertainty of future flows, but rather are incorporating it directly into our model, it does not seem appropriate to use a risk-free rate. In their study mentioned earlier, Gibson and Haynes argue that the rate of discount in Fisherian models should reflect the firm's best estimate of its 'cost of capital', although they are vague about what this term encompasses.[38] The problem of measuring the cost of equity capital, either as an average or at the margin, is complex. Further, average cost of capital is not conceptually appealing in the current study because it emphasises the cost of funds supplied rather than the opportunity value of the funds to be released.

A third position suggests that discounting should be at the 'internal rate of return' or what Keynes called the 'marginal efficiency of capital'. [39] Although this approach may be acceptable for purposes of reflecting 'depreciation' on specific long-lived assets, its applicability here is questionable for two reasons. First, there is no evidence that the concept is even operational at the level of a firm as a whole. Second, even if the internal earning rate could be measured for a firm, the result of using it to discount future flows is to reflect a rate of return on investment equal to the average earning rate inherent in the firm's investment purchase decisions. This is not connected with our intent, namely, discounting in order to reflect the time value of future flows.

In summary, none of the usually mentioned alternatives, the risk-free rate, the cost of capital or the internal rate seem to be clearly appropriate. Although any earnings measure based on a Fisherian valuation model certainly involves the choice of a discount rate or rates as well as a calculational schema for treating future flows adjusted by the rate(s), the problem of choosing the rate(s) is beyond the scope of this research. We will use a constant rate of 10 per cent when necessary for purposes of illustration. If the overall approach suggested here gains wider acceptance, the discount rate question would need to be studied further.

Given a discount rate, we must next consider how to incorporate the rate into a discounted measure of the expected net realisable value of the tree inventory. The undiscounted expression for the net realisable value of a tree now in transient state i, v_i, was given by:

$$v_i = h_i + \Sigma_j q_{ij} v_j \,.$$

Table 3.3

The matrix $(I - DQ)^{-1}$

	0–1	1–2	2–3	3–4	4–5	5–6	6–7	7–8	8–9	9–10
0–1	1·098	·820	·654	·562	·500	·417	·311	·231	·160	·081
1–2	0	1·101	·879	·755	·672	·560	·417	·310	·215	·109
2–3	0	0	1·098	·943	·840	·700	·521	·387	·268	·137
3–4	0	0	0	1·103	·982	·818	·609	·453	·313	·160
4–5	0	0	0	0	1·104	·919	·685	·509	·352	·180
5–6	0	0	0	0	0	1·092	·813	·605	·418	·213
6–7	0	0	0	0	0	0	1·094	·813	·563	·287
7–8	0	0	0	0	0	0	0	1·096	·758	·387
8–9	0	0	0	0	0	0	0	0	1·101	·562
9–10	0	0	0	0	0	0	0	0	0	1·047

The flows represented by h_i are all next period flows which do not require discounting. Thus, the only change we must make in the recursion relation to allow for discounting is to acknowledge that the one period hence values, v_j, have a present value of only Dv_j, where D is the discount factor, $1/1 + d$, for a given discount rate, d. Incorporating this change, we have the following present value expression:

$$v_i = h_i + \Sigma_j q_{ij} (Dv_j).$$

Since D is a constant, it can be factored outside the summation to produce the following result:

$$v_i = h_i + D \Sigma_j q_{ij} v_j .$$

Switching to vector notation, we have:

$$V = H + DQV .$$

Solving for V, we have,

$$
\begin{aligned}
V - DQV &= H, \\
(I - DQ) V &= H, \\
V &= (I - DQ)^{-1} H.
\end{aligned}
$$

This result can now be substituted in the dot product $W.V$ to yield a present value measure of the net realisable value of the inventory stock at any point in time. Earnings for a period would still be computed as realised flows ± the change in $W.V$ over the period. The only change is the substitution of a discounted measure of V. Using the data reproduced in Tables 3.3 and 3.4, we can illustrate the earnings model with discounting for the nursery for 1968. Realised flows for the period were receipts of $5,135·50 and costs of $2,901·50. The discounted measures of net realisable value at the beginning and end of the period, $W.V_{67}$ and $W.V_{68}$, were $17,103·38 and $16,861·20, respectively. Based on these figures, we would show earnings of $(5,135·50 − 2,901·50) + (W.V_{68} − W.V_{67}) = $2,234·00 + $(− 242·18) = $1,991·82. Although it is true that this model does make somewhat arbitrary judgements concerning the uncertainty of future costs, future revenues and of an appropriate discount rate, it is argued that the systematic manner in which it incorporates the predominant uncertainty facing the test firm, the uncertainty of the development process itself, establishes it as superior to existing accounting or economic models for purposes of measuring periodic accomplishment of the firm. The anticipated objection that this represents pure speculation which has no place in an accounting statement can be countered by arguing that such statements already incorporate much speculation which is not nearly

96

as well founded upon the specific character of the uncertainty underlying the operating process of the particular firms involved.[40] Before attempting to evaluate the proposed model more fully let us illustrate it in comparison with current practice in the industry.

A comparison between the proposed model and current practice

Table 3.5 summarises earnings calculations for the test firm for 1968 under two models representing current practice and the one from this research. The first column of the table represents a cash-basis computation which is the approach actually used by the test firm.

As we noted earlier, the special problems of nursery accounting have not received much attention in the accounting literature. No mechanism has been developed for treating inventory valuation or cost of goods sold within the conventional cost–based accrual framework. There is no problem on the input side, since all production costs can readily be charged to inventory instead of expense as incurred. When a tree is sold, however, there is no established method for separating the inventoried costs associated with it for purposes of charging costs of goods sold. Further there is no established method for valuing the 'in-process' inventory at any point in time to provide a check on the accuracy of the inventory carrying amount or cost of goods sold. The combination of the lack of attention to

Table 3.4

Test firm data for illustrating the stochastic model

States	$\bar{s}_i$	$\bar{g}_i$	$\bar{o}_i$	h_i	v_i
0–1	\$ 0	\$ ·015	\$ ·038	\$ (·053)	\$ ·148
1–2	0	·009	·041	(·050)	·277
2–3	0	·005	·064	(·069)	·416
3–4	0	·001	·079	(·080)	·574
4–5	·066	·002	·082	(·018)	·744
5–6	·211	·001	·084	·126	·906
6–7	·252	·005	·148	·099	1·035
7–8	·364	·003	·150	·211	1·249
8–9	·636	·002	·129	·505	1·478
9–10	1·658	·006	·011	1·641	1·718

the problems of inventory accounting for a Christmas tree nursery and the fact that the cash basis is accepted by the Internal Revenue Service has resulted in the cash-basis constituting 'generally accepted accounting' in this situation.

The basic problem in developing a cost-based accrual inventory model for a firm such as the test nursery is that most costs cannot be specifically related to any particular tree. Except for the cost of the seedlings themselves, the situation is a classic example of the joint cost dilemma. For purposes of illustration, however, we will speculate that in applying a conventional accrual framework to the nursery, a logical starting point would be informally developed standards such as those reflected in Table 3.2. Using this information we can develop estimated 'in-process' costs for the trees which are consistent with the conventional accrual framework. This hypothetical measure reflects the sum of the costs of the transitions the tree must undergo to arrive at its current height. The fact that the transition path is really a random variable rather than a fixed constant cannot be incorporated in the conventional framework. To reflect absorption costing, we must also set up some convention for charging depreciation to the inventory. For purposes of this illustration, we will assume that each tree on hand at the beginning of the year should carry an equal share of the depreciation expense for the year. To simplify the calculations, we will also assume that the inventory averages about 25,000

Table 3.5

A comparison of earnings calculations

		Cash basis	Conventional accrual basis	Proposed model with discounting
(1)	Revenues	$5,135·50	$ 5,135·50	$ 5,135·50
(2)	Costs and expenses			2,901·50
(3)	Product costs	2,851·50	2,851·50	
(4)	Period costs	50·00	50·00	
Inventory valuation				
(5)	Beginning	–	12,202·67	17,103·38
(6)	Ending	–	12,077·97	16,861·20
Period earnings		$2,234·00[a]	$ 2,109·30[b]	$ 1,991·82[c]

[a] Earnings = (1) − (3) − (4).
[b] Earnings = (1) − [(5) + (3) − (6)] − (4).
[c] Earnings = [(1) − (2)] + [(6) − (5)].

trees. Depreciation expense for each year is about $60. Using this approach, an eight-foot tree will carry a depreciation charge of:

$$8 \text{ yrs} \times 1/25{,}000 \times \$60/\text{yr} = \${\cdot}0192 .$$

Using this information and the variable costs shown in Table 3.2 we can compute 'in-process' costs estimates for use in inventory valuation as shown in Table 3.6. The product cost column is just the sum of variable cost and depreciation.

In this hypothetical conventional accrual model, the cost valuation of the tree inventory at any time, T, is represented by the dot product $W_T.K$. Cost of goods sold can be calculated according to the familiar formula: beginning inventory plus product costs incurred during the period less ending inventory. Since there are no credit sales for the test firm, sales revenue for purposes of this model is the same as cash collections. Net income for 1968 for the nursery under this model is shown in the second column of Table 3.5.

Table 3.6

Estimated in-process product costs

Size category	Variable cost*	Depreciation	Total product cost
0–1	$ ·160	$·002	$ ·162
1–2	·205	·005	·210
2–3	·273	·007	·280
3–4	·353	·010	·363
4–5	·441	·012	·453
5–6	·541	·014	·555
6–7	·717	·017	·734
7–8	·907	·019	·926
8–9	1·110	·022	1·132
9–10	1·325	·024	1·349

* If we denote the variable cost for a tree in size category i by b_i, the the values in this column are determined as follows:

$$b_i = {\cdot}115 + \sum_{j=1}^{i} c_{j,\,j+1} \, ,$$

where ·115 represents the cost of the seedling and the labour to plant it. We will denote by k_i the total product cost for a tree in size category i.

Finally, the model proposed in this paper is shown as column three in the table. Although we will not attempt to make any broad generalisations based only upon the reflected differences among these approaches over the time span of one year, it does seem justifiable to conclude that the stochastic earnings model is preferable to either of the alternatives representing current practice because neither of them allows for changes in the expected net realisable value of the inventory.

Summary

Before attempting to draw any conclusions from the research let us review its major features. We adopted as a theoretical framework the Hicksian concept of periodic income or earnings as being the change in well-offness over the period, arguing that such a view is externally useful as a measure of overall firm performance. Within this framework, we adopted as our goal Irving Fisher's approach to measuring well-offness, although it was orginally intended as a model for situations in which future events are known with certainty. We argue that the goal of earnings determination under conditions of uncertainty should be to reflect as closely as possible the conceptual accounting and economic models developed for situations in which uncertainty is not a factor. We modified Fisher's model in two significant ways. First, we dealt only with the tree inventory as the wealth or well-offness stock for the test firm. Although this is not the same thing as the overall wealth stock for an entity which Fisher envisioned, it does represent a more manageable first step away from the conventional accounting model for purposes of a preliminary study such as this. Also, for the particular test firm involved, the inventory wealth stock is a rather close surrogate for the overall wealth stock. Cash is not allowed to accumulate within the firm, all receipts by the firm are the result of inventory transactions, and nearly all expenditures are directly relatable to the inventory as variable costs. [41] The second modification involves limiting the wealth stock to future flows attributable only to those trees currently standing, not considering as well the flows from anticipated future trees as would a pure Fisherian model. This restriction was adopted, first, because it is deemed to be much more operational and objective. Second, it represents a valuation which reflects both a fair selling price for the tree inventory and a fair purchase price for any prospective buyer, assuming the discount rate used is appropriate. In this sense, the restricted wealth stock reflects market considerations and thus has meaning as a potential exchange value as well as a value in use. Third, this restriction is more in

100

keeping with the author's impression of the limits which the accounting sources quoted in the first section of the paper as favouring a Fisherian conceptual model would place upon such a model, in terms of its relevance to accounting.

Further, in using this Fisherian net realisable value measure of inventories to assess periodic performance, we adopted the view that capital gains are earnings of the period in which they are discovered. We argue that this is the least unreasonable treatment of this troublesome item under the overall change in the well-offness criterion applied to the problem of firm performance in general. Finally, we emphasised the accrual of earnings prior to actual realisation by means of a stochasic expectation model. The goal is to allow formally in the earnings model for the increasing probability of realisation as a unit moves through the Markovian development process.

The proposed stochastic earnings model based on this framework incorporates a stochastic net realisable value measure of the tree inventory in terms of expected future cash flows. This cash flow orientation means that the model is well suited for discounting to allow for the time value of future flows. Although the model does deal deterministically with some of the uncertain elements involved in the earnings computations, it incorporates systematically the uncertainty of development and sale itself which is the predominant uncertainty facing the firm. The model is appealing from three standpoints. First, the stochastic measure of net realisable value upon which it is based approximates very closely, for the test firm at least, to the theoretical goal for inventory valuation proposed by Sprouse and Moonitz. [42] Second, it measures earnings in terms of realised flows ± the change in net realisable value which is also consistent with the goal proposed by Sprouse and Moonitz. Finally, it is fully operational. Floyd Windal has aptly observed that the problem of earnings measurement is to determine the earliest point at which the change in assets or liabilities from a collection of inputs to an expected realisation is sufficiently 'definite' and 'objective' to warrant recognition in the accounts. [43] As mentioned earlier, the model is certainly 'objective' in the Ijiri/Jaedicke sense. It also reflects 'definite' outcomes if one interprets the concept in a formal, probabilistic sense.

Conclusions

Considering the advances of recent years in the area of incorporating business uncertainty into planning and decision-making models, many firms should also be able to incorporate such uncertainty into operational and objective performance evaluation models. Specifically, performance evaluation in terms of periodic earnings could be improved by first developing an appropriate stochastic analysis of the firm's environment and operating process and then formally incorporating this analysis into the earnings model. This was illustrated for the test firm, a Christmas tree nursery. As mentioned earlier, the specification of a different stochastic model or a different theoretical structure might dictate some changes in the earnings model. This would not, however, detract from the overall intent of this research which was only to show that it is possible to construct an operational earnings model for a test firm which allows systematically for the particular form of its operating uncertainty and is consistent with some given theoretical structure.

It is hoped that the stochastic income model developed for the test firm will illustrate the potential superiority of this general approach over existing accounting models to the extent that accountants will consider incorporating in their earnings measurements the particular characteristics of the uncertainty underlying the operations of firms or industries for whom, unlike nurseries perhaps, there is a degree of urgency for improvement in financial reporting. In attempting to translate the complex and multifaceted question of periodic performance evaluation for an ongoing business firm into a one-dimensional measure such as net income, one must consider in one way or another many elements of uncertainty. We are not suggesting that all the elements can be treated simultaneously in a rational manner, but rather that income models which attempt to identify and incorporate systematically the major forms of uncertainty present in a specific situation should have more merit than those which do not.

Colin Cherry has observed that the study of the history of science shows over and over again the cyclic nature of its evolution — ideas and theories coming to a stop because of a lack of technique, and the later reciprocal effect of new techniques upon revival and extension of earlier theory.[44] Accountants long ago decided that such problem areas as measuring the future benefit from research and development or advertising programmes, measuring goodwill or measuring the accretion in value of a stand of timber were beyond their skills and thus should not be reported. It is likely that no one will ever develop verifiable 'correct' answers to these questions in an absolute sense because of the prospective nature of the data upon which such answers must be based. Moonitz has argued persuasively, however, that such information would be appropriate for inclusion in financial statements if it could be measured.[45] This research study has explored the extension of accounting measurement skills with respect to quantifying business uncertainty in order to make possible the inclusion in earnings determination models of this significant and relevant variable, previously considered unmeasurable.

Notes

1 Reprinted by kind permission from *The Accounting Review* vol. 46, 1971, pp. 57–74.
2 See, for example, Solomons [38], Schattke [34] and Storey [42].
3 Bierman and Davidson [7], p. 241.
4 See also, Edwards [14], p. 80, and Alexander [1], p. 159.
5 Sprouse and Moonitz [39], p. 24.
6 1957 AAA Statement [2], p. 4.
7 Although there is no more agreement among economists about what constitutes earnings than there is among accountants, the ideas of Irving Fisher [15] constitute the basis for what will here be called 'economic' earnings. Further, although the terms 'income' and 'earnings' are not synonymous to an economist, accountants tend to use them interchangeably. They will be used interchangeably in this paper.
8 Borch [10], p. 172.
9 A notable example is the work by Alexander [1]. See also Hansen [18], and Bodenhorn [9].
10 See, for example, Grant and Ireson [17], Chapter 13; Bierman and Smidt [8], Chapter 9; Morris [30], pp. 210–13; Robichek and Myers [33], Chapters 2 and 5.
11 Hendriksen [19], p. 201.
12 Since the incorporation of prospective data results in a closer approximation to the stated conceptual goal, movement toward such models should be considered as progress as long as it is operational and objective.
13 See, for example, Schlaifer [35], Borch [10], Spurr and Bonini [40], and Bierman, Bonini, Fouraker and Jaedicke [6].
14 See Sterling [41] for a good description of the kinds of predictions inherent in the measurement of conventional accounting income. Boulding [11] has also stressed this point.
15 See Ijiri and Jaedicke [22]. They define objectivity in terms of dispersion among measures made by accountants using a generally accepted measurement rule rather than in terms of verifiability.
16 See Gibson and Haynes [16], p. 23.
17 More precisely, let D_n represent the stage a tree is in at time n. Then, $p_{ij} = pr(D_n = j/D_n = i)$. This is read, p_{ij} equals the probability that the

process is in stage j at time n, given that it was in stage i at the time $n-1$.

18 More precisely, $pr(D_n = j/D_1 = d_1, D_2 = d_2, ... , D_{n-1} = i) = pr(D_n = j/D_{n-1} = i)$, for all $d_1, d_2, ... , d_{n-2}$. Another way of stating this is to say that the future transitions a tree may undergo are determined, probabilistically, by the stage at which the tree stands now and are not influenced at all by the transitions it went through to arrive at its current position.

19 More precisely, $pr(D_m = j/D_{m-1} = i) = pr(D_n = j/D_{n-1} = i)$ for all m and n.

20 See, for example, Maffei [28], Kuehn [24], Bierman [5], Cyert, Davidson and Thompson [13], and Lee, Cain and Judge [25].

21 Hicks [20], p. 172.

22 Hicks [20], p. 172 and following.

23 See Nelson [31] for four other alternatives.

24 Nelson [31], p. 3.

25 The assumption of constant price levels is based partly on the relative stability of prices in this industry, partly on the fact that this research is focusing upon internal operating uncertainty rather than uncertainties, such as price levels, which are external to the firm, and partly upon analytical convenience.

26 Alexander [1], p. 143.

27 Alexander [1], p. 185.

28 Alexander [1], p. 199.

29 Howard [21], particularly chapter 2.

30 Although an 'indefinite' life span is not really the same thing as an 'infinite' life span, it is argued that using the limiting form of $V(n)$ is more appropriate than selecting any particular fixed time horizon.

31 See, for example, Lloyd [27], Chapter 8.

32 See Storey [42]. For an earlier reference, see Nelson [32].

33 In support of the accuracy of these estimates, at least in the short-run, it can be noted that actual variable costs incurred for 1968 differ by less than 5 per cent from what would have been predicted using the C matrix and the actual inventory level.

34 See, for example, Kemeny and Snell [23], Chapter 4.

35 See, for example, Robichek and Myers [33], or Bierman and Smidt [8].

36 Snavely [37], p. 345.

37 Shwayder [36], p. 306.

38 Gibson and Haynes [16], p. 31.

39 See, for example, Bierman [4].

40 Consider, for example, the valuation of inventories at expected

selling price less expected costs to complete and sell less expected normal profit under the lcm rule. The stochastic nature of these variables is not incorporated in the rule at all.

41 In 1968, out of $2,901·50 expended, variable costs accounted for $2,791·50 or 96 per cent.

42 Sprouse and Moonitz [39], p. 28.

43 Windal [43], p. 257.

44 Cherry [12], p. 40.

45 Moonitz [29].

References

1 Alexander, S., 'Income measurement in a dynamic economy', reprinted in W.T. Baxter and S. Davidson (eds), *Studies in Accounting Theory*, Richard D. Irwin, Inc., 1962.

2 American Accounting Association, *Accounting and Reporting Standards for Corporate Financial Statements and Preceding Statements and Supplements*, School of Commerce, University of Wisconsin, 1957.

3 Anderson, T.W., and Goodman, L.A., 'Statistical inference about Markov chains' *Annals of Mathematical Statistics* vol. 28, 1957, pp. 89–110.

4 Bierman, H., Jr 'Depreciable assets — timing of expense recognition' *The Accounting Review*, October 1961.

5 Bierman, H., Jr 'The bond refunding decision as a Markov process' *Management Science*, August 1966.

6 Bierman, H., Jr, Bonini, C., Fouraker, L., and Jaedicke, R., *Quantitative Analysis for Business Decisions*, Richard D. Irwin, Inc., 1965.

7 Bierman, H., Jr, and Davidson, S., 'The income concept — value increment or earnings predictor' *The Accounting Review*, April 1969.

8 Bierman, H., Jr, and Smidt, S., *The Capital Budgeting Decision*, The Macmillan Co., 1960.

9 Bodenhorn, D., 'A cash flow concept of profit' *The Journal of Finance*, March 1964.

10 Borch, K., *The Economics of Uncertainty*, Princeton University, 1968.

11 Boulding, K., 'Economics and Accounting: the uncongenial twins' in W.T. Baxter and S. Davidson (eds), *Studies in Accounting Theory*, Richard D. Irwin, Inc., 1962.

12 Cherry, C., *On Human Communication*, The MIT Press, 1966.

13 Cyert, R., Davidson, J., and Thompson, G.L., 'Estimation of the allowance for doubtful accounts by Markov chains' *Management Science*, April 1962.

14 Edwards, R.S., 'The nature and measurement of income', reprinted in W.T. Baxter and S. Davidson (eds), *Studies in Accounting Theory*, Richard D. Irwin, Inc., 1965.

15 Fisher, I., *The Nature of Capital and Income*, Macmillan, 1906.

16 Gibson, J.L., and Haynes, W., *Accounting in Small Business*, University of Kentucky Press, 1963.

17 Grant, E., and Ireson, W.G., *Principles of Engineering Economy*, 4th ed., The Ronald Press, 1960.

18 Hansen, P., *The Accounting Concept of Profit*, North-Holland Publishing Co., 1966.

19 Hendriksen, E.S., *Accounting Theory*, Richard D. Irwin, Inc., 1966.

20 Hicks, J.R., *Value and Capital*,Oxford University Press, 1946.

21 Howard, R., *Dynamic Programming and Markov Processes*, John Wiley and Sons, 1960.

22 Ijiri, Y., and Jaedicke, R., 'Reliability and objectivity of accounting measurement' *The Accounting Review*, July 1966.

23 Kemeny, J., and Snell, J.L., *Finite Markov Chains*, D. Van Nostrand, 1960.

24 Kuehn, A.A., 'A model for budget advertising' *Journal of Business*, April 1961.

25 Lee, T.C., Judge, G.G., and Cain, R.L., 'A sampling study of the properties of estimators of transition probabilities' *Management Science*, March 1969.

26 Lindahl, E., 'The concept of income' in *Economic Essays in Honor of Gustav Cassel*, Allen and Unwin, 1963.

27 Lloyd, C., *Microeconomic Analysis*, Richard D. Irwin, Inc., 1957.

28 Maffei, R., 'Brand preferences and simple Markov processes' *Operations Research*, March–April 1960.

29 Moonitz, M., 'Some critical areas in the development of accounting principles' *The Florida CPA*, November 1963.

30 Morris, W.T., *Engineering Economy*, Richard D. Irwin, Inc., 1960.

31 Nelson, C.L., 'Introduction to income measurement', unpublished working paper, Columbia University.

32 Nelson, E.G., 'The relationship between the balance sheet and the profit and loss statement' *The Accounting Review*, April 1942.

33 Robichek, A., and Myers, S.C., *Optimal Financing Decisions* Prentice-Hall Inc., 1965.

34 Schattke, R., 'Expected income – a reporting challenge' *The Accounting Review*, October 1962.

35 Schlaifer, R., *Probability and Statistics for Business Decisions*, McGraw-Hill, 1959.

36 Schwayder, K., 'The capital maintenance rule and the net asset valuation rule' *The Accounting Review*, April 1969.

37 Snavely, H.J., 'Current costs for long-lived assets: a critical view' *The Accounting Review*, April 1969.

38 Solomons, D., 'Economic and accounting concepts of income' *The Accounting Review*, July 1961.

39 Sprouse, R., and Moonitz, M., 'A tentative set of broad accounting principles for business enterprises' *Accounting Research Study no. 3*, AICPA, 1962.

40 Spurr, W., and Bonini, C., *Statistical Analysis for Business Decisions*, Richard D. Irwin, Inc., 1967.

41 Sterling, R., 'The going concern: an examination' *The Accounting Review*, July 1968.

42 Storey, R.K., 'Cash movements and periodic income determination' *The Accounting Review*, July 1960.

43 Windal, F., 'The accounting concept of realisation' *The Accounting Review*, April 1961.

Some Time Series Properties of Accounting Income[1]

Introduction

The time series behaviour of corporate incomes has generated considerable interest. The early work of Little [28] suggests that succesive changes in corporate incomes in the UK are independent. Subsequent empirical work suggests that the same conclusion applies to corporate incomes in the US. This artcle applies different methods from those of previous researchers, but the conclusion is unchanged. We conclude that, in general, measured annual accounting incomes for US corporations follow either a submartingale or some very similar process.[2] Because of small sample problems this conclusion is based on mean and median results; no attempt has been made to determine whether specific firms are systematic outliers.

The conclusion that corporate incomes are submartingales has important implications for forecasters and researchers in accounting and finance. For example, it implies that attempts to smooth corporate incomes in the manner suggested in the accounting and finance literatures are not successful. It also affects the interpretation of the growth and decline of firms.

The smoothing of income

The accounting and finance literatures are replete with the suggestion that accountants smooth the incomes of firms. That is, it is commonly hypothesised that accountants manipulate their income-measuring techniques in order to soften the effect of hard times upon income and, conversely, in order to diminish the extent to which good times are contemporaneously reflected in income.

The hypothesis that accountants do smooth income and the belief that they should smooth income have existed for decades. Hepworth [25], Gordon [21], [22], Gordon et al. [23], Schiff [36], Dopuch and Drake [14], Copeland [10], Copeland and Licastro [11], and Gagnon [20] all investigate income smoothing. To our knowledge, no study has addressed the possible futility of alleged smoothing practices.

As it is presented in the literature, smoothing is an attempt to reduce the variance of income around its expectation.Income is assumed to be generated by a process whose expectation is constant or is a deterministic function of time.[3] For example, Schiff writes [36, p. 66]:

> Some years ago, Boulding referred to the 'homeostasis of the balance sheet — that there is some desired quantity of all the various items in the balance sheet, and that any disturbance of this structure immediately sets in motion forces which restore the 'status quo'. It can be suggested that we now have a 'homeostasis of earnings per share' and that the application of generally accepted accounting principles facilitates the reporting of earnings per share in a constant or rising pattern ....

Gordon writes [22, p. 223]:

> If the variations of the observations around the curve are smaller [when accountants adopt a specific accounting practice], income smoothing has been the consequence ....

Copeland says essentially the same thing [10, p. 102]:

> Income smoothing involves the repetitive selection of accounting measurement or reporting rules in a particular pattern, the effect of which is to report a stream of income with a smaller variation from trend than would otherwise have appeared.

These and other sources imply that the expectation of income is a function of time or is constant. Smoothing implies a return to good times, on average, after bad times, during which income decreases are artificially reduced by smoothing practices. It implies that many increases in income are also temporary, and can therefore be smoothed in order to avoid the impression of permanence.

Apart from ignoring the substantial evidence that the market can decide for itself whether in fact income changes are permanent or temporary,[4] the smoothing of income by the accounting profession would seem to ignore the possibility that good times are not followed, on average, by bad times. A submartingale implies that a firm is stuck with good and bad times (deviations of realised incomes from expectations) when they occur since a submartingale, by definition, is a process in which any one observation becomes the basis for the expectation of the next. Given the uncertainty of the world, there is always a probability distribution around the expectation. But the behaviour of the expectation of a submartingale over time would be such as to make nonsense of the notion of income smoothing.[5]

One could initially be tempted to argue that this is not true, because the evidence of independence of income changes applies only to measured income numbers — which are observed *after* accountants have decided upon which measurement rules to use. This argument does not go far enough, for smoothing of a series generated by a process with an expectation that is constant or a deterministic function of time produces another series of the same form.[6] Since the observed series is not of this form, smoothing of this type does not appear to occur. If accountants try to smooth in the manner which we outline, then they attempt a futile exercise.[7]

Growth and decline

The interpretation of growth and decline (and their extreme counterparts, survival and failure) depends heavily upon the income-generating process. Growth in a martingale mechanism occurs as frequently as decline; and either, once experienced, is permanent, on average. Growth in a process whose expectation is constant over time is nonexistent.[8]

The implications of income variability for the survival of a firm depend upon the process which generates income. A constant-expectation finite-variance process implies the relative insignificance of variability in income. Deviations of income from the expectation are then *once-and-for-all* increments or decrements in the value of the firm. Value changes are relatively small — the value of the firm changes in the order of the size of the deviation in income, given the (known) expectation of the process. If the expectation of income is known and stationary (and it surely would become known), then investors face very little risk. It is difficult to see why individual firms would ever fail; even the possibility of gambler's ruin and its consequential reorganisation costs seem to be avoidable by borrowing when the expectation of income is constant. While borrowing is not without cost, it is then difficult to see the *ex ante* importance of variability to the valuation of the firm, conditional upon a (known) long-run expectation.

In contrast, a process whose expectation is not constant or a deterministic function of time implies the importance of variability. For a martingale (that is, ignoring trend), there is a finite probability, which is a function of the variability of the process, that the expectation of income at some future time will be negative or zero, and that the firm will on

111

average fail. The expectation of *all* future incomes is changed with each observation. Hence, investors face greater risk than under the other type of income process. The value of the firm should change in the order of a normal proportionality factor times the change in income, reflecting the changed expected profitability.

The interpretation of decline and growth processes and of income variability is therefore significantly different when income is generated by a submartingale mechanism.

Given that the nature of the income process has importance both for the successful smoothing of income and for the interpretation of growth in the incomes of firms, what is the prior evidence and what does it imply about the income generating process?

Prior evidence

The original work of Little [28] and the later and larger study of Little and Rayner [29] indicate that successive growth rates in the incomes of British companies are random. Both studies use percentage changes in incomes to measure growth rates and are concerned with the period-to-period stability of those growth rates. As the authors recognise, the use of such period-to-period percentage changes biases the results towards randomness.

Lintner and Glauber [27] also investigate the relationship between growth rates in successive periods. However, the periods are longer, namely five to ten years, and the sample consists of the 309 US corporations on the Compustat industrial tapes with positive dividends in each of the years 1946 to 1965 inclusive. Using log arithmetic data, growth is measured as the slope coefficient in the regressions of various income variables on time over the five ten years periods.[9] Although they find very small cross-sectional correlation between the growth rates of successive periods, Lintner and Glauber are not prepared to accept the hypothesis that the successive growth rates are independent: 'any conclusion to the effect that nothing but a table of random numbers is relevant to growth in the real world itself would be premature and unwise' [27, p. 8].

Brealey [6 and 7] follows Lintner and Glauber in studying the incomes of US corporations. However, he investigates changes in incomes instead of growth rates in incomes. From cross-sectional correlations of changes in incomes for various lags, runs tests and financial analysts' predictions based on past accounting data only, Brealey effectively concludes that incomes follow a martingale [6, p. 13]. In his later book Brealey [7] reviews his own study and that of Lintner and Glauber and does not change his conclusions.

Other evidence comes from less direct analyses. Fama and Babiak [17] note in their dividend study that signs of earnings changes are nearly independent over time. Ball and Brown [2] find that changes in earnings capture the new information which the stock market sees in an income number. Ball and Brown [3] find that the assumption $E(Y_t) = Y_{t-1}$, where Y_t is the income number in year t, leads to less error in measurement of the expectation of Y than using an average of past Ys[10].

This evidence suggests that incomes conform to the specific kinds of non-randomness which are implicitly assumed by using specific tests. In our examination of the incomes of US corporations, we do not impose such restrictive assumptions since it is difficult to hypothesise a specific form of time series behaviour for incomes. While the theory of efficient markets may yield specific hypotheses for the time series behaviour of market prices of securities, there is no such theory for firms' incomes. The theory of the firm is comparative static rather than stochastic, and the properties of accounting measurement rules are not well understood. Consequently, our investigation is essentially a descriptive exercise and it uses a number of different tests.

Since we are concerned with the income generating process *per se*, we do not use the cross-sectional approach of Brealey, Little, and Little and Rayner.

Our analysis is deliberately confined to the expectations of the probability distributions of change, ignoring other distributional features. [11]

Data

Data are from Standard and Poor's *Compustat* file for the twenty years 1947–66. [12] Firms with less than twenty years of data are excluded from the sample because the estimating procedures are sensitive to both few and missing observations. As a consequence, the incomes of fewer than the approximately 900 firms on the S & P file are investigated, the number differing according to the specific definition of net income which is used.

The effect of our sample selection procedure probably is to over-estimate the importance of trends which are imposed upon expectations. Because the S & P file contains only survived firms, because it contains only large firms which are presumably older survivors than average, and because we do not accept firms without early data and are presumably left with even older survivors than the S & P average, we probably have fewer average decreases in income in our sample than have occured over the time period under study. Failed firms represent an obvious bias; age represents another. A proportion of unexpected positive deviations from expectation will appear to constitute an *expectation* of upward trend, since a proportion of offsetting chance negative deviation will have been removed by the selection of only surviving and older firms. [13]

The importance of this upward bias in income relative to genuine expectations of trend (due, say, to reinvestment) cannot be determined within the selected sample of firms. In an extension of this study we consider the effects of these biases by investigating different samples of firms over different time periods. Preliminary results indicate that the effects are minimal.

Four definitions of 'income' in year t, Y_t, are studied. They are:

1   Net income, after income taxes, as defined by Standard and Poor's. [14]
2   Adjusted earnings per share, adjusted for stock splits and dividends.
3   Net income, deflated by total assets, which might reduce reinvestment effects.
4   Net sales, which is chosen because of its possible dominance of the income series, and because it could be less affected by income 'smoothing' practices of accountants.

Test and results

As we suggested above, this study is a descriptive exercise since we do not have theories of the firm or of the measurement of income. Further, due to our limited number of observations for each firm, the results we obtain may be sensitive to violations of the assumptions of each test. Analytical results for most tests are for 'large' samples. [15] We attempt to avoid both issues by subjecting the income data to a number of different tests. Some of their characteristics are noted below; conclusions are based upon their broad tenor. [16]

Average changes. One indication of trend in a series is the number of increases relative to decreases [29, p. 390]. However, the test assumes symmetrically-distributed changes. An alternative test for trend is to investigate changes for the *average* firm; that is, to aggregate incomes over firms and then to look at signs of changes in the aggregate series. The test is sensitive to asymmetry, but the asymmetry possibly has been removed by the averaging process.

114

Table 3.7 shows the time series of average net income and earnings per share (EPS) for 1947—65. The averages are those used in [8]. Average net income is calculated as a single average over 451 Compustat firms. Average EPS is a weighted average over the same firms, the weights being the adjusted number of common shares outstanding at the end of each year for each firm.

Table 3.7

Time series of income averaged over 451 *Compustat* firms

Year	Net income		EPS	
	Levels ($m)	Changes ($m)	Levels ($PS)	Changes ($PS)
1947	11·17		1·207	
1948	14·43	+3·26	1·550	+0·343
1949	13·12	−1·31	1·399	−0·151
1950	17·27	+4·15	1·829	+0·430
1951	15·96	−1·31	1·646	−0·183
1952	15·32	−0·64	1·551	−0·095
1953	16·93	+1·61	1·696	+0·145
1954	18·18	+1·25	1·775	+0·079
1955	23·72	+5·54	2·250	+0·475
1956	24·57	+0·85	2·259	+0·009
1957	24·63	+0·06	2·221	−0·038
1958	21·27	−3·36	1·867	−0·354
1959	25·26	+3·99	2·188	+0·321
1960	25·16	−0·10	2·143	−0·045
1961	25·59	+0·43	2·143	0·000
1962	28·66	+3·07	2·393	+0·250
1963	32·17	+3·51	2·659	+0·266
1964	37·08	+4·91	3·020	+0·361
1965	42·47	+5·39	3·420	+0·400
Increases		13		11
Decreases		5		6

Source: Brown and Ball [8, p. 61]. The 451 firms were those which met the more stringent data requirements of those authors.

An *ex post* upward trend in both series is apparent. Unfortunately, the sample cannot reveal the importance of an *ex post* sample selection bias against decreases in income, relative to an *ex ante* expectation of increase.

Runs tests. A 'weak' test of independence is afforded by comparing the actual and expected numbers of runs in a series. The test is 'weak' because it tests for independence conditional upon known probabilities of increases and decreases in income, which must be estimated from the sample itself. Thus is tends to fit the data too closely to the distribution which is assumed to generate the observations.[17] Furthermore, it tests a specific form of independence: the randomness of the sequential arrangement in signs of deviations within a finite series.

Wald and Wolfowitz [38] calculate the exact distribution of the number of runs, R, under the assumption of independence, and show that:

$$\mu_R = \frac{2N_1 N_2}{N} + 1 ,$$

and

$$\sigma_R^2 = \frac{2N_1 N_2 (2N_1 N_2 - N)}{N^2 (N + 1)} ,$$

Table 3.8

Runs in signs of income changes

	Mean	Decile								
		·1	·2	·3	·4	·5	·6	·7	·8	·9
Net income										
Z value	−0·03	−1·37	−0·94	−0·49	−0·22	−0·12	0·34	0·50	0·74	1·20
EPS										
Z value	−0·04	−1·22	−0·04	−0·61	−0·22	−0·13	0·25	0·39	0·72	1·01

	Net income		EPS	
	Number	per cent	Number	per cent
Firms with more runs than expected under independence	348	48·7	326	48·0
Firms with fewer runs than expected under independence	366	51·3	353	52·0
	714	100·0	679	100·0
Total runs in sample	6522	100·0	6338	99·8
Total expected runs, assuming independence	6524	100·0	6350	100·0

where μ_R and $\sigma^2{}_R$ are the expectation and variance of R respectively, N_1 is the number of cases when $Y_t > Y_a$ (for any Y_a), N_2 is the number of cases when $Y_t < Y_a$, and $N = N_1 + N_2$. Further assuming that both N_1 and N_2 are 'large', the statistic

$$ Z = \frac{R - \mu_R}{\sigma_R} $$

is normally distributed, with limiting distribution normal (0, 1). The normal approximation holds 'closely' for N_1, $N_2 > 10$ ([13], p. 289; [31], pp. 414–16), which requires at least five more observations than our sample possesses. [18]

Results for $Y_a = Y_{t-1}$ (that is, for runs in signs of changes) are reported in Table 3.8. The table gives the deciles of the cross-sectional distribution of Z scores for the 714 firms with net income data and the 679 firms with EPS data. It also gives two comparisons of the observed number of runs in the series with the expected number of runs under the assumption of independence.

The runs tests reveal that, on average, changes in both net income and EPS are essentially independently distributed. The mean Z for both series is extremely close to zero. [19] The actual number of runs is very close to the expected number under the assumption of independence.

Serial correlation. The analytical serial covariance of *changes* in equally-lagged drawings from an independently-distributed process is zero. The expectation of the computed serial correlation coefficient of 'large' samples from an independent process also is zero. With 'large' samples, the computed coefficient is insensitive to non-normality [26]. With 'small' samples, and assuming normality,

$$ \mu_s = -\frac{1}{N-1}, $$

and

$$ \sigma_s^2 = \frac{T-2}{(T-1)^2}, $$

where μ_s and σ_s^2 are the expectation and variance of the computed coefficient S, N is the number of changes in the series, and T is N less the size of the lag ($N - 1$ for successive differences). The distribution of S is approximately normal [20] and hence the statistic

$$ Z = \frac{S - \mu_s}{\sigma_s} $$

is approximately normal (0, 1).

Table 3.9

Distribution of serial correlation coefficients, net income changes
Lag 1

	Mean	Decile								
		·1	·2	·3	·4	·5	·6	·7	·8	·9
Net income										
Coefficient	−0·030	−0·386	−0·286	−0·233	−0·150	−0·075	0·009	0·085	0·213	0·388
Z value	+0·01	−1·45	−1·01	−0·78	−0·41	−0·08	0·29	0·62	1·18	1·94
EPS										
Coefficient	−0·200	−0·453	−0·371	−0·307	−0·247	−0·198	−0·151	−0·090	−0·036	0·057
Z value	−0·42	−1·74	−1·38	−1·10	−0·84	−0·62	−0·42	−0·15	−0·09	0·49

Table 3.10

Distribution of serial correlation coefficients, net income changes
Lags 2–5

	Mean	Decile								
		·1	·2	·3	·4	·5	·6	·7	·8	·9
Net income										
Lag 2	−·040	−·368	−·275	−·197	−·129	−·067	−·002	+·087	+·209	+·315
3	+·006	−·306	−·202	−·131	−·068	+·001	+·053	+·120	+·205	+·321
4	−·007	−·320	−·221	−·128	−·070	−·013	+·050	+·111	+·184	+·313
5	+·055	−·277	−·165	−·085	−·008	+·047	+·118	+·193	+·262	+·403
EPS										
Lag 2	−·076	−·375	−·255	−·182	−·131	−·081	−·030	+·020	+·098	+·208
3	−·061	−·331	−·231	−·163	−·115	−·073	−·027	+·035	+·132	+·259
4	+·023	−·300	−·163	−·150	−·088	−·052	−·009	+·069	+·159	+·319
5	+·010	−·346	−·150	−·140	−·079	−·024	+·031	+·096	+·200	+·318

Estimated coefficients are presented in Table 3.9 for net income and EPS with lag of one (that is, for successive first differences), and in Table 3.10 for lags of two to five. The tables once again give cross-sectional data. Table 3.9 also gives the cross-sectional distribution of the standard normal deviate Z, calculated on the assumption of independence.

The serial correlation coefficients are in agreement with the tenor of the runs tests, indicating that net income changes are essentially independent and that there is only a very low probability of a compensating mechanism for EPS. Most mean and median coefficients are very close to the expectation for an independent normal process. For example, with lag one, $N = 19$ and assuming independence and normality, the expectation of the computed coefficient is -0.056 and its standard deviation is 0.228. The mean coefficient for net income is -0.075, and for EPS it is -0.198. Table 3.10 reveals that the coefficients for lags two and five are even closer to their expectations than those for lag one. The most extreme mean or median coefficient in either table is -0.200. This is not only an extreme observation; it also implies a mere 4 per cent explanatory power for an autoregressive prediction model. [21]

Mean squared successive difference (MSSD). Runs tests give some indication of the source of any non-randomness in a series. An excess of actual over expected runs suggests a compensating mechanism, while a deficit is evidence of either persistence, or of a mixture of processes with alternating parameter values. [22] The serial correlation coefficient has the added advantage of being sensitive to the size of successive differences and not merely their sign. The ratio of the mean squared successive difference to an estimate of the variance possesses some of the characteristics of both of these tests.

   Define

$$\delta^2 = \sum_{t=1}^{N-1} (Y'_{t-1} - Y'_t)^2 / 2 \, (N-1),$$

where Y'_t are successive differences. Then δ^2 is an unbiased estimate of the variance of Y' if Y' is identically and independently distributed with finite variance.

   Define

$$s^2 = \sum_{t=1}^{N} (Y'_t - \overline{Y}')^2 / N,$$

where $\overline{Y}'$ is the average difference. Then s^2 is the usual estimate of the variance under the same assumptions. If the assumptions are violated, then the ratio δ^2 / s^2 measures the strength and sources of the violation. If, for

120

example, a persistent trend exists, then the ratio will be small, or if the series fluctuates highly, then the ratio will be large. Hart and von Neumann show that under the assumption of an identically and independently distributed process with defined variance, and for 'large' N, $\epsilon = \delta^2 / s^2$ has

$$\mu_\epsilon = 1$$

$$\sigma_\epsilon^2 = \frac{N - 2}{N^2 - 1}$$

and is distributed approximately normally. [23] Hence the statistic

$$Z = \frac{1 - \epsilon}{\sigma_\epsilon}$$

is normal (0, 1).

Values for the standardised ϵ value are reported in Table 3.11. Zero would indicate an independent process, while positive and negative values would indicate persistence and fluctuations, respectively. The results are, on the whole, consistent with previous tests. The median estimated ϵ for net income is $+0.22$ standard deviations from its expected value, assuming independence, and is -0.73 standard deviations from its conditional expectation for EPS. Once again, independence of changes in income is suggested.

It is helpful to bear in mind that the computed serial correlation coefficients do not constrain the average change to be zero, and therefore linearly detrend the income series. Further, the MSSD tests are conducted on changes in income, and the runs tests do not constrain the probabilities of increases and decreases to be equal. Hence, each of these three tests is a different test of the independence of deviations from a constant trend mechanism. Taken together with the observed trends in the aggregate time series of Table 3.7, the tests consistently imply that net income and EPS behave, on average, as a submartingale. [24]

Partial adjustment models. We initially distinguished two extreme types of processes: with means which are a deterministic function of time and submartingales. The first type implies the independence of the expectation of income from the *observed* past incomes; in contrast, a submartingale implies total dependence in the sense that the expected value becomes the most immediate past observed income.

Partial adjustment models provide a natural method of determining the extent of dependence of the expectation of income upon past income. Let $\hat{Y}_t$ represent a forecast of income in period t. Then let $\hat{Y}_t$ be a function of

121

Table 3.11

Ratio of MSSD to estimated variance (standardised)*

	Mean	Decile								
		·1	·2	·3	·4	·5	·6	·7	·8	·9
Net income	+0·366	−1·37	−0·86	−0·48	−0·13	0·22	0·63	1·04	1·67	2·36
EPS	−0·584	−1·91	−1·44	−1·15	−0·92	−0·73	−0·45	−0·18	0·26	0·84

* Expressed as standard normal deviates

the prior period's forecast $\hat{Y}_{t-1}$, and the observed income Y_{t-1}.

$$\hat{Y}_t = \alpha Y_{t-1} + (1 - \alpha)\hat{Y}_{t-1}, \quad 0 \leqslant \alpha \leqslant 1.$$

Our objective is to estimate α from the income data. The α which produces, *ex post* and on average, the 'best' forecast of income is deemed to characterise the *ex ante* degree of dependence of the expectation of income upon past observed values. That is, we define:

$$\hat{Y}_t^o = E(Y_t/Y_o, \dots, Y_{t-1})$$

where $\hat{Y}_t^o$ is the optimal forecast of Y_t on average.[25] An α of unity implies a martingale. An α of zero implies a process with a constant expectation. Intermediate values of α provide a linear measurement of the extent to which the time series can be described by a process with a constant expectation.

Two complications immediately arise. First, there is the problem of specifying what a 'best' average forecaster of income would be. We choose mean absolute error as a measure of forecasting accuracy,

$$\sum_t |e_t| = \sum_t |Y_t - \hat{Y}_t|,$$

in order to avoid assumptions concerning the distribution of the errors. However, mean absolute error gives almost identical results to those of mean squared error (unreported).

Second, there is the problem of growth in incomes óver time. The partial-adjustment models described above do not perform well under the upward trend of the past twenty years. For example, a process with an expectation which is a strong positive function of time would be best fitted by the model which gives the most weight to the most recent observation: by a martingale. In order to accommodate trends, and therefore to avoid biasing the estimate of α upward, the range of smoothing models is generalised beyond the simple partial-adjustment models which assume that variables are unrelated to time. As well as these 'constant' models we investigate models which allow for linear and quadratic dependence on time. [26] Detailed proofs and some explanation of the models are given by Muth [32] and Brown [9].

Values of α ranging between zero and one and with increments of 0·05 are used in making forecasts of Y_t. These twenty-one values of α, combined with the three levels employed, give sixty-three forecasting models which are tested. Thus, sixty-three forecasts of income are generated for each firm and each year. For α equal to zero or unity, the three broad models degenerate into a process with a constant mean and a martingale, respectively, for both of which time is not an argument. Thus, we are left with fifty-nine sub-models overall, although there are twenty-one sub-models within each broad class.

Results from partial adjustment models – actual data

Forecasts in a given year are based upon actual observations in the series up to the previous year. The 1948 forecast is the actual value for 1947, since that is the only prior observation available. [27] Forecasts for subsequent years employ progressively more observations.

For each firm and each variable, the sub-models are then ranked on their total absolute errors over the nineteen forecasts. Two sets of rankings are computed for each firm: an overall ranking of the fifty sub-models and individual rankings of the twenty-one sub-models within each of the three broad classes of models. The ranks of each sub-model are then summed over all firms, giving two sets of sums of ranks for each of the four income variables. The final procedure is to rank these sums, giving ranks of one through fifty-nine overall and one through twenty-one for each class of models.

The sub-model which ranks first on the basis of overall rankings is shown in Table 3.12. Except for sales, the generating process which best fits the data is close to a martingale. A martingale is indicated for net income, and a slight degree of serial dependence in changes in EPS and deflated net income is indicated. The most recent observation in the time series appears if we take the results at face value and concentrate on expected values, to contain 100 per cent, 95 per cent, and 90 per cent of all the predictive information in the series, for net income, EPS and deflated net

Table 3.12

Sub-models ranked first for each variable
on the basis of minimum sum of overall ranks over N firms
Ranks for each firm are based on mean absolute errors

Variable	Model	α	Firms
Net income	Constant	1·00	714
Earnings per share	Constant	0·95	679
Deflated net income	Constant	0·90	669
Sales	Linear	0·55	690

income respectively. [28] The fact that models which incorporate growth are not selected, except for sales, probably reflects a misspecification of the growth process. Evidence is presented below that this interpretation is reasonable. These results are consistent with those for the average series (Table 3.7).

The rankings of the models change slightly when computed within each group. Ranking models one through fifty-nine attaches a greater penalty to large forecast errors than does within-class ranking of one through twenty-one.

Table 3.13

Sub-models ranked first in each class for each variable
on the basis of minimum sum of ranks within each class
Ranks for each firm are based on mean absolute error

Variable	αs			Firms
	Constant	Linear	Quadratic	
Net income	0·95	1·00	1·00	714
Earnings per share	0·95	1·00	1·00	679
Deflated net income	0·85	1·00	1·00	669
Sales	1·00	0·60	0·35	690

Table 3.13 presents the rankings on a within-group basis. Again, the extreme relative importance of the most recent observation is indicated, except for sales. The best 'linear' and 'quadratic' models for each of the income variables all have αs of unity, and therefore collapse into the martingale model. The best constant model for sales is a martingale, but middle-sized αs outperform the martingale in both the linear and quadratic models, as well as overall. Since a linear model with $\alpha = 0.6$ gives a weight of 1·2 to Y_{t-1}, sales might be similar to a submartingale (with a trend). We present more evidence on this point later.

The partial-adjustment models confirm that net income is, on average, a martingale or a similar process. However, since the analytical properties of partial adjustment models are not well known, we cannot place full reliance upon them. Further, the availability of relatively few observations for the forecasts of early years biases the findings against low αs. The importance of such a bias is difficult to treat analytically. We therefore adopt further tests in the following section.

Results from partial adjustment models – simulated data

Data are simulated for twenty observations and four different generating processes:

(a)   a constant process, with stationary expectation and error term distributed normally;

(b)   a linear process, with linearly increasing expectation and error term distributed normally;

(c)   a specific type of martingale, namely a random walk process with error distributed normally; and

(d)   a specific type of submartingale, namely a random walk with normally-distributed error, and with a linear trend through time. [29]

Table 3.14

Sub-models ranked first for each simulated process
on the basis of minimum sum of overall ranks for N simulated firms
Ranks for each firm are based on mean absolute error

Simulated process	Model	α	N
Constant with noise	Constant	·20	200
Linear with noise	Linear	·20	200
Martingale	Constant	·90	714
Submartingale with trend	Constant	·95	200

Table 3.15

Sub-models ranked first in each class for each simulated process
on the basis of minimum sum of ranks within each class
Ranks for each firm are based on mean absolute error

Simulated process	αs			N
	Constant	Linear	Quadratic	
Constant with noise	·20	·10	·05	200
Linear with noise	·55	·20	·15	200
Martingale	·90	1·00	1·00	714
Submartingale with trend	·95	1·00	1·00	200

Tables 3.14 and 3.15 contain the rankings of the models, with simulated firms ranked overall and within groups respectively. The partial adjustment models discriminate submartingales from other processes even with only twenty observations available. There is some bias against low αs, as expected, since α is estimated at 0·20 for a simulated stable and constant process (that is, with $\alpha = 0$). Whether this constitutes an effective bias in favour of the αs close to unity is another question. The high α of 0·55 which the constant model gives to the process whose expectation is a deterministic function of time shows that more recent observations capture trend information. This is removed by the linear and quadratic models.

While these results establish the discriminating power of the techniques, they give no appealing measure of that power, and they do not assist in solving the equation of unconsidered forms of generating functions. [30] Thus, we compare the rankings given the various models under the four actual income series and the four simulated series. Table 3.16 quantifies the

Table 3.16

Rank order correlation coefficients
between the rankings of the four variables and the rankings
of four simulated processes based on minimum sum of overall ranks

Variable or process	Actual variables				Simulated processes			
	NI	EPS	DI	S	C	L	M	ST
Net income	1·0000							
Earnings per share	·9210	1·0000						
Deflated net income	·9015	·9952	1·0000					
Sales	·7528	·4798	·4327	1·0000				
Constant with noise	−·0270	·2405	·2974	−·5342	1·0000			
Linear with noise	·5467	·7181	·7406	·0751	·6135	1·0000		
Martingale	·9742	*·9788*	·9671	·6232	·0932	·6325	1·0000	
Submartingale with trend	*·9950*	·9272	·9063	*·7436*	−·0586	·5389	·9802	1·0000

Note: The italicised numbers represent the highest correlation between the ranks of the particular variable and the simulated processes.

The hypothesis that there is no relationship between the rankings of two variables cannot be rejected if $|r| \geqslant 0.22$ at the 95 per cent level, and if $|r| \geqslant 0.302$ at the 99 per cent level.

comparisons by reporting the computed matrix of rank order correlation coefficients between the rankings of the models when fitted to first the actual and then the simulated series. Rankings are computed overall (one through fifty-nine).

We draw the following conclusions from the table:

1 Deflated net income and EPS behave very similarly to the simulated martingale series, and the correspondence between the rankings for net income and the simulated submartingale with a linear trend is amazingly close. The deflated and undeflated income variables do not look like processes with means which are deterministic functions of time.

2 Sales correspond most closely to a submartingale with a trend, as we earlier speculated. However, the association is not as strong as that for the other variables. One interpretation of the 'low' rank order correlation of 0·74 between the rankings given to the sales series and the simulated submartingale with a trend is that partial-adjustment models do not perform well for such series. Table 3.16 presents some evidence in this regard: the trend in a simulated submartingale with a trend is not identified by the partial-adjustment models.

3 The actual net income data give similar rankings to both a martingale and a submartingale with a trend. This is most likely due to the higher growth rate in net income and the consequential selection of high α models which we referred to earlier.

4 The partial-adjustment class of forecasting models differentiates processes with expectations which are constant or deterministic functions of time from submartingale processes. Hence the simulation results add credence to our earlier conclusions. Their discriminatory power is greatest in nontrend situations, as evidenced by the rank order correlations of 0·09 and −0·06 between the rankings given to simulated submartingale processes and the simulated stationary constant mean process.

In general, the simulations support the previous section. In that section it was concluded that net income is best described by a martingale. However, that section did not fit submartingales with trends to the net income time series and the simulation data suggests that those processes may also be good descriptions of net income. Consequently, our conclusion from both sections is that income can be characterised on average as a submartingale or some similar process. The term submartingale includes the martingale process.

Summary of results

The evidence of independence in detrended income changes is compelling. Results from a variety of testing procedures lead us to the conclusion that measured accounting income is a submartingale or some very similar process. We do not investigate income which is calculated in ways which differ from conventional accounting practice. Further, our conclusions are necessarily based upon mean and median results (because of small-sample problems) and do not investigate whether specific firms are systematic outliers. Subsequent research addresses the latter issues. [31]

The conclusion that measured income is a submartingale is consistent with the earlier research reported at the beginning of this paper. This conclusion has important implications, some of which are spelled out above.

Notes

[1] Reprinted by kind permission from *The Journal of Finance* vol. 27, 1972, pp. 663–81. The authors are indebted to Philip Brown, Eugene Fama, Nicholas Gonedes, Merton Miller, Robert Officer and a referee for their assistance. An earlier version of this paper was delivered at the Workshop in Accounting Research and the Workshop in Finance at the University of Chicago on 23 April 1968.

[2] Let Y_1, Y_2 ... be random variables with expectations. Then the sequence $\{Y_t\}$ is a submartingale if

$$E\,(Y_{t+1}/Y_o, \dots, Y_t) \geqslant Y_t \quad \text{for all } t \,,$$

where E is an expectation operator.

The martingale is a specific case of a submartingale.
The sequence $\{Y_t\}$ is a martingale if

$$E\,(Y_{t+1}/Y_o, \dots, Y_t) = Y_t \quad \text{for all } t \,.$$

[3] If Y_1, Y_2 ... are random variables with expectations, the assumption is

$$E\,(Y_{t+1}/Y_o, \dots, Y_t) = \Psi \quad \text{for all } t \,,$$

where Ψ is a constant or

$$E\,(Y_{t+1}/Y_o, \dots, Y_t) = f\,(t + 1)$$

where $f(t + 1)$ is some function of $t + 1$, and which incorporates trends in expectations in an analogous fashion to a submartingale.

[4] See the theory and evidence summarised by Fama [16]. Some specific studies of market ingenuity in reacting to information, such as income, are [2] and [18].

[5] Attempting to smooth an underlying submartingale mechanism would *increase* the variance of future income changes, simply by making the probability distribution of changes asymmetric.

[6] The variance of income changes and higher moments are reduced, but the covariance of successive changes is reduced in the same order. Hence, the correlation coefficient for successive changes is roughly the same for the observed and unsmoothed series. We observe essentially zero serial correlation.

[7] Of course, other types of smoothing can be investigated. In a paper which provides valuable insights in other ways, Beaver [4] adopts a different definition of 'smoothing'. He hypothesises a non-manipulative type of smoothing, different from that which exists in the literature, and demonstrates its consistency with our results.

[8] Either process, when superimposed with a trend, produces growth. A submartingale therefore can exhibit either or both of two kinds of growth: on average, due to the expectation of trend; and by chance, in spite of the zero expectation of non-trend change.

[9] The income variables used by Lintner and Glauber are sales, operating income, earnings before interest and taxes, aggregate dollar earnings, earnings per share and dividends per share.

[10] Specifically, a covariance between Y and another series is measured with less error in first differences (which assumes $E(Y_t) = Y_{t-1}$) than in levels (which averages Y over the whole time series).

[11] For example we do not test directly whether incomes arise from a single constant process. The more general form $g(Y_{t+1}/Y_0, \dots, Y_t)$, where g is the distribution function for Y_{t+1}, is not considered.

[12] Tape used is dated 7 July 1967.

[13] Any competitive situation with selection of succeeding entities faces this same *ex post* sample selection bias, unless records are available of failures after they drop out. The construction of an unbiased sample of firms is thus a delicate procedure. We do not use log transformations in this paper because we do not wish to eliminate zero and negative incomes.

[14] S & P exclude 'extraordinary items' which are shown in company reports net of tax. Where gross figures are available, extraordinary items are included. Using *Moody's Industrial Manual* as a reference, it would appear that S & P thereby include most extraordinary items.

[15] Kendall and Stuart [26].

[16] Bennett and Franklin [5, p. 688] also suggest this procedure.

[17] Roberts [35], Chapter 5, p. 24. Partly for this reason, the distribution of runs by length of run is not considered. Another reason for the omission is the sensitivity of this test to discontinuities in a series.

[18] An adjustment for the normal approximation to the binomial distribution [37, p. 280] is omitted because we are describing the data, not testing a specific hypothesis.

[19] The median z is sensitive to the fact that R is an integer. However, it should also be noted that there will be cross-sectional correlation in firms' incomes.

[20] Anderson [1, p. 7] and Malinvaud [30, pp. 292–4].

[21] The analytical serial correlation coefficient for first differences in a stable stationary process is -0.5. The computed coefficients clearly are of a lesser magnitude.

[22] See Roberts [35, pp. 5–13].

[23] Hart and von Neumann [24, p. 211]. Note the close similarity with the familiar tests for autocorrelation in regression analysis, where Y' is constrained to equal zero.

[24] Some of the tests assume normal distributions, in which case the implication would be a random walk with an upward trend, i.e. a submartingale with a normal distribution. The term submartingale includes random walks and martingales (see note 1).

[25] The identity is also conditional upon the class of forecasting models used to calculate the various $\hat{Y}_t$.

[26] There are reasons for confining the analysis to the three broad classes of constant, linear, and quadratic models: we doubt whether, given the available data, one could differentiate between a large number of models; and the estimation procedures make it desirable to limit the study from a computational point of view.

[27] As discussed below, this 'starting problem' biases our estimate of α. This is met in two ways. First, the simulations reported below assess this bias to be minimal. Second, in an unreported analysis, the forecasting models rank in essentially the same order over only the last fifteen observations, giving the low α models time to 'settle down'.

[28] Since the best sales forecast model under this criterion falls with the linear class, there is no similarly natural interpretation for the sales variable. Note, however, that the absolute weight given by the linear model to the most recent observation is *twice* the value of α for that model.

[29] The generating equations are:

$$\text{(a)} \quad y_t = z_t$$
$$\text{(b)} \quad y_t = 8(t-1) + 4z_t$$
$$\text{(c)} \quad y_t = y_{t-1} + 4z_t$$
$$\text{(d)} \quad y_t = y_{t-1} + 4z_t + 1$$

where z_t is drawn from the standardised normal distribution, and $t = 1, ..., 20$. The expectations, variance and trends are roughly estimated from a random sample of fifty of the actual firms. Specification of the distribution of z_t implies (c) and (d) are random walks. Experimenting with several variances for the error terms reveals that the results are not sensitive to the size of the variance.

[30] See note 24.

[31] In a subsequent paper Watts [39] investigates the incomes of thirty-two firms over the thirty-eight year period 1927–1964. He uses an identification and estimation technique which allows a much broader range of processes than the partial adjustment models we use. For six of the thirty-two firms Watts is able to reject at the ·01 probability level the hypothesis that the incomes of those firms are random walks with or without trend.

References

1 Anderson, R.L., 'Distribution of the serial correlation coefficient' *Annals of Mathematical Statistics* 13, 1942, pp. 207–14.

2 Ball, R., and Brown, P., 'An empirical evaluation of accounting income numbers' *Journal of Accounting Research* vol. 6, no. 2, Autumn 1968, pp. 159–78.

3 Ball, R., and Brown, P., 'Portfolio theory and accounting' *Journal of Accounting Research* vol. 7, no. 2, Autumn 1969, pp. 300–23.

4 Beaver, W.H., 'Time series behaviour of earnings', paper presented at the Conference on Empirical Research in Accounting, Graduate School of Business, University of Chicago, 21 May 1970.

5 Bennett, C.A., and Franklin, N.L., *Statistical Analysis in Chemistry and the Chemical Industry*, John Wiley and Sons, Inc., New York 1954.

6 Brealey, R.A., 'Statistical properties of successive changes in earnings', unpublished paper, March 1967, Keystone Custodian Funds, p. 13.

7 Brealey, R.A., *An Introduction to Risk and Return from Common Stocks*, MIT Press, Boston 1969.

8 Brown, P., and Ball, R., 'Some preliminary findings on the association between the earnings of a firm, its industry and the economy' *Empirical Research in Accounting: Selected Studies* (1967) (supplement to *Journal of Accounting Research* vol. 5), pp. 55–77.

9 Brown, R.G., *Smoothing, Forecasting and Prediction of Discrete Time Series*, Prentice-Hall, Englewood Cliffs, NJ, 1962.

10 Copeland, R.M., 'Income smoothing' *Empirical Research in Accounting: Selected Studies* (1968) (supplement to *Journal of Accounting Research* vol. 6), pp. 101–16.

11 Copeland, R.M., and Licastro, R.D., 'A note on income smoothing' *The Accounting Review* vol. 43, no. 3, July 1968, pp. 540–5.

12 Cragg, J.Y., and Malkiel, B.Y., 'The consensus and accuracy of some predictions of the growth of corporate earnings' *Journal of Finance* vol. 23, no. 1, March 1968, pp. 67–84.

13 Dixon, W.J., and Massey, F.J., Jr, *Introduction to Statistical Analysis* 2nd ed., McGraw-Hill, New York 1957.

14 Dopuch, N., and Drake, D., 'The effect of alternative accounting rules for non-subsidiary investments' *Empirical Research in Accounting: Selected Studies 1966* (supplement to *Journal of Accounting Research* vol. 4), pp. 192–219.

15 Fama, E.F., 'The behavior of stock market prices' *Journal of Business* vol. 38, January 1965, pp. 34–105.

16 Fama, E.F., 'Efficient capital markets: a review of theory and empirical work' *Journal of Finance* vol. 25, no. 2, May 1970, pp. 383–417.

17 Fama, E.F., and Babiak, H., 'Dividend policy: an empirical analysis' *Journal of the American Statistical Association* 63, December 1968, pp. 1132–61.

18 Fama, E.F., Fisher, L., Jensen, M.C., and Roll, R., 'The adjustment of stock prices to new information' *International Economic Review* 10, February 1969, pp. 1–21.

19 Fisher, L., 'Some new stock market indices' *Journal of Business* vol. 39 (supplement 1966), pp. 191–225.

20 Gagnon, J.-M., 'Purchase versus pooling of interests: the search for a predictor' *Empirical Research in Accounting: Selected Studies, 1967* (supplement to *Journal of Accounting Research* vol. 4), pp. 187–204.

21 Gordon, M.J., 'Postulates, principles and research in accounting' *The Accounting Review* vol. 39, no. 2, April 1964, pp. 251–63.

22 Gordon, M.J., Discussion of Dopuch and Drake [14], in *Empirical Research in Accounting: Selected Studies, 1966* (supplement to *Journal of Accounting Research* vol. 4), pp. 220–3.

23 Gordon, M.J., Horwitz, B.N., and Myers, P.T., 'Accounting measure-

ments and normal growth of the firm' in R.K. Jaedicke, Y. Ijiri and O. Nielsen (eds), *Research Accounting Measurement*, American Accounting Association, Evanston, Ill. 1966.

24 Hart, B.I., and von Neumann, J., 'Tabulation of the probabilities of the ratio of the mean square difference to the variance' *Annals of Mathematical Statistics* 13, 1942, pp. 207–14.

25 Hepworth, S.R., 'Smoothing periodic income' *The Accounting Review* vol. 28, no. 1, January 1953, pp. 32–9.

26 Kendall, M.G., and Stuart, A., *The Advanced Theory of Statistics* vol. III, Charles Griffin and Co., London 1966.

27 Lintner, J., and Glauber, R., 'Higgledy piggledy growth in America? ', paper presented to the Seminar on the Analysis of Security Prices, Graduate School of Business, University of Chicago, 11–12 May 1967.

28 Little, I.M.D., 'Higgledy piggledy growth' *Institute of Statistics, Oxford* vol. 24, no. 4, November 1962.

29 Little, I.M.D., and Rayner, A.C., *Higgledy Piggledy Growth Again*, Basil Blackwell, Oxford 1966.

30 Malinvaud, E., *Statistical Methods of Econometrics*, Rand McNally, Chicago, Ill ., 1966.

31 Mood, A.M., and Graybill, F.A., *Introduction to the Theory of Statistics*, McGraw-Hill, New York 1963.

32 Muth, J.F., 'Optimal properties of exponentially weighted forecasts' *Journal of the American Statistical Association* vol. 55, no. 290, June 1960, pp. 299–306.

33 Praetz, P.D., 'Australian share prices and the random walk hypothesis' *Australian Journal of Statistics* vol. 11, no. 3, November 1969, pp. 123–39.

34 Press, S.J., 'Security prices and the compound Poisson process', Report no. 6707, Center for Mathematical Studies in Business and Economics, Graduate School of Business, University of Chicago, 1967.

35 Roberts, H.V., 'Statistical inference and decision', mimeographed, University of Chicago, 1966.

36 Schiff, M., 'Accounting tactics and the theory of the firm' *Journal of Accounting Research* vol. 4, no. 1, Spring 1966, pp. 62–7.

37 Schlaiffer, R., *Probability and Statistics for Business Decisions*, McGraw-Hill, New York 1959.

38 Wald, A., and Wolfowitz, J., 'On a test of whether two samples are from the same population' *Annals of Mathematical Statistics* 11, pp. 147–62.

39 Watts, R., Appendix A to 'The informational content of dividends', unpublished paper, Graduate School of Business, University of Chicago, October 1970.

Working Capital

In this section a means is suggested of analysing the risk-return trade-off for a firm under differing liquidity conditions and differing debt compositions. The risk of insolvency is examined for alternative strategies, the opportunity costs of which are also found. The author thereby provides a model enabling the firm to rationally attain a working-capital position giving the required safety margin relative to the cost of reaching that position.

A Risk-Return Analysis of a Firm's Working-Capital Position[1]

Introduction

The appropriate levels of current assets and current liabilities for a firm, which determine its level of working capital, are the result of fundamental decisions concerning the firm's liquidity and the maturity composition of its debt. In turn, these decisions are influenced by a trade-off between profitability and risk. The purpose of this paper is to develop a framework for evaluating decisions affecting the firm's working-capital position, so that optimal decisions can be made more readily. As working-capital management is an area largely lacking in theoretical perspective, [2] it is hoped that the framework presented will place the subject in a clearer conceptual light. In this regard, we examine separately the level of the firm's liquid assets and the maturity composition of its debt in order to illustrate the respective trade-offs between profitability and risk. We then combine these decision variables in the subsequent development of a framework for analysing the overall problem. The major input for the method is a cash budget, expressed in probabilistic terms.

Decision variables

In a broad sense, the appropriate decision variable to examine on the asset side of the balance sheet is the maturity composition, or liquidity, of the firm's assets – i.e., the turnover of these assets into cash. Decisions that affect the asset liquidity of the firm include: the management of cash and marketable securities; credit policy and procedures. Inventory management and control; and the administration of fixed assets. As we wish to reduce the problem to workable proportions, however, we shall hold constant the last three factors. These factors represent separate but important means by which to improve the efficiency of the firm and to change its liquidity.[3] As the purpose of this paper is to provide an underlying theory of working-capital management, however, this theory is developed exclusive of the above factors. The decision variable then becomes the

141

amount of liquid assets held by the firm; these assets are defined as cash and marketable securities. Moreover, our concern is with only the total amount of these two assets and not with the optimal split between them.[4]

Determining the appropriate amount of cash and marketable securities held by the firm (hereafter called liquid assets) involves a trade-off between risk and profitability. All other things the same, the lower the level of liquid assets, the greater the risk of being unable to meet current obligations. For our purposes, risk is defined as the probability of technical insolvency. Legally, insolvency occurs whenever the assets of a firm are less than its liabilities and the net worth is negative. Technical insolvency, on the other hand, occurs whenever a firm is unable to meet its cash obligations.[5]

The risk of running out of cash can be reduced or even eliminated, of course, by maintaining a high proportion of liquid assets. However, there is a cost involved. This cost is the profit foregone on the investment of these funds in other assets.[6] However cost is measured, it is clear that there exists a trade-off between risk and profitability.

The maturity structure of the firm's debt also involves a trade-off between risk and profitability, similar to that affecting its level of liquid assets. A decision here determines the proportion of current assets financed with current liabilities. For purpose of analysis, we assume an established policy with respect to payment for purchases, labour, taxes, and other expenses. These liabilities finance a portion of the assets of the firm and tend to fluctuate with the firm's production schedule, and in the case of taxes, with profits. Our concern is with how assets, not supported by accounts payable and accruals, are financed.[7] We assume also that the firm maintains the existing portion of total debt to equity. Our attention is centred only on the maturity composition of the debt, not on the capital-structure problem.[8]

Depending upon the synchronisation of the repayment of debt with the firm's schedule of expected future cash flows, different debt instruments will be more or less risky. The shorter the maturity schedule of the debt in relation to expected future cash flows, the greater the risk of inability to meet principal and interest payments, all other things the same. Generally, the longer the maturity schedule of debt, the less risky the debt financing of the firm. However, the longer the maturity schedule, the more costly is likely to be the financing. For one thing, the explicit cost of long-term financing usually is more than that of short-term financing.[9] In periods of very high interest rates, however, the rate on short-term corporate borrowings actually may exceed that on long-term borrowings. In general, this occurence is not the case; the firm typically pays more for long-term borrowings, particularly if they are negotiated privately. In addition, if intermediate and long-term financing is used to finance short-term funds requirements, the firm may well pay interest on debt during times when it is not needed. In particular, this situation would hold if there were a seasonal component to the business. Thus, generally, there is an inducement to finance funds requirements, less payables and accruals, on a short-term basis. Offsetting this incentive, of course, is the added risk.

If a firm's future cash flows were known with certainty, it would be able to arrange its maturity schedule of debt to correspond exactly with its schedule of future net cash flows. Because of this synchronisation, there would be no need to hold liquid assets. When cash flows are subject to uncertainty, however, the situation is changed. To provide a margin of safety the firm can: (a) increase its level of liquid assets; and/or (b) lengthen the maturity schedule of its debt. To analyse the appropriate margin of safety, management must have information about the expected future cash flows of the firm and possible deviations from these expected outcomes. We turn now to a discussion of how this information can be provided, followed by an evaluation of the use of the information in determining an appropriate margin of safety.

Cash-forecast information

In order to assess possible adverse deviations in net cash flows, cash forecasts must be prepared for a range of possible outcomes, with a probability attached to each. An initial cash budget should be prepared based upon the expected value of outcomes in each future period. This budget is prepared in the usual manner by: estimating and totalling all cash receipts for each future period; doing the same for cash disbursements; subtracting total disbursements from total receipts to obtain the net cash flow for each period; and calculating the ending cash balance for each period without additional financing. Instead of the cash balance, however, we wish to calculate the liquid-asset balance, the sum of cash and marketable securities. For longer-term forecasts, it is not feasible to prepare detailed cash budgets. Here, estimates of liquid-asset balances based upon major sources and uses of funds probably will be sufficient.

Given an initial cash budget, assumptions with respect to sales, average collection period, production schedule, purchasing, and expenses should be varied by management in keeping with possible deviations from expected conditions. For each change in assumptions, a new set of liquid-asset balances reflecting the change can be generated. Thus, management

143

formulates subjective probabilities of possible future liquid asset balances. These balances are treated as subjective random variables. In determining the effect of a change in assumptions on the liquid-asset balance, simulation techniques can be very helpful in reducing or even eliminating the detail work involved.[10]

In summary, changes in assumptions are tne bases for alternative outcomes in liquid-asset balances. For each of these outcomes, management attaches the probability of occurrence of the associated change in assumptions. For example, suppose that management felt that there were a 0·10 probability of a 20 per cent drop in sales accompanied by a slowing in the average collection period from thirty to forty days for all periods. Suppose further that production were expected to be cut back only after a month's delay. Given these changes in assumptions, a new set of liquid-asset balances for all periods would be determined, the probability of this outcome being 0·10. It is not necessary that the decline in sales or the slowing in collections be the same percentage amount for all months. If different changes over time are expected to occur, these changes should be used to determine the new set of liquid-asset balances.

By varying assumptions in this manner, management formulates subjective probability distributions of liquid-asset balances for various future periods; these distributions encompass a range of possible outcomes. To illustrate a probabilistic cash budget, consider the example in Table 4.1.

Table 4.1

Possible liquid-asset balances without additional financing
(in thousands)

Probability	19X1								
	Jan.	Feb.	March	April	May	June	July	Aug.	Sept.
·02	−$200	−$300	−$400	−$500	−$700	−$900	−$900	−$800	−$700
·03	−100	−200	−300	−400	−600	−800	−800	−700	−600
·05	0	−100	−200	−300	−500	−700	−700	−600	−500
·10	100	0	−100	−200	−400	−600	−600	−500	−400
·15	200	100	0	−100	−300	−500	−500	−400	−300
·20	300	200	100	0	−200	−400	−400	−300	−200
·18	400	300	200	100	−100	−300	−300	−200	−100
·12	500	400	300	200	0	−200	−200	−100	0
·07	600	500	400	300	200	−100	−100	0	100
·05	700	600	500	400	300	0	0	100	200
·03	800	700	600	500	400	100	100	200	300

144

Here, discrete probability distributions of ending liquid-asset balances without additional financing are shown. These balances are reported on a monthly basis for one year, followed by quarterly forecasts for the next two years. We note that the probability of occurrence of a particular liquid-asset balance in one period corresponds to specific liquid-asset balances in all other periods. For simplicity of illustration, absolute changes in liquid-asset balances are made equal over time. While the realism of this example may be questionable, it is meant only to illustrate the framework for analysis.

Level of liquid assets

As discussed earlier, the level of liquid assets and the maturity composition of debt determine the margin of safety of the firm in relation to possible adverse deviations in net cash flows. The level of liquid assets is affected by: (1) the future cash flows of the firm exclusive of new financing; and (2) changes in the total financing of the firm. These factors jointly determine the expected value of liquid assets of the firm. To illustrate, consider in Table 4.1 the liquid-asset balance for January 19X1. The expected value of this balance can be found by

$$\overline{LB_1} = \sum_{i=1}^{11} L_{i1} P_{i1}, \qquad (1)$$

19X1 (continued)			19X2				19X3			
Oct.	Nov.	Dec.	March	June	Sept.	Dec.	March	June	Sept.	Dec.
−$700	−$600	−$500	−$600	−$1,000	−$700	−$500	−$700	−$1,000	−$700	−$600
−600	−500	−400	−550	−950	−650	−450	−600	−900	−600	−500
−500	−400	−300	−500	−900	−600	−400	−550	−850	−550	−450
−400	−300	−200	−400	−800	−500	−300	−500	−800	−500	−400
−300	−200	−100	−300	−700	−400	−200	−400	−700	−400	−300
−200	−100	0	−200	−600	−300	−100	−300	−600	−300	−200
−100	0	100	−100	−500	−200	0	−200	−500	−200	−100
0	100	200	0	−400	−100	100	−100	−400	−100	0
100	200	300	100	−300	0	200	0	−300	0	100
200	300	400	200	−200	100	300	100	−200	100	200
300	400	500	300	−100	200	400	200	−100	200	300

145

where L_{i1} is the ith possible balance, and P_{i1} is the probability of occurrence of that balance at the end of period 1. Thus, the expected value of liquid-asset balance for period 1 is

$$\overline{LB_1} = -200(\cdot02) - 100(\cdot03) + 0(\cdot05) + 100(\cdot10) + 200(\cdot15)$$
$$+ 300(\cdot20) + 400(\cdot18) + 500(\cdot12) + 600(\cdot07) \qquad (2)$$
$$+ 700(\cdot05) + 800(\cdot03) = \$323,000.$$

If the firm were to increase its total financing by \$150,000, the expected value of liquid-asset balance at the end of the period would be \$473,000. If we assume a liquid-asset balance of \$400,000 at time 0, there would be a \$73,000 net increase in the expected value of liquid assets for the period.

A decision to change the total financing of the firm will affect all probability distributions in Table 4.1. For simplicity of illustration, we assume that changes in total financing occur in exactly the same proportions of debt and equity as in the existing capital structure of the firm and that any new debt financing involves perpetual debt. Changes that involve other than perpetual debt are taken into account in the last section of this paper when we consider the total information needed to evaluate alternatives. In our example, then, a decision to increase total financing by \$150,000 at time 0 will increase the liquid-asset balance in Table 4.1 by \$150,000 for each probability for each of the periods.[11] As a result, there is obviously a reduced risk of cash insolvency.[12]

For each contemplated change in total financing, we can determine its effect on the probability distributions of possible liquid-asset balances shown in Table 4.1. In order to evaluate the trade-off between risk and profitability, however, we must have information about the effect of a change in liquid assets on profitability. To determine the cost of a change in liquid assets, we multiply the cost of carrying liquid assets (expressed as a percentage) by the change. First, however, we must define a change. While different interpretations are possible, we shall define it as

$$C_j = \sum_{t=1}^{12} (\overline{LB_t} - LB_A)/12 \qquad (3)$$

where C_j = change in liquid-asset balance for alternative j
$\overline{LB_t}$ = expected value of liquid-asset balance in period t for alternative j
LB_A = average liquid-asset balance during previous twelve months.

In words, our measured change in the liquid-asset balance represents an average of the expected values of liquid-asset balances for the forthcoming

146

twelve months, less the average of liquid-asset balances for the previous twelve months. If LB_A is not considered typical or appropriate, a more suitable liquid-asset balance may be substituted. The expected value of liquid-assset balance at time t is found with equation (1).

To illustrate the use of equation (3), consider the probability distribution of possible liquid-asset balances for April 19X1 in Table 4.1. Suppose that the firm increases its total financing by $200,000. The new probability distribution of possible liquid-asset balances for April is found by adding $200,000 to each of the eleven liquid-asset balances for that month. The new expected value of liquid-asset balance is

$$\overline{LB}_4 = -300,000(\cdot02) - 200,000(\cdot03) - 100,000(\cdot05) + 0(\cdot10)$$
$$+ 100,000(\cdot15) + 200,000(\cdot20) + 300,000(\cdot18) + 400,000(\cdot12)$$
$$+ 500,000(\cdot07) + 600,000(\cdot05) + 700,000(\cdot03) = \$214,000. \quad (4)$$

If LB_A, the average liquid-asset balance of the firm during the previous year, were $200,000, the change in liquid-asset balance for period t would be $214,000 − 200,000 = $14,000. Similarly, we are able to calculate the expected value of change in the liquid-asset balance for the other eleven months of the year. With equation (3), we then average the changes for the twelve months; this average represents our measure of the change in liquid assets of the firm for a specific change in total financing.

Given our measured change in liquid-asset balance, C_j, this change is multiplied by the opportunity cost of maintaining liquid assets, expressed as a percentage, in order to obtain the total cost of the change. Within a limited range, the opportunity cost of an increase in liquid assets might be approximated by the firm's cost of capital, on a before-tax basis. The product of the above multiplication represents our measure of the impact on profitability of a change in the level of liquid assets of the firm. We defer specific evaluation of the trade-off between profitability and risk until we have considered the effect of changes in the maturity composition of the firm's debt on profitability and risk.

Maturity composition of debt

Similar to the case for liquid-asset changes, we are able to compute the effect of changes in the maturity composition of the firm's debt on the probability distributions of liquid-asset balances shown in Table 4.1. To illustrate the impact of a change in maturity composition, suppose that the firm had in its existing debt structure a three-year term loan which called for monthly principal payments of $25,000. These payments are

147

assumed to be embodied in the figures in Table 4.1. If the firm renegotiated the term loan into one of $7\frac{1}{2}$ years with equal monthly payments, the principal payment per month would be reduced from $25,000 to $10,000. We can recalculate easily the probability distributions shown in Table 4.1 by adding $15,000 to the liquid-asset balance for each probability for each monthly period.[13] Thus, the probability of running out of cash is reduced for three years as a result of this debt lengthening. Of course, for years 4 through $7\frac{1}{2}$, the firm will be faced with a $10,000 increment in monthly principal payments. For other changes in the maturity composition of existing debt, we likewise can recompute the probability distributions shown in Table 4.1.

A flexible borrowing arrangement for meeting short-term funds requirements is a bank line of credit. A line of credit enables a firm to borrow up to some maximum amount over a period of time, usually one year. With a line of credit, we must recompute the probability distributions in Table 4.1. To illustrate, suppose that the firm increases its total financing by $400,000, of which $200,000 represents a line of credit. Assume further that the firm will borrow upwards to the whole line to maintain a liquid-asset balance of $250,000. For April, the probability distribution of possible liquid-asset balances after financing becomes that shown in Table 4.2. For possibilities 1 through 4, the firm would utilise the full $200,000 under the line. For possibility 5, it would borrow $150,000 under the line; for possibility 6, $50,000. For possibilities 7 through 11, it would borrow nothing under the line; but, of course, there would be $200,000 in regular financing.

With a line of credit, the firm typically is required by a bank to pay off loans for a length of time during the year, perhaps two months. This requirement creates a problem with respect to risk. During the period of expected seasonal slack, the firm must assume the absence of the line so that it is out of debt during the 'clean-up' period. For our example in Table 4.1, we see that peak expected liquid-asset balances without additional financing occur in December and January. If the required 'clean-up' period were two months, we would not adjust the probability distributions to reflect the availability of the line of credit during this period.

In our cash-flow evaluation, there is an obvious horizon problem. We have estimated cash flows for only three years hence. Given this horizon, an optimal strategy might call for all debt maturing in three years, one month. Under most circumstances, such a strategy would not be appropriate, for the firm will have funds requirements beyond three years. These requirements no doubt will preclude the paying off of all debt at that time. Consequently, the firm must arrange maturities beyond the

148

cash-budget horizon on the basis of general estimates of future funds requirements and ability to service debt. We might point out, however, that the principles of risk and profitability are the same as those that govern debt maturities falling within the cash-budget horizon.

The opportunity cost of a change in maturity composition of debt must be estimated. If long-term borrowings command an interest rate different from that on short-term borrowings, usually higher, there exists a measurable explicit cost for the operation.[14] Suppose that, in our previous example, the three-year term loan required an interest rate of 6 per cent, while the $7\frac{1}{2}$ year loan required a rate of $6\frac{1}{2}$ per cent. The difference, $\frac{1}{2}$ per cent, represents the additional cost of lengthening the debt. If debt were assumed in perpetuity and the amount of the term loan were $900,000, the oppertunity cost of debt lengthening would be $900,000 × 0·5 per cent = $4,500 annually.

The second explicit cost involved with debt lengthening is the payment of interest on debt when it is not needed. Suppose that at 1 January a firm had a short-term loan of $600,000, of which $200,00 matured on 31 August, $200,000 on 31 October, and $200,000 on 31 December. To reduce the risk of running out of cash, the firm might consider changing its borrowing accommodation to a one-year loan, maturing 31 December. If the interest rate were 6 per cent on both loans, the firm would pay additional interest on $200,000 for four months and on $200,000 for two months. The additional interest cost would be:

Table 4.2

Liquid-asset balance with new financing of $400,000

Possibility i	Liquid-asset balance	Probability of occurrence
1	−$100,000	·02
2	0	·03
3	100,000	·05
4	200,000	·10
5	250,000	·15
6	250,000	·20
7	300,000	·18
8	400,000	·12
9	500,000	·07
10	600,000	·05
11	700,000	·03

$$\cdot 06 \times \$200,000 \times \tfrac{4}{12} = \$4,000$$
$$\cdot 06 \times \$200,000 \times \tfrac{2}{12} = \underline{2,000}$$

Total $6,000

The opportunity cost of a line of credit relates principally to the requirement of compensating balances. This requirement, frequently 15 per cent of the line, increases the cost of borrowing if balances must be maintained in excess of those ordinarily maintained. One way to measure the cost is to take the interest rate on borrowings times the increase in balances necessary to compensate the bank. This notion assumes that the firm will have to borrow under its line to maintain balances considered compensating.

To summarise, for each feasible change in the composition of the firm's debt, we determine the effect of the change on the probability distributions of expected future liquid-asset balances. In addition, we estimate the incremental explicit cost of the particular alternative. Again, we must point out that we have limited our attention to explicit costs. No consideration has been given to the effect of changes in the maturity composition of debt on the way investors at the margin value the firm's stock. Having taken up the effect of changes in liquid assets and debt composition individually, we now must combine the two factors.

Combination of factors and selection

In reducing the risk of running out of cash, the firm can select a combination of changes in liquid assets and in maturity composition of its debt. With a combination, we must estimate the joint effect of the two factors on the probability distributions of expected liquid-asset balances as well as the opportunity cost of the combination. Before proceeding, however, we must digress to relax an assumption made previously. It will be recalled that we assumed that debt issued in connection with an increase in total financing was perpetual. When such is not the case, we must take account of the effect of principal payments on the schedule of expected future cash flows. For example, suppose that the firm obtained a $540,000 three-year term loan payable monthly and that this loan represented new debt. Because the liquid-asset balances previously computed to reflect the change in total financing assumed perpetual debt, we would need to reduce these balances by $15,000 ($540,000/36) for each probability for each monthly period over three years. In addition, we must take account of the effect of the change on explicit costs. Both of these changes should be incorporated into the information provided for evaluating alternatives.

150

Table 4.3

Schedule of alternatives for reducing risk of running out of cash

Alternative	Description	Opportunity cost
1	$400,000 increase in total financing	$5,100
2	$500,000 increase in total financing	15,100
3	$600,000 increase in total financing	25,100
4	$700,000 increase in total financing	35,100
5	$800,000 increase in total financing	45,100
6	$900,000 increase in total financing	55,100
7	$1,000,000 increase in total financing	65,100
8	Conversion of term loan maturing $200,000 quarterly through three years into six-year term loan with $100,000 quarterly payments	9,000
9	Conversion of term loan into ten-year term loan maturing from year four through ten	16,000
10	Alternatives 1 and 8	14,100
11	Alternatives 2 and 8	24,100
12	Alternatives 3 and 8	34,100
13	Alternatives 4 and 8	44,100
14	Alternatives 1 and 9	21,100
15	Alternatives 2 and 9	31,100
16	Conversion of term loan from three to six years and refunding of mortgage maturing May 19X1 into ten-year note maturing quarterly	23,800
17	Alternative 1, and refunding mortgage	19,800
18	Alternative 2, and line of credit of $250,000	17,400
19	Alternative 2, line of credit of $250,000, and extending $1 million in notes from three-year loan to $4\frac{1}{2}$-year loan	26,200
.	.	.
.		.
.		.
32	Alternative 1, and refund intermediate-term loan into long-term loan	21,700

For each feasible alternative for reducing the risk of cash insolvency, a revised schedule of probability distributions of expected future liquid-asset balances should be prepared, accompanied by the estimated opportunity cost of the alternative. Instead of providing the entire probability distribution, it may be suitable to specify only the probability of running out of cash during each future period. The total opportunity cost for each alternative should be denoted on a total annual dollar basis.[15] In this regard, it may be helpful to show not only the total opportunity cost, but also the opportunity cost of each of the changes comprising the alternative. An example of a schedule of possible alternative is shown in Table 4.3. The probabilities of running out of cash for these alternatives are shown in Table 4.4.

Given information similar to that found in Tables 4.3 and 4.4, the firm must determine the best alternative by balancing the risk of running out of cash against the cost of providing a solution to avoid the possibility. If the cost of running out of cash were known, the best alternative could be determined easily by comparing the expected cost of a cash stockout with the opportunity cost of a particular solution to avoid that stockout. [16] The expected cost of a cash stockout is the cost associated with a particular stockout times its probability of occurrence. The optimal solution could be found by a comparison of the reduction in the expected cost of cash stockout accompanying a particular solution with the opportunity cost of implementing that solution.

The difficulty, of course, is in estimating the cost of a cash stockout. When a firm does not have a sufficient liquidity cushion to cover a cash drain, it may be forced to convert other assets into cash. Frequently, these assets can be converted only at a significant price concession. This concession can be thought to represent the cost of illiquidity; and we would expect it to increase at an increasing rate with the amount of assets to be converted. However, many assets cannot be converted into cash on short notice. The measurement of the cost of illiquidity in this case is very difficult, for it does not involve tangible considerations. The cost will depend upon which obligations cannot be paid — that is, whether they are payments to suppliers, wages to employees, tax payments, bank loans, or other obligations. Because of the obvious difficulties in measuring the cost of a cash stockout and applying it consistently, the method is seldom used.

A more practical method is for decision-makers to specify a risk tolerance for running out of cash. For example, this risk tolerance might be 5 per cent, meaning that the firm would tolerate upwards to a five per cent probability of not being able to pay its bills in a future period. Given

Table 4.4

Probabilities of running out of cash for various alternatives

Alternative	19X1												19X2				19X3			
	Jan.	Feb.	March	April	May	June	July	Aug.	Sept.	Oct.	Nov.	Dec.	March	June	Sept.	Dec.	March	June	Sept.	Dec.
1	·00	·00	·02	·05	·20	·55	·55	·35	·20	·20	·10	·05	·20	·85	·35	·10	·35	·85	·35	·20
2	·00	·00	·00	·02	·10	·35	·35	·20	·10	·10	·05	·02	·10	·73	·20	·02	·20	·73	·20	·05
3	·00	·00	·00	·00	·05	·20	·20	·10	·05	·05	·02	·00	·02	·55	·10	·00	·05	·55	·05	·02
4	·00	·00	·00	·00	·02	·10	·10	·05	·02	·02	·00	·00	·00	·35	·02	·00	·02	·35	·02	·00
5	·00	·00	·00	·00	·00	·05	·05	·02	·00	·00	·00	·00	·00	·20	·00	·00	·00	·20	·00	·00
6	·00	·00	·00	·00	·00	·02	·02	·00	·00	·00	·00	·00	·00	·10	·00	·00	·00	·05	·00	·00
7	·00	·00	·00	·00	·00	·00	·00	·00	·00	·00	·00	·00	·00	·02	·00	·00	·00	·02	·00	·00
8	·10	·20	·20	·35	·73	·85	·85	·73	·35	·35	·20	·05	·10	·55	·02	·05	·00	·02	·00	·00
9	·10	·20	·10	·20	·55	·55	·55	·35	·05	·05	·02	·00	·00	·00	·00	·00	·00	·00	·00	·00
10	·00	·00	·00	·02	·10	·20	·20	·10	·02	·02	·00	·00	·00	·02	·00	·00	·00	·00	·00	·00
11	·00	·00	·00	·00	·05	·10	·10	·05	·00	·00	·00	·00	·00	·00	·00	·00	·00	·00	·00	·00
12	·00	·00	·00	·00	·02	·05	·05	·02	·00	·00	·00	·00	·00	·00	·00	·00	·00	·00	·00	·00
13	·00	·00	·00	·00	·00	·02	·02	·00	·00	·00	·00	·00	·00	·00	·00	·00	·00	·00	·00	·00
14	·00	·00	·00	·00	·05	·05	·05	·02	·00	·00	·00	·00	·00	·00	·00	·00	·00	·00	·00	·00
15	·00	·00	·00	·00	·02	·02	·02	·00	·00	·00	·00	·00	·00	·00	·00	·00	·00	·00	·00	·00
16	·00	·00	·02	·05	·10	·15	·15	·13	·12	·08	·06	·04	·07	·16	·00	·00	·00	·02	·00	·00
17	·00	·00	·02	·05	·04	·04	·04	·04	·03	·02	·01	·01	·02	·04	·02	·00	·02	·05	·04	·00
18	·00	·04	·05	·07	·09	·10	·09	·09	·05	·04	·04	·06	·06	·10	·08	·07	·06	·12	·09	·08
19	·00	·04	·04	·05	·06	·07	·06	·06	·04	·03	·04	·03	·05	·08	·05	·04	·04	·09	·06	·04
32	·00	·00	·02	·05	·10	·10	·08	·05	·02	·00	·00	·00	·02	·08	·05	·02	·00	·06	·00	·00

an acceptable level of risk, the firm then would seek the least costly solution to reducing the probability of running out of cash to that level. This is done simply by taking those feasible alternatives that provide a probability of cash stockout of approximately 5 per cent or less and picking the least costly. We see in Tables 4.3 and 4.4 that this alternative would be number 17. For this alternative, there is a 5 per cent probability of running out of cash in April 19X1, and a 5 per cent probability for June 19X3. We note that the alternative has a total annual opportunity cost of $19,800.

Another way that decision-makers might select an alternative would be for them to formulate risk tolerances on the basis of the opportunity cost involved in reducing the risk of cash stockout to various tolerance levels. It could well be that the specification of a low risk tolerance would result in a very high cost to provide a solution. If management had information about the cost associated with reducing risk to other levels, it might pick a higher tolerance level that could be implemented at considerably less cost. For example, the least costly alternative in our hypothetical example that will reduce the probability of running out of cash to 2 per cent is number 15, involving a total annual cost of $31,100. This compares with a cost of $19,800 to reduce the probability to 5 per cent. On the basis of this information, management might not feel that the additional $11,300 to reduce the probability of running out of cash from 5 to 2 per cent was justified. Accordingly, we see that it may be useful to prepare a shedule showing the least costly solution to reducing risk to various levels. In this way, decision-makers can better evaluate the trade-off between risk and profitability.

Even here, however, there is the problem of not providing enough information. For example, a certain alternative may result in a probability of running out of cash in only one future period, whereas another might result in that probability being reached in several periods. In Table 4.4, we note that for alternative 17, there is a 5 per cent probability of running out of cash in two periods, a 4 per cent probability in six periods, a 3 per cent probability in one period, a 2 per cent probability in five periods, and a 1 per cent probability in two periods. On the other hand, for alternative 14, there is a 5 per cent probability of running out of cash in three periods, and a 2 per cent probability in one period. Thus, there are considerably more periods in which the firm may run out of cash with alternative 17 than with alternative 14. As the total cost of alternative 14 is only $21,000, compared with $19,800 for alternative 17, the firm might regard alternative 14 as more favourable.

Therefore, a strong case can be made for providing decision-makers with information about the probability distributions of liquid-asset balances for all future periods for each alternative and the opportunity cost of the alternative. In this way, the firm is able to evaluate the maximum probability of running out of cash and the number of future periods in which there is a chance for a cash stockout. With this additional information, it then can assess more realistically the trade-off between the risk of running out of cash and the opportunity cost of reducing this risk. On the basis of this assessment, it would select and implement the most appropriate alternative. The actual implementation will determine the liquid-asset level of the firm and the maturity composition of its debt. In turn, these factors will determine the working-capital position of the firm, given the assumptions listed earlier. This position should be the one most appropriate with respect to considerations of risk and profitability.

Conclusions

In this paper, we have proposed a framework by which management can evaluate the level of liquid assets and the maturity composition of the firm's debt. Employing certain probability concepts, the framework allows a realistic appraisal of the risk of running out of cash for various levels of liquid assets and different debt compositions. Given the opportunity cost of a change in liquid assets and/or maturity composition of the firm's debt, decision-makers are able to evaluate the trade-off between profitability and risk. The method proposed is designed to provide them with certain necessary information on which to make a decision. However, the decision itself will depend upon management's preferences with respect to risk borne by the firm. The decision itself will determine the current assets and current liabilities of the firm, given the assumptions of the model. The result should be the most desirable working-capital position for the firm.

Notes

¹ Reprinted by kind permission from *The Engineering Economist* vol. 14, no. 2. 1969, pp. 71–89. The author is grateful for the suggestions of Gerald A. Feltham and Charles T. Horngren.

² Exceptions include Berenek [4], Burton [5], and Walker [8].

³ See Van Horne [7], Chapters 2–5, 17 and 18.

⁴ For a discussion of the latter issue, see Baumol [2]; and Miller and Orr [6].

⁵ See Walter [9].

⁶ If the firm does not engage in capital rationing, a case can be made that the appropriate opportunity cost is the cost of capital, particularly if the firm increases its proportion of liquid assets to total assets.

⁷ Delaying payment on accounts payable and accruals can be a decision variable for financing. However, there are limits to the extent to which a firm can 'stretch' its payables. For simplicity, we assume a definite and consistent policy with respect to payment of current obligations. Consequently, payables and accruals are not active decision variables.

⁸ For a review and analysis of this problem, see Van Horne [7], Chapter 7.

⁹ We ignore consideration of implicit costs that might be associated with short-term financing. These implicit costs in part may be embodied in management's decision, a subject we take up later.

¹⁰ We have developed a programme for cash budgeting using a time-sharing system. The programme allows one to judge the effects of a change in one or more assumptions on cash balances without having to rework the cash budget. See also 'Probabilistic Projections', unpublished paper, Amos Tuck School of Business Administration, Dartmouth College, 1967.

¹¹ For ease of exposition, we ignore the effect of the payment of interest on new debt and dividends on new stock issued on the cash budget. These factors could be incorporated in the revised cash budget simply by deducting expected new interest and dividend payments in each future period from the $150,000 increase in liquid assets.

¹² Archer [1] advocates computing the average daily transactions cash balance for a month and the standard deviation about this average. On the basis of this probability distribution, he suggests that the firm should add to its cash balance until the risk of running out of cash is reduced to an acceptable level.

¹³ For simplicity of exposition, we ignore again the effect of interest payments on the cash flows.

[14] Again, we must recognise the possibility of short-term rates higher than long-term rates when interest rates in general are very high.

[15] If there is a change in the average cost of debt financing accompanying a change in total financing, it is necessary to multipy the change in average cost by the total amount of debt financing after the change in total financing.

[16] This assumes that the two costs are comparable.

References

1   Archer, S.H., 'A model for the determination of firm cash balances' *Journal of Financial and Quantitative Analysis* vol. I, March 1966, pp. 1–11.
2   Baumol, W.J., 'The transactions demand for cash: an inventory theoretic approach' *Quarterly Journal of Economics* vol. LXVI, November 1952.
3   Beranek, W., *Analysis for Financial Decisions*, Richard D. Irwin, Inc., Homewood, Ill., 1963, Chapter 11.
4   Beranek, W., *Working Capital Management,* Wadsworth Publishing Company, Belmont 1966.
5   Burton, J.C., 'The management of corporate liquid assets' unpublished doctoral thesis, Columbia University, 1962.
6   Miller, M.H., and Orr, D., 'A model of the demand for money by firms' *Quarterly Journal of Economics* vol. LXXX, August 1966, pp. 413–35.
7   Van Horne, J.C., *Financial Management and Policy*, Prentice-Hall, Inc., Englewood Cliffs, NJ, 1968.
8   Walker, E.W., 'Towards a theory of working capital' *The Engineering Economist* vol. 9, no. 2, January–February 1964, pp. 21–35.
9   Walter, J.E., 'Determination of technical insolvency' *Journal of Business* vol. 30, January 1957, pp. 30–43.

Capital Budgeting

There is little doubt that capital budgeting and the topics relating to it occupy one of the larger portions of academic financial literature. Indeed, one might be forgiven for concluding that the importance of the subject has been over-emphasised, and that some of the more sophisticated current models lack practicality. Although this criticism may occasionally be justified, the value of investigating and formulating procedures upon which an organisation can base a rational capital investment policy is clearly immense.

During the last few years an increasing number of writers have examined the subject from a probabilistic rather than a deterministic approach. This should occasion no surprise since many other traditional financial models have come under similar scrutiny, and have been modified in view of the more realistic assumption of an uncertain future.

The paper in this section has been chosen to illustrate an unusual aspect of capital budgeting under uncertainty, in which the take-over of one company by another is considered as a large-scale investment consistent with the assumptions underlying the standard theory.

The Take-over in the Context of a Capital Budgeting Framework[1]

Introduction

Over recent years there has been a marked increase in amounts spent by companies on mergers and acquisition in the UK. This trend reached a peak in 1968 when over £2,000m. was laid out for this purpose. Whilst to date this figure has not been exceeded, it does seem that the takeover has become an accepted part of corporate strategy.

In practice, the most frequent methods of estimating the price that an acquiring company is prepared to pay in a take-over include the stock market value, some multiple (generally based on the stock market Price/ earnings (P/E) rating for comparable companies) of prospective sustainable earnings, or a price related to asset value [16]. Generally speaking the acquiring company estimates the impact of the acquisition upon its prospective reported earnings per share over a fairly short period. In doing this, estimates are made of rationalisation potential, proceeds of realising surplus assets, cutting out losers and selling off some divisions. An earnings per share projection of this type also assumes that the target company prepares its accounts in line with the accounting practices of the acquiring company — often this means changed depreciation policy, revaluation of assets, revised treatment of profit on long-term contracts and the like, which can make substantial differences to reported profits.

However, as various writers ([1], [13], [22]) have pointed out, the acquisition is essentially a capital budgeting decision capable of fundamental analysis in the same way as any other investment opportunity. This would suggest that if a firm appraises possibilities for the commitment of capital via the Discounted Cash Flow (DCF) criterion, there would appear to be no reason why it should not look at acquisitions on the same basis. On this score, the results of empirical research are surprising. In his study of the takeover criteria and subsequent post-acquisition performance of thirty-eight companies making acquisitions in 1967 and 1968, Newbould [16] points out that not one such company used DFC for evaluation purposes.

With this background the objective of this paper is to indicate how capital budgeting criteria may be applied in take-over analysis. The approach is on two planes. First, at a somewhat theoretical level, the use of portfolio analysis [9] and subjective probability estimates in acquisition appraisal is explained. But given that neither of these two techniques, particularly portfolio analysis, is widely encountered in practical capital budgeting, least of all in the evaluation of take-over candidates, this section is perhaps of academic interest. The business-based reader may well wish to skip this section, which he may do without any loss of continuity. The second part of this paper is concerned with the application of more usual capital budgeting evaluation techniques to the take-over, and the related and very significant topic of earnings per share projections for the period following acquisition — this section is therefore directed at the financial manager.

A theoretical approach to the acquisition as a capital budgeting decision

Using portfolio analysis as an aid to descision-making presupposes that the firm has defined its views on risk and investment payoff. The selection of the most desirable portfolio of investments will depend upon the preferences of management with respect to net present value, on the one hand, and variance or standard deviation as a measure of risk, on the other. The company's management, or at least the dominant members of the coalition that forms the management [4], will have made explicit its trade-off between risk and return in a series of indifference curves, in a form similar to Figure 5.1.

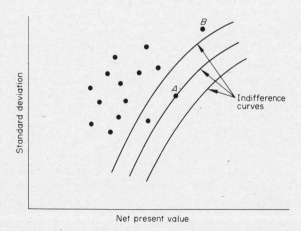

Fig. 5.1 Indifference curves representing company's risk—return trade-off

Moving to the right in Figure 5.1 means that one is moving towards a higher level of present value. The company would choose the portfolio of investments that lies on the indifference curve furthest to the right. Each dot in the figure represents a combination of investment opportunities located in terms of net present value versus standard deviation. The optimal portfolio occurs at the intersection of a dot with the most advantageous curve. In Figure 5.1, this occurs at point A which represents the portfolio of existing capital projects under consideration that possesses the most desirable characteristics in terms of net present value and risk. It will be observed that the portfolio represented by point B promises a higher net present value than A, but its risk characteristics are clearly greater.

For the purpose of summarising the use of portfolio analysis as a capital budgeting decision-aid, it is assumed that the specification of the firm's indifference curves has already been made.[2] It is next necessary to estimate future cash flows and outlays for all investment projects (including the acquisition) under consideration. In order to build a risk profile of the investments, subjective probabilities are attached to anticipated cash flows enabling the standard deviation and the expected value of the net present value for each series of investment project portfolios to be calculated.[3] Then having plotted points representing standard deviation versus net present value on a chart similar to Figure 5.1, it is simply a matter of selecting the optimal portfolio.

Portfolio analysis may be used to evaluate a potential acquisition either assuming that the purchase price is known or where the consideration is not fixed but it is desired to estimate the maximum feasible bid price.

In both cases the purchasing company will estimate future net of tax cash flows that the acquisition is likely to add including synergistic economies (which are discussed in the context of the take-over later in this article). Generally it is preferable to do this assuming that merely the equity of the target company is to be acquired; thus on the other side of the equation, the purchase price will be the consideration necessary to acquire the equity of the take-over candidate. Expected incremental cash flows will be accompanied by subjective probabilities and will include anticipated cash to be derived from realising surplus assets, and selling off divisions (if applicable). Full allowance must of course be made in respect of any new investment that the acquiring company believes is necessary to achieve the expected cash inflows. All of these forward forecasts will be on the basis that the potential acquisition company is developed in the manner most profitable to the purchaser.

The various net of tax cash flow series, together with their probability of occurrence, will than be discounted at the risk free rate (probably with the aid of a computer) to give a probability distribution of possible outcomes for the acquisition — for example Figure 5.2. The expected value and standard deviation of this distribution can easily be determined, as can the expected value of the net present value of the acquisition (by deducting the purchase consideration).

It is now possible (again via computer) to calculate, for various permutations of investment projects the prospective net present value and standard deviation, and to select that portfolio which is most in keeping with the firm's risk/return requirements. If the acquisition is in such a portfolio the implication is that the acquisition should be undertaken.

In most cases, of course, the purchase price will not be fixed at the above stage, and in these circumstances portfolio analysis is potentially a valuable tool in setting a maximum feasible purchase consideration. How this is done is now set out.

The procedure, in terms of estimation of likely cash flows, is exactly as outlined above. It is clearly possible to take the analysis up to the probability distribution showing present value — but not net present value because purchase consideration is unknown — versus probability of occurrence.

Now the lowest theoretical purchase price is zero; in this case the net present value is the same as the present value. At the other extreme the maximum price is given by the expected value of the present value; in this instance the expected value of the net present value will be zero. If the acquisition is feasible the purchase price will fall between these two extremes. To determine the maximum price that the firm can feasibly pay, net present value against standard deviation is calculated for all possible

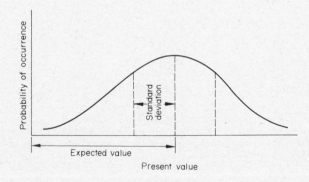

Fig. 5.2   Probability distribution of possible outcomes for acquisition

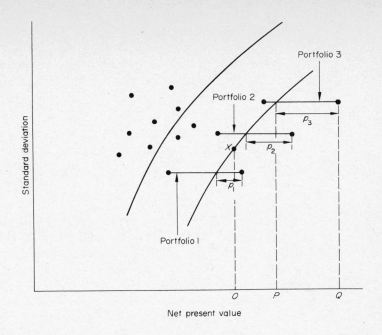

Fig. 5.3
Possible portfolios represented in terms of NPV and standard deviation

portfolios. In the case of those portfolios which include the acquisition, net present value is determined both on the basis of a nil purchase price and on the basis of paying the expected value of the present value for the take-over. Figure 5.3 shows the form of results of this procedure.

According to Figure 5.3, of those portfolios excluding the acquisition, that portfolio represented by point X is the best choice. But if the take-over consideration is zero, clearly all of the portfolios which include the acquisition (i.e., portfolios 1, 2 and 3) will, since they lie on indifference curves to the right of the curve on which X appears, be preferred to portfolio X. With the notation in the figure, in which only portfolios 1, 2 and 3 include the acquisition, and $p_3 > p_2 > p_1$, clearly if p_1 is the amount of the take-over consideration, the firm will be indifferent between portfolio X and portfolio 1. But since both p_2 and p_3 are greater than p_1, the firm would clearly prefer portfolio 3. Using this line of reasoning, it is evident that up to a purchase consideration of p_3 the acquisition is feasible and portfolio 3 should be selected. This distance given by p_3 is the maximum limit to the purchase price.

167

A practical approach to the acquisition as a capital budgeting decision

Given that there are considerable limitations to the practical application of portfolio analysis to capital budgeting in the complex modern business organisation, it is appropriate to look at a more straightforward method of appraising the take-over. In essence the presentation outlined here involves the estimation of probable future cash flows (either with or without subjective probabilities) and discounting them to produce a present value, which represents the maximum purchase price. In projecting future outturns it is advisable to approach the problem piecemeal. Most companies are not one-product companies and analysis should be in terms of each distinct business entity. This necessarily involves an in-depth study of all of the target company's activities, broken down, for example, by production capacity, mode of marketing, determinants of demand, nature of competition, innovation in the industry, management strengths and past financial performance. The key objective of this analysis is the development of a comprehensive understanding of the nature of the business and the tactics necessary for success. This analysis will lead to estimates of future results on the assumption that the business is developed in the manner most profitable to the purchasing company.

At this stage it is essential to assess whether the candidate's business is an entrepreneurial one, dependent upon the flair of one or more of the proprietors. Frequently these entrepreneurial situations involve specialist skills in the areas of salesmanship and innovation. It is important to recognise where profit stems from this source, because continued profit performance depends upon the continued motivation of the entrepreneur(s). The company making the acquisition ought, in these circumstances, to make the purchase consideration contingent upon achievement of specified profit levels over a period of time [18].

This whole process of estimating future results and assessing strengths and weaknesses is clearly facilitated where access to figures and to people is possible; in other cases the exercise must be completed from the outside looking in.

This pre-acquisition analysis will form the cornerstone for valuing the equity capital of the take-over candidate. In financial terms, five categories of projection should be set out, namely:

1   an estimate of likely incremental future net of tax cash flows assuming that the target company is acquired and the potential new subsidiary is operated in the manner most profitable to the purchasing company. Incremental cash flows include net cash outflows – for example on addi-

tional investment — necessary to achieve the most profitable development of the potential new subsidiary;

2   a valuation of all surplus assets, that is, assets not required in running the main business activities of the take-over target company;

3   a valuation, on a break-up basis, of the business's operating assets;

4   an estimate of the necessary timing of replacement and the cost thereof in respect of all non-surplus assets;

5   the timing and amount of any loan redemptions which are to be repaid from normal cash flow, as opposed to the proceeds of a replacement debt issue.

The operative statement in making the above projections is that 'the potential new subsidiary is operated in the manner most profitable to the purchasing company'.

In the estimation of future cash flows under (1) above, the analyst should be concerned with the *incremental* flows — this necessarily includes, besides cash flows that may accrue to the company being taken over, higher profit that may be earned in the area of the acquiring company's existing operations as a result of economies arising from the acquisition. It also includes allowance for losses that would occur in the absence of the take-over. For example, if company A does not buy out company B, allowing company C to merge with B, then A's profit would fall. In these circumstances, company A should calculate incremental cash flows on the basis of (cash flows with the acquisition of B) less (cash flows accruing to A on the basis of B merging with C).

Assuming that the acquired firm will continue to be operated into the foreseeable future, and that surplus assets are realised, it is possible by taking (1), (2), (4) and (5) together to determine the cash flows resulting from the acquisition. Now using the discounted flow technique, the present value of the target company may be obtained.

The acquired company may have only a limited economic life. Given the above estimates, comparison of the present value of items (1) and (5) with the present value of item (4) indicates whether this is so. Clearly if the present value of the costs of replacement exeeds that of net income, the business can be viewed as being only to limited economic viability. This does not mean to say that it is not worth buying but it should be seen as an investment with a limited life. In this case, however, the present value of the target company should be calculated by aggregating the discounted estimates of (1) — taken over the economic life of the business — (2) and (5).

The take-over target, either in total or in respect of individual divisions, should be viewed as one without an economic life if the break-up value (or the amount for which it can be sold off) – (3) above – exeeds the net present value of future cash flows. This type of investment – the asset situation – can be especially attractive where the purchase price is less than the asset value, and such assets can readily be disposed of.

Clearly difficulties exist in estimating future cash flows especially when there are hostilities surrounding the acquisition and access to information is limited. Even in the cases of agreed bids where access to the target company's books, management, production and marketing facilities is given, a pragmatic view should be adopted. For example where a loss-making division is due, according to the vendor, to move into profit, business logic ought to underpin the forecast. In any case, having seen the vendor's future projections, his management and other capabilities, the purchaser is always advised to base caculations on his own estimates of likely future outturns.

The estimation of future cash flows involves appraising all possible ways that the firm might be developed and choosing the one that maximises the present value of the future net incremental cash flows. Economies based on rationalisation of manufacturing, purchasing, distribution, marketing facilities and general overheads, etc., should all be evaluated. From the incremental income so derived should be deducted corporate taxation and the discounted value of any capital investment necessary to maintain and expand the business. In estimating rationalisation and synergy gains – and here synergy means real economic improvement rather then puffery and vague notions of super-marketing, etc. – it is wise to take a somewhat sceptical view.

This is because, in assessing potential economies of scale and sources of synergy release, research [8] indicates significant differences between theory and practice. It is generally considered that the production function is the most likely source of achieving synergy gains through longer manufacturing runs, increased raw materials purchasing leverage, the justification of more efficient plant and machinery, and the opportunity to rationalise manufacturing facilities. The second most profitable area, in terms of synergy release, is often reckoned to be research and development through the elimination of duplicated effort. Similarly there is potential for more efficient marketing effort where product line, distribution channels and sales forces can be combined. Organisational gains are ranked fourth; these involve economies of scale that eliminate duplicated functions and release 'human creativity through improved motivation'. Finally financial economies of scale, where new money is raised on uncharged assets, or where asset backing for borrowing is increased, are generally

170

ranked below other functional pay-offs.

In practice — and this is of utmost relevance in projecting and planning for future results following a merger — these theoretcal rankings are almost completely reversed. Synergy is most easily released in financial areas, and next comes the marketing function. Production and research and development gains, which are usually thought to be the most easily won sources of synergy, turn out to be the hardest economies of scale to release in the real world.

For the acquisition-minded company, these findings suggest that a certain amount of scepticism in respect of manufacturing and technological economies of scale would not be unhealthy. If the challenge of such potential gains is to be reaped then it comes as a reward for real management effort. Synergy is certainly not automatically inherent in a situation — it is the prize not entitlement!

The valuation of assets at the time of an acquisition is clearly one of the key aspects from both purchaser's and seller's standpoint.

The first objective of this part of the exercise is to identify and to value those assets required to carry on the business and assets that are surplus to business operations. For those assets that are to be retained, the purchaser should be interested mainly in their value on a replacement cost basis. However in terms of the valuation procedure he should require details first of their resale value and second of their estimated remaining life and cost of subsequent replacement. The analysis of when assets are likely to become worn out and their replacement cost is often approached by setting out total figures for various classes of assets, e.g., plant and machinery, vehicles, etc., and looking at single assets only where their cost is large in relation to the total business.

In respect of surplus assets, the valuation should aim at providing an estimate of their resale value. If it is likely that the surplus assets will appreciate in value, an indication of likely movements in value should be obtained. Thus if the rate of appreciation exceeds the purchaser's cost of capital, the assets may be worth holding for resale at some later time.

The above valuation procedure should be backed if possible by an evaluation of net current assets verified through undertaking a balance sheet audit.

Having carried out the above investigation the purchaser will be in a position to value the business of the vendor. The minimum value of the business to the vendor should be the sum of all assets at break-up value. If the purchaser can buy the whole of the business for an amount less than this, clearly he can reap immediate short-term gains merely by liquidating all assets.

At this stage of the financial analysis, the purchaser will have estimates of all of the key areas mentioned above. Estimates of likely future net of tax incremental cash flows − suitably adjusted where necessary for replacement of worn out assets − taken with realisations of surplus assets and loan redemptions will provide information, which when discounted at the cost of capital will provide a reasoned valuation of the business to be acquired.

Except in the case of the asset situation it is this price that should be set as the maximum price that the purchaser is prepared to pay. By contrast, the minimum price, in the case of a company with a stock market quotation will generally be set by the stock exchange share price.[4] In fixing the bid price the purchasing company will have in mind the value based on the stock market price, the break-up value and the discounted net present value.

Earnings per share considerations

The modern theory of financial management is based on the objective of maximising the present value of the ultimate owners' stake in the corporation, but according to empirical studies of companies' actual behaviour, the indication is that managers frequently pursue other goals. This may be owing to the development of the modern corporate entity, with divorce of ownership and control. It is frequently asserted that managers, with minimal equity stakes in the company, are less motivated than the owner-manager. This factor has beed noted by various writers ([3], [7], [17], [23]. Others ([5], [19]) have suggested that economic survival may take priority in terms of being the goal of a business. Alternatively, cases are instanced [2] where firms try to maximise sales subject to the constraint that a satisfactory rate of return on invested capital should be earned.

This approach is well borne out by the concept of satisficing developed by Herbert Simon [20] from his observations of the workings of administrative systems. Instead of 'economic man', Simon talks of 'administrative man'. Whilst 'economic man' maximises − selecting the best course of action available − 'administrative man' satisfices − that is, he selects a course of action which is satisfactory or good enough. In business terms, 'administrative man' seeks adequate profit rather than maximum profit; a fair price rather than maximum price.

An alternative concept concerning convictions about the proper role of the company in the economic and social system is reflected in the pursuit of somewhat ideological goals. This view can be summarised [12] as conducting 'the affairs of the corporation in such a way as to maintain an equitable and working balance amongst the claims of the various interested groups — stockholders, employees, customers and the public at large'. Stating explicitly how the compromise is to be achieved may vary from one firm to another, but the mere fact that a balance is involved presupposes a conflict with the goal of profit maximisation.

The interpretation of the firm's goals as consisting of a collection of various interacting motives of the interested parties is endorsed by the research of Cyert and March [4] who argue 'that the goals of a business firm are a series of more or less independent constraints imposed on the organisation through a process of bargaining among potential coalition members and elaborated over time in response to short-run pressures. Goals arise in such a form because the firm is, in fact, a coalition of participants with disparate demands, changing foci of attention, and limited ability to attend to all organisational problems simultaneously'. 'In the long run, studies of the goals of a business firm must reflect the adaptation of goals to changes in the coalition structure.' This concept, the behavioural theory of the firm, implies that it is meaningless to talk of a single organisational goal. It is the participants who have personal objectives, and organisational goals can mean only the goals of the dominant members of the coalition.

A not dissimilar picture of the firm has been suggested in the theory of managerial capitalism [10], which implies that 'top management, owning little or no equity in the firm, has three main motives: (i) growth, because growth provides job satisfaction, job expansion, higher salaries, higher bonuses and prestige; (ii) continuity of employment, which means for the management team as a whole, avoidance of involuntary take-over; and (iii) reasonable treatment of shareholders and generally good relations with the financial world' [11].

All of the above theories of corporate objectives tend to suggest the imposition of constraints upon the maximising objective, the conclusion being that the fiscal goal might be restated as the maximisation of the present value of the firm to the shareholders, subject to certain constraints, which vary from company to company and from time to time. In any case, even if behaviourally the economist's concept of profit maximisation does not appear to be universally true, this approach can be justified since from the standpoint of business efficiency the company should know what it foregoes by pursuing some policy other than the profit maximising one.

Despite these objections it is, for the purpose of this exposition, proposed to look upon corporate objectives in terms of maximising the present value of the equity owners' stake in the corporation. The value of this investment is reflected in cash flows that accrue to ordinary share-holders, both in terms of dividends and capital gains realised when the shareholder sells out. Thus this corporate objective may be restated as maximising long-term growth in share price and dividend.

Generally speaking the share price of a company reflects the stock market's opinion of the company's existing level of earnings per share and potential for future earnings per share growth, although, of course, other factors may be at work in determining the market price, for example, underlying asset value, rumours of take-over bids, etc.

An acquisition can make a considerable impact of earnings per share for various reasons. This may be because of changed accounting practices, or financing, or via an advantageous purchase price. How changes in depreciation policy, profit on long-term contracts and the like can affect reported earnings is well known. Financing an acquisition by debt as opposed to equity may increase short-term earnings per share or earnings per share growth. It may also tend towards the minimisation of the weighted average cost of capital[5] issued by the company. Acquisition-orientated companies generally[6] aim to issue as much debt as possible in a take-over financing package.[7] In terms of an advantageous purchase consideration, this may arise where the candidate company, because of short-term prospects, is lowly valued despite significant growth prospects in the longer term which are not taken into account by the market price (which may be more concerned with the nearer time horizon).

If an acquisition increases both short-term earnings per share and, at the same time, longer-term earnings per share growth prospects of the company making the acquisition, this appears to be a favourable deal to the purchaser (assuming that it gives rise to incremental cash flows which when discounted exceed the purchase consideration). Whilst this situation sometimes arises in acquisitions of private unquoted companies where the vendor is prepared for tax reasons to accept a price favourable to the purchasing company, this type of occurrence is less regular where public companies are being bought. What is more usual is the situation where either short-term earnings per share are diluted but growth prospects enhanced or short-term earnings per share are increased although growth prospects are reduced.

Recent empirical studies [1] of stock market behaviour in these situations are interesting. In theory, at least in the short term, following an acquisition the total valuation of the surviving company should be equal to the sum of the values immediately prior to the acquisition of the purchasing company and the vendor company. In practice, Newbould's research tends to indicate otherwise. In those situations where the surviving

174

company experienced an immediate boost to earnings per share, the value of the corporation was generally higher than the theoretical one. Conversely immediate earnings dilution was accompanied by an actual value below the theoretically calculated one.

But does this mean that a company making an acquisition should never allow immediate earnings to be diluted? If not, how should it quantify the relative merits in earnings per share terms of such an acquisition *vis-à-vis* other possible acquisitions?

The answer to the first question is undoubtedly no. This is because in the longer term earnings per share may be enhanced – and in terms of the present value of earnings per share, the acquisition which causes immediate dilution may give a higher present value. Table 5.1 instances such a case. Company P can take over company Q or company R: in the former case short-term earnings rise, but in the longer term fall, whilst in the latter example short-term earnings are diluted but in the longer term, they rise. It can be seen that if earnings per share are discounted at the cost of equity capital (for the purpose of the example taken as 10 per cent) the latter acquisition is preferable viewed on the criterion of present value of earnings per share.

If this type of analysis is used, the result can clearly be affected by the

Table 5.1

Incremental earnings per share gains resulting from acquisition by P Ltd of Q Ltd and R Ltd discounted to present value

Year	Discounted factor at 10 per cent	Impact on earnings per share (new pence)			
		P Ltd takes over Q Ltd		P Ltd takes over R Ltd	
		Impact of takeover	Discounted	Impact of takeover	Discounted
0	1·000	+2·5	+2·5	−1·7	−1·7
1	0·909	+2·1	+1·9	−0·5	−0·5
2	0·826	+1·5	+1·2	+1·1	+0·9
3	0·751	+0·8	+0·6	+3·4	+2·5
4	0·683	+0·1	+0·1	+6·4	+4·4
5	0·621	−1·0	−0·6	+10·5	+6·5
Net present value of gain in projected earnings per share			+5·7		+12·1

discount rate chosen, but more significantly by the time horizon of projections. Thus where it is adopted it is imperative to specify these two factors. The discount rate, since one is concerned with earnings available for equity shareholders, should be the cost of equity capital. As regards the time horizon this should, if stock market confidence is not to be undermined, be fairly short. The take-over situation where immediate earnings per share are massively diluted but things come right if a very long-term view is taken will clearly be suspect in stock market terms.

Conclusions

Writers on financial management regard the take-over basically as a capital budgeting decision capable of analysis in the same way as any other investment opportunity. At the theoretical level this would enable all of the techniques in the armoury of project analysis to be applied to the aquisition, for example, at this level portfolio analysis is a valuable tool. But at the practical level of the complex business organisation there are difficulties in specifying the trade-off between risk and return. These difficulties should not preclude the use of the discounting process to estimated future cash flows, although in practice this is not frequently done. Nevertheless it is a recommended practice.

In determining the financing of an acquisition, the most usual procedure involves assessing the effect on earnings per share. This is undoubtedly a valuable method, but it does not mean that the appraisal should focus only upon immediate earnings per share implications. It is preferable for earnings per share projections to cover a specified time horizon with calculations in terms of the present value of anticipated earnings per share increments.

The procedure advocated in this paper involves, then, selection of an acquisition dependent either upon whether it is included in the portfolio of investments that meets the firm's risk/return requirements, or whether it is sufficiently attractive in terms of the present value of anticipated future cash flows. Accompanied by an analysis which focuses upon the present value of earnings per share increments over a period to be specified by management, this should enable the firm to make a logical choice from take-over opportunities which present themselves.

Notes

[1] Reprinted by kind permission from *Journal of Business Finance* vol. 4, no. 2, pp. 37–46. ©1972 Mercury House Business Publications Ltd.

[2] In practice this is an extremely difficult process. It is perhaps less complex in the case of the one-man business, where it is required only to establish the proprietor's risk/return trade-off. But in the modern complex business organisation where ownership and control are divorced, and decisions, according to Cyert and March, flow from a coalition which varies from time to time, specifying risk/return indifference curves clearly has problems.

[3] For a summary of the necessary calculations here see, for example, reference [24].

[4] However there are exeptions, for example the succesful bid by Lines Brothers Ltd for Meccano Ltd.

[5] This is because debt is generally the cheapest form of finance. The net of corporation tax cost of a $10\frac{1}{2}$ per cent debenture is $6 \cdot 3$ per cent because debenture interest is an allowable expense in calculating corporation tax payable. By contrast the dividend payable on preferred capital is viewed, for tax purposes, as an appropriation of profit, not a charge against profit. Thus the net of corporation tax cost of capital raised via $10\frac{1}{2}$ per cent preference shares is $10\frac{1}{2}$ per cent. Fixing the cost of equity capital is more complex, and opinion is divided as to the best method of assessment. Approaches include:

the earnings yield basis, i.e., the current earnings per share dividend by share price;
the dividend yield plus an allowance for growth (either of future dividends or share price);
the opportunity cost approach;
the earnings yield plus an allowance for growth.

Usually the cost of equity capital works out as being in excess of the cost of debt.

[6] In those cases where they view their equity as being overvalued, the incentive to issue equity increases proportionally.

[7] The reasoning is that debt tends to affect, besides earnings per share, the total value of the corporation. But the literature on this subject is by no means in agreement. The proponents of the 'traditional' theory of financial managment — see for example [21] — suggest that the judicious use of debt will enhance the total stock market value of the company. By contrast the original studies of Modigliani and Miller [14] indicated that

the total value of the corporation is independent of capital structure. In a subsequent paper — following a reply by David Durand [6] — Modigliani and Miller modified their opinion to the effect that where interest is deductible for taxation purposes, the total value of the company may be. enhanced by the use of debt — but only by virtue of the taxation treatment of debt interest [15].

References

1 Alberts, W.W., and Segall, J.E. (ed)., *The Corporate Merger*, The University of Chicago Press, Chicago and London 1966.
2 Baumol, W.J., *Business Behaviour, Value and Growth*, Macmillan 1959.
3 Berle, A.A., and Means, G.C., *The Modern Corporation and Private Property*, Macmillan, 1932.
4 Cyert, R.M., and March, J.G., *A Behavioural Theory of the Firm*, Prentice Hall, 1963.
5 Drucker, P.F., 'Business objectives and survival needs: notes on a discipline of business enterprise' *Journal of Business*, April 1958.
6 Durand, D., 'The cost of capital in an imperfect market: a reply to Modigliani and Miller' *American Economic Review*, June 1959.
7 Gordon, R.A., *Business Leadership in the Large Corporation*, The Brookings Institute, Washington 1945.
8 Kitching, J., 'Why do mergers miscarry'? *Harvard Business Review*, November–December 1967.
9 Markowitz, H.M., *Portfolio Selection: Efficient Diversification of Investments*, John Wiley and Sons, Inc., New York 1959.
10 Marris, R.L., *The Economic Theory of Managerial Capitalism*, Macmillan, 1964.
11 Marris, R.L., 'Profitability and growth in the individual firm'. *Business Ratios*, Spring 1967.
12 Mason, E.S., 'The apologetics of managerialism' *Journal of Business*, January 1958 (quotes Abrams, F.).
13 Merrett, A.J., and Sykes, A., *The Finance and Analysis of Capital Projects*, Longmans, 1964.
14 Modigliani, F., and Miller, M.H., 'The cost of capital, corporate finance and the theory of investment' *American Economic Review* vol. 48, no.3, 1958.
15 Modigliani, F., and Miller, M.H., 'Corporate cost of capital: a correction' *American Economic Review*, July 1963.

16 Newbould, G.D., *Managment and Merger Activity,* Guthstead Ltd, 1970
17 Penrose, E.T., *The Theory of the Growth of the Firm,* Oxford University Press, 1959.
18 Reum, W.R., and Steele, T.A., 'Contingent payouts cut acquisition risks' *Harvard Business Review,* March—April 1970.
19 Rothschild, K.W., 'Price Theory and Oligopoly' *Economic Journal,* September 1947.
20 Simon, H.A., *Administrative Behaviour,* Macmillan, 1960.
21 Solomon, E., *The Theory of Financial Management,* Columbia University Press, 1963.
22 Van Horne, J.C., *Financial Management and Policy,* Prentice Hall, 1968.
23 Veblen, T., *Absentee Ownership,* Macmillan, 1923.
24 Weston, J.F., and Brigham, E.F., *Managerial Finance,* Holt, Rinehart and Winston, 1970.

Additional references

Capital budgeting is an immense subject, including as it does aspects of portfolio analysis and investment analysis. The following lengthy list is intended to provide the interested reader with a starting point into the many avenues that he might explore. In providing these references particular emphasis has been placed on published work which involves a statistical or probabilistic element.

Adelson, R.M., 'Discounted cash flow — can we discount it? A critical examination' *Journal of Business Finance* vol. 2, no. 2, 1970, pp. 50–66.

Amey, L.R., 'Interdependences in capital budgeting: a survey' *Journal of Business Finance* vol. 4, no. 3, 1972, pp. 70–86.

Baker, J.C., and Beardsley, L.J., 'Multinational companies' use of risk evaluation and profit measurement for capital budgeting decisions' *Journal of Business Finance* vol. 5, no. 1, 1973, pp. 38–43.

Barron, M.J., 'Investment decisions under uncertainty' *Journal of Business Finance* vol. 5, no. 1, 1973, pp. 3–9.

Bernhard, R.H., 'A comprehensive comparison and critique of discounting indices proposed for capital investment evaluation' *The Engineering Economist* vol. 16, no. 3, 1971, pp. 157–86.

Bhaskar, K.N., 'Rates of return under uncertainty' *Accounting and Business Research* no. 9, 1972, pp. 40–52.

Bierman, H., Jr, and Smidt., S., *The Capital Budgeting Decision*, 2nd ed., Macmillan, 1966.

Bierman, H., Jr, and Hausmann, W.H., 'The resolution of investment uncertainty through time' *Management Science (Applications)* vol. 18, no. 12, 1972, pp. 654–62.

Bierman, H., Jr, and Hass, J.E., 'Capital budgeting under uncertainty — a reformulation' *Journal of Finance*, vol. 28, no. 1, 1973, pp. 119–30.

Brennan, J.F., 'A short cut to capital budgeting forecasting for public utilities' *The Engineering Economist* vol. 14, no. 3, 1969, pp. 151–8.

Bromwich, M., 'Capital budgeting — a survey' *Journal of Business Finance* vol. 2, no. 3, 1970, pp. 3–26.

Brumelle, S.L., and Schwab, B., 'Capital budgeting with uncertain future opportunities — a Markovian approach' *Journal of Financial and Quantitative Analysis* vol. 8, no. 1, 1973, pp. 111–22.

Bussey, L.E., and Stevens, G.T., Jr, 'Formulating correlated cash flow streams' *The Engineering Economist* vol. 18, no. 1, 1972, pp. 49–70.

Economos, A.M., 'A financial simulation for risk analysis of a proposed subsidiary' *Management Science (Applications)* vol. 15, no. 12, 1968, pp. 675–82.

Godfrey, J.T., and Spivey, W.A., 'Models for cash flow estimation in capital budgeting' *The Engineering Economist* vol. 16, no. 3, 1971, pp. 187–210.

Greer, W.R., Jr, 'Capital budgeting analysis with timing of events uncertain' *The Accounting Review* vol . 45, 1970, pp. 103–14.

Hackett, W., 'The discounting of single and multiple pulses of distributed cash flow' *Journal of Business Finance* vol. 4, no. 4, 1972, pp. 25–33.

Hertz, D.B., Risk analysis in capital investment' *Harvard Business Review* January– February 1964, pp. 96–106.

Hillier, F.S., 'The derivation of probabilistic information for the evaluation of risky investments' *Management Science* vol .9, April 1963, pp. 443–57.

Hillier, F.S., 'A basic model for capital budgeting of risky interrelated projects' *The Engineering Economist* vol. 17, no. 1, 1971, pp. 1–30.

Jones-Lee, M., 'Portfolio adjustments and capital budgeting criteria' *Journal of Business Finance* vol. 1, no. 2, 1969, pp. 47–54.

Keeley, R., and Westerfield, R., 'A problem in probability distribution techniques for capital budgeting' *Journal of Finance* vol. 27, 1972, pp. 703–10.

Kim, S., 'Capital appropriations and investment behaviour' *Journal of the American Statistical Association* no. 331, 1970, pp. 1181–94.

Knoblett, J.A., 'The gambler's ruin model as an aid in capital budgeting decisions' *Management Adviser*, March–April 1973, pp. 49–54.

Kryzanowski, L., Lustzig, P., and Schwab, B., 'Monte Carlo simulation and capital expenditure decisions – a case study' *The Engineering Economist* vol. 18, no. 1, 1973, pp. 31–48.

Laughhunn, D.J., and Petersen, D.E., 'Computational experience with capital expenditure programming models under risk' *Journal of Business Finance* vol. 3, no. 4, 1971, pp. 43–8.

Levy, H., and Sarnat, M., 'Diversification, portfolio analysis and the uneasy case for conglomerate mergers' *Journal of Finance* vol. 25, 1970, pp. 795–802.

Levy, H., and Sarnat, M., 'The portfolio analysis of multiperiod capital investment under conditions of risk' *The Engineering Economist* vol. 16, no. 1, 1970, pp. 1–20.

Litzenberger, R.H., and Rao, C.U., 'Portfolio theory and industry cost of capital estimates' *Journal of Financial and Quantitative Analysis* vol. 7, no. 2, 1972, pp. 1442–68.

Lockett, A.G., and Freeman, P., 'Probabilistic networks and R & D portfolio selection' *Operational Research Quarterly* vol. 21, pp. 353–9.

Ma, R., and Tydeman, J., 'Project selection criteria, wealth maximisation, and capital rationing' *Journal of Business Finance* vol. 4, no. 4, 1972, pp. 34–43.

Mao, J.C.T., and Helliwell, J.F., 'Investment decision under uncertainty: theory and practice' *Journal of Finance* vol. 24, 1969, pp. 323–38.

Michelsen, D.L., Commander, J.R., and Snead, J.R., 'Risk allowance in original capital investments' *The Engineering Economist* vol. 5, no. 3, 1969, pp. 137–58.

Miller, V.V., Anderson, L.P., and Josephs, S.S., 'A probability distribution of discounted payback for evaluating investment decisions' *Journal of Financial and Quantitative Analysis* vol. 7, no. 2, 1972, pp. 1439–43.

Oakford, R.V., 'The prospective growth rate as a measure of acceptability of a proposal' *The Engineering Economist* vol. 15, no. 4, 1970, pp. 207–16.

Pegels, C.C., 'A comparison of decision criteria for capital investment decisions' *The Engineering Economist* vol. 13, no. 4, 1968, pp. 211–20.

Reisman, A., and Rao, A.K., 'Stochastic cash flow formulae under conditions of inflation' *The Engineering Economist* vol. 18, no. 1, 1972, pp. 49–70.

Ross, M.H., 'Probability, games, regret and investment criteria' *The Engineering Economist* vol. 18, no. 3, 1973, pp. 191–8.

Salazar, R.C., and Sen, S.K., 'A simulation model of capital budgeting under uncertainty' *Management Science (Applications)* vol. 15, no. 4, 1968, pp. 161–79.

Stapleton, R.C., 'Portfolio analysis, stock valuation, and capital budgeting decision rules for risky projects' *Journal of Finance* vol. 26, 1971, pp. 95–117.

Tuttle, D.L., and Litzenberger, R.H., 'Leverage, diversification, and capital market effects on the risk adjusted capital budgeting framework' *Journal of Finance* vol. 23, 1968, pp. 427–43.

Van Horne, J.C., 'Capital budgeting decisions involving combinations of risky assets' *Management Science B* vol. 13, no. 2, 1966, pp. 84–91.

Van Horne, J.C., 'The analysis of uncertainty resolution in capital budgeting for new products' *Management Science (Applications)* vol. 15, no. 8, 1969, pp. 376–86.

Van Horne, J.C., 'Capital budgeting under conditions of uncertainty as to the project's life' *The Engineering Economist* vol. 17, no. 3, 1972, pp. 189–99.

Wagle, B., 'A statistical analysis of risk in capital investment projects' *Operational Research Quarterly* vol. 21, 1967, pp. 353–9.

Weingarter, H.M., 'Capital budgeting of interrelated projects: survey and synthesis' *Management Science (Applications)* vol. 12, no. 7, 1966, pp. 485–516.

Wilkes, F.M., 'Inflation and capital budgeting decisions' *Journal of Business Finance* vol. 4, no. 3, 1972, pp. 46–53.

Williamson, R.N., 'Uncertainty present value calculations' *Management Adviser* January–February 1973, pp. 25–7.

Wilson, R., 'Investment analysis under uncertainty' *Management Science (Applications)* vol. 15, no. 12, 1969, pp. 650–64.

Estimation

One of the most important practical uses of statistical methodology, as opposed to statistical modelling, is in estimation and hypothesis testing. The great majority of theory rests on the 'classical' assumption of normality in the underlying probability distributions, and — although normal distributions rarely appear in practice — the statistical procedures based on this assumption are sufficiently robust for small deviations from true normality to be far from critical. The following article illustrates two estimation situations in which normal theory can be used to reveal some rather unexpected pitfalls awaiting the accountant.

Problems of Estimation in Accounting

Introduction

The purpose of this article is to examine some statistical implications of the calculation of index numbers in inflation accounting, and of the solution of a specific problem in break-even (CVP) analysis. In particular, it is intended to illustrate how the same, quite sophisticated, analysis can intrude unexpectedly upon two apparently dissimilar areas of financial and management accounting. Although the algebraic detail may be a little difficult for the mathematically unskilled, it is hoped that the inclusion of numerical examples will clarify the conclusions.

Index numbers and accounting for price-level changes

The formation of an index number relating the price of, say, a commodity at time t to its price at some arbitrary base date, 0, by calculating the ratio of the prices is a very familiar process. In a similar manner, a more broadly based general index can be designed in order to take into account price changes in a wide range of different commodities. Moonitz [7] has recently considered, in detail, the use of such indices in accounting for price-level changes, and comments that an 'average of index numbers is bound to be biased to some extent or other unless the individual numbers in the series are carefully weighted'. It is with some explanation of this phenomenon — and indeed with the biasedness of ratios in general — that we shall be concerned initially. Subsequently, a method is suggested which enables the bias to be substantially reduced in a large number of cases.

Let us begin with the simple example of a commodity whose price, X_i ($i = 1, \ldots, n$) has been ascertainted at n outlets at time zero. Subsequently, at time t, the prices at the same outlets are Y_i ($i = 1, \ldots, n$).

Two methods for calculating the index suggest themselves:

(1)
$$\hat{I}_1 = (\sum_{i=1}^{n} Y_i)/(\sum_{i=1}^{n} X_i)$$

and

$$(2) \qquad \hat{I}_2 = \sum_{i=1}^{n} (Y_i/X_i)/n$$

Almost instinctively, one feels that probaby $\hat{I}_1$ represents the more 'accurate' (in some sense) index, although the rationale underlying this choice is not immediately obvious. Certainly $\hat{I}_1$ and $\hat{I}_2$ are not generally equal — a fact which is clearly demonstrated in Table 6.1

Thus,
$$\hat{I}_1 = 415 \cdot 8/244 \cdot 6$$
$$= 1 \cdot 700$$

and
$$\hat{I}_2 = 22 \cdot 936/12$$
$$= 1 \cdot 911 \ .$$

The two questions to be answered then, are: (a) Which index do we use?; and (b) Why should one index be any 'better' than the other? As we shall see, both are subject to a systematic bias, although the bias of $\tilde{I}_1$ is less than that of $\tilde{I}_2$.

To approach the problem theoretically, it is not unreasonable to assume that Y_i ($i = 1, ..., n$) and X_i ($i = 1, ... , n$) are both random samples from normal distributions of prices at times t and zero respectively. The value calculated for I_1 is then seen as a sampling estimate of the true value of the index, and the estimator

$$\tilde{I}_1 = (\Sigma \, \tilde{Y}_i)/(\Sigma \, \tilde{X}_i)$$

is the ratio of two normally distributed random variables. If the expected value of price at time t is Y, and at time zero is X, and if the corresponding variances are $\sigma_{yy} = \sigma_y^2$ and $\sigma_{xx} = \sigma_x^2$ respectively, then the numerator is $N(nY, n\sigma_{yy})$ and the denominator is $N(nX, n\sigma_{xx})$. Typically, the two price distributions will be quite highly correlated, and we shall denote the covariance between them by $\sigma_{xy} = \rho\sigma_x\sigma_y'$ where ρ ($-1 \leqslant \rho \leqslant 1$) is the correlation coefficient. Consequently, the covariance between the numerator and denominator of $\tilde{I}_1$ is $n\sigma_{xy}$.

The distribution of such a ratio has been examined extensively in the statistical literature, notably by Fieller [2], Geary [3], Hinkley [5], and Merrill [6]. It displays the peculiar theoretical property of having an expected value of infinity or zero, and an infinite variance. Fortunately, this theoretical consideration can be avoided in a practical situation (Fieller, *op. cit.*) since a necessarily finite amount of empirical data cannot include infinite values, nor can it have infinite mean or variance. Accordingly, by considering the distribution of the denominator to be truncated (or, more

190

Table 6.1

Price data for different outlets and different times

i	X_i	Y_i	Y_i/X_i	X_iY_i	X_i^2
1	14·5	46·0	3·172	667·00	210·25
2	17·8	41·4	2·326	736·92	316·84
3	20·4	33·9	1·662	691·56	416·16
4	16·6	47·5	2·861	788·50	275·56
5	13·6	20·1	1·478	273·36	184·96
6	27·8	1·0	0·755	583·80	772·84
7	14·5	2·5	2·241	471·25	210·25
8	37·8	37·5	0·992	1417·50	1428·84
9	24·8	19·3	0·778	478·64	615·04
10	13·2	42·9	3·250	566·28	174·24
11	19·8	38·3	1·934	758·34	392·04
12	23·8	35·4	1·487	842·52	566·44

$\Sigma X_i = 244\cdot6$ $\Sigma Y_i = 415\cdot8$ $\Sigma (Y_i/X_i) = 22\cdot936$ $\Sigma X_iY_i = 8275\cdot67$ $\Sigma X_i^2 = 5563\cdot46$

precisely, to be greater than zero), we can obtain the expected value of I_1 as (approximately),

$$E(\tilde{I}_1) = (Y/X) \left\{ 1 + \left(\frac{\sigma_{xx}}{nX^2} - \frac{\sigma_{xy}}{nXY} \right) \right\}.$$

This result was first obtained by Merrill [6]. The percentage bias in $\tilde{I}_1$ is therefore:

$$100 \left(\frac{\sigma_{xx}}{nX^2} - \frac{\sigma_{xy}}{nXY} \right).$$

Directing our attention now to $\tilde{I}_2$, we note that the ratio Y_i/X_i will have an expected value of:

$$(Y/X) \left\{ 1 + \left(\frac{\sigma_{xx}}{Y^2} - \frac{\sigma_{xy}}{XY} \right) \right\}. \tag{1}$$

Since $\tilde{I}_2$ is just the average of n such variables,

$$E(\tilde{I}_2) = (Y/X) \left\{ 1 + \left(\frac{\sigma_{xx}}{X^2} - \frac{\sigma_{xy}}{XY} \right) \right\}$$

and the percentage bias in $\tilde{I}_2$ is seen to be greater than that in $\tilde{I}_1$ by a factor of n.

Unfortunately, in practice one does not have available exact values of σ_{xx}, σ_{yy} and σ_{xy} with which to calculate the bias. However, estimates of these quantities can, of course, be obtained from the data.

Returning now to Table 6.1

σ_{xx} is estimated by

$$\frac{\Sigma X_i^2 - (\Sigma X_i)^2/n}{(n-1)} = \frac{5563 \cdot 46 - 4985 \cdot 76}{11} = 52 \cdot 25$$

σ_{yy} is estimated by

$$\frac{\Sigma Y_i^2 - (\Sigma Y_i)^2/n}{(n-1)} = \frac{15475 \cdot 88 - 14407 \cdot 47}{11} = 97 \cdot 12$$

192

σ_{xy} is estimated by

$$\frac{\Sigma X_i Y_i - (\Sigma X_i)(\Sigma Y_i)/n}{(n-1)} = \frac{8275 \cdot 67 - 8475 \cdot 39}{11} = -18 \cdot 16$$

X is estimated by $\qquad \Sigma X_i/n = 20 \cdot 38$

Y is estimated by $\qquad \Sigma Y_i/n = 34 \cdot 65$

The estimated percentage bias in $\tilde{I}_1$ is therefore:

$$100 \left\{ \frac{52 \cdot 25}{12 \, (20 \cdot 38)^2} + \frac{18 \cdot 16}{12 \, (20 \cdot 38)(34 \cdot 65)} \right\} = 1 \cdot 26 \text{ per cent}$$

and in $\tilde{I}_2$ is $15 \cdot 15$ per cent.

In fact, both these are underestimates of the biases, since the sets of prices, X_i and Y_i were randomly drawn from two independent normal distributions with expected values 20 and 35, and variances 100 and 100 respectively. Thus,

$$\begin{aligned}
\sigma_{xx} &= \sigma_{yy} = 100 \\
X &= 20 \\
Y &= 35 \\
\sigma_{xy} &= 0 \; .
\end{aligned}$$

The true percentage bias in $\tilde{I}_1$ is therefore:

$$100 \left\{ \frac{100}{12 \, (20)^2} \right\} = 2 \cdot 08 \text{ per cent}$$

and in $\tilde{I}_2$ is $25 \cdot 00$ per cent.

A further point can be usefully mentioned at this stage. It might be thought that a correction could be made to the estimated values of the indexes by using the estimated values of the biases. Thus, knowing that I_1 is estimated as $1 \cdot 700$ and that the estimated bias of $\tilde{I}_1$ is $1 \cdot 26$ per cent, one might suggest $\dfrac{1 \cdot 700}{1 \cdot 0126} = 1 \cdot 679$ as an improved estimate for the index. In a like manner, the improved version of the second index would be $\dfrac{1 \cdot 911}{1 \cdot 1515} = 1 \cdot 660$. Bearing in mind that the true value of the index (which we know only because the data has been artificially generated) is $\frac{35}{20} =$ 1·75, the correction for bias can be seen to have worsened the first estimate and improved the second. This ambivalent behaviour is explained by the fact that the bias, and the calculated value of $\hat{I}_1$ and $\hat{I}_2$, are all estimates.

The choice of the estimator, $\tilde{I}_1$, rather than $\tilde{I}_2$ is now an obvious one, using the criterion of percentage bias. It is worth noting that Geary [4] has questioned the applicability of this criterion, particularly in situations where the values of Y_i are disparate, and the ratios Y_i/X_i have a low dispersion. Dickinson [1] has also examined this problem in the estimation of weights in a portfolio of investments, and has used the so-called jack-knife statistic — originally due to Quenouille [8] — to reduce the bias. In the present context, the method is essentially to define the n estimators

$$\tilde{I}^j = \frac{\tilde{Y}_1 + \ldots + \tilde{Y}_{j-1} + \tilde{Y}_{j+1} + \ldots + \tilde{Y}_n}{\tilde{X}_1 + \ldots + \tilde{X}_{j-1} + \tilde{X}_{j+1} + \ldots + \tilde{X}_n} = \frac{\tilde{Y}^j}{\tilde{X}^j} \ , \text{say,} \ (j = 1, \ldots, n)$$

and then to define the composite estimator:

$$\tilde{I}^* = n\tilde{I}_1 - \left(\frac{n-1}{n}\right) \sum_{j=1}^{n} \tilde{I}^j \ .$$

The expected value of $\tilde{I}^*$ can be found as follows:

$$E(\tilde{I}^*) = nE(\tilde{I}_1) - \left(\frac{n-1}{n}\right) \sum_{j=1}^{n} E(\tilde{I})^j$$

$$\doteq n(Y/X) \left\{ 1 + \frac{\sigma_{xx}}{nX^2} - \frac{\sigma_{xy}}{nXY} \right\}$$

$$- \left(\frac{n-1}{n}\right) n(Y/X) \left\{ 1 + \left[\frac{\sigma_{xx}}{(n-1)X^2} - \frac{\sigma_{xy}}{(n-1)XY} \right] \right\}$$

$$= Y/X$$

Thus the bias in $\tilde{I}^*$ is zero to $0(1/n)$, and can in fact be shown to be $0(1/n^2)$. The calculation of $\tilde{I}^*$ is illustrated below in Table 6.2 using the same data as in Table 6.1.

Table 6.2
Derivation of jack-knife estimates

i	X^i	Y^i	Y^i/X^i
1	230·1	369·8	1·6071
2	226·8	374·4	1·6508
3	224·2	381·9	1·7034
4	228·0	368·3	1·6154
5	231·0	395·7	1·7130
6	216·8	394·8	1·8210
7	230·1	383·3	1·6658
8	206·8	378·3	1·8293
9	219·8	396·5	1·8039
10	231·4	372·9	1·6115
11	224·8	377·5	1·6793
12	220·8	380·4	1·7228
Total	—	—	20·4233

$$\hat{I}^* = 12 \times 1\cdot700 - \tfrac{11}{12} \times 20\cdot4233$$

$$= 20\cdot400 - 18\cdot721$$

$$= 1\cdot679 \ .$$

In this particular example, the point estimate of the index is worse using the estimator $\tilde{I}^*$ than it is using $\tilde{I}_1$. This is mainly due to the fact that sampling errors are large because n is small. In repeated use, however, $\hat{I}^*$ will be a better estimate overall than will $\hat{I}_1$.

A final point concerns the variance of the ratio estimators. Taking the ratio Y_i/X_i, for example, it is not difficult to show (Merrill, op.cit.) that

$$\text{Var}\,(Y_i/X_i) \doteq \left(\frac{Y}{X}\right)^2 \left\{ \frac{\sigma_{yy}}{Y^2} - \frac{2\sigma_{xy}}{XY} + \frac{\sigma_{xx}}{X^2} \right\} \qquad (2)$$

and this general expression can be simply adapted to give the variances of ratios $\tilde{I}_1, \tilde{I}_2$, and $\tilde{I}^*$. Although only an estimate of the variance can be found — using the sample values — it does give some indication of the reliability of the estimate, and facilitates the construction of approximate confidence intervals for the value of the index. For example, taking $\tilde{I}_1$,

$$\text{Var } \tilde{I}_1 \doteq (Y/X)^2 \left\{ \frac{\sigma_{yy}}{nY^2} - \frac{2\sigma_{xy}}{nXY} + \frac{\sigma_{xx}}{nX^2} \right\}$$

$$\doteq \left(\frac{34 \cdot 65}{20 \cdot 38} \right)^2 \left\{ \frac{97 \cdot 12}{12 \, (34 \cdot 65)^2} + \frac{2 \, (18 \cdot 6)}{12 \, (34 \cdot 65)(20 \cdot 38)} + \frac{52 \cdot 25}{12 \, (20 \cdot 38)^2} \right\}$$

$$= 0 \cdot 06217$$

(The true value of var $\tilde{I}_1$ is $0 \cdot 07987$.)

The preceding discussion has taken place in the context of the estimation of a comparatively simple index. However, the essential point — that natural ratio estimators are subject to a systematic bias — is clearly of much broader interpretation. Indeed, any index — either specific or general — or average index will typically be subject to a systematic bias in exactly the same way.

A problem in CVP analysis

Let us now turn to a problem in CVP analysis which is quite dissimilar at first sight. Suppose a certain product can be manufactured by two processes and that each has a pattern of fixed and variable costs. The problem is to determine the level of production at which, say, the first process becomes more costly than the second. Alternatively, we may consider two separate products with distinct manufacturing costs, and require the level of production below which the second, say, is more costly to produce than the first. In either case, we may denote the total costs associated with the first process (or product) by y_{i1} ($i = 1, \dots, n_1$), and with the second by y_{i2} ($i = n_1 + 1, \dots, n_1 + n_2$).

Then,

$$y_{i1} = \alpha_1 + \beta_1 x_{i1} + \epsilon_i \qquad i = 1, \dots, n_1$$

and $\qquad y_{i2} = \alpha_2 + \beta_2 x_{i2} + \epsilon_i \qquad i = n_1 + 1, \dots, n_1 + n_2$

where $\alpha_1, \alpha_2, \beta_1, \beta_2$ are unknown parameters (representing fixed and variable costs), x_{i1}, x_{i2} are production levels, and ϵ_i are assumed to be independent normally distributed random variables, each with mean zero and variance σ^2.

Graphically, the two theoretical patterns might appear as in Figure 6.1. Here y'_{i1} and y'_{i2} denote the theoretical total costs, and the intersection of

196

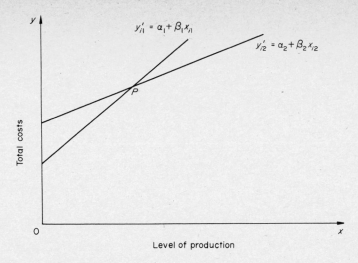

Fig. 6.1 Linear cost functions associated with two products or processes

the two lines, P represents the focus of our interest. On the basis of this model, the coordinates of P are $\left\{ \dfrac{\alpha_1 - \alpha_2}{\beta_2 - \beta_1}, \dfrac{\alpha_1 \beta_2 - \beta_1 \alpha_2}{\beta_2 - \beta_1} \right\}$. In a practical situation, of course, one has data giving the total costs at various production levels, and the parameters $\alpha_1, \alpha_2, \beta_1, \beta_2$ are estimated by the fitting of least-squares regression lines. Denoting these estimates by a_1, a_2, b_1, b_2 respectively, we have

$$a_1 = \sum_{i=1}^{n_1} (y_{i1} - b_1 x_{i1})/n_1 \tag{3}$$

$$a_2 = \sum_{i=n_1+1}^{n_1+n_2} (y_{i2} - b_2 x_{i2})/n_2 \tag{4}$$

$$b_1 = \frac{\left\{ n_1 \sum_{i=1}^{n_1} x_{i1} y_{i1} - \left(\sum_{i=1}^{n_1} x_{i1} \right) \left(\sum_{i=1}^{n_1} y_{i1} \right) \right\}}{\left\{ n_1 \sum_{i=1}^{n_1} x_{i1}^2 - \left(\sum_{i=1}^{n_1} x_{i1} \right)^2 \right\}} \tag{5}$$

$$b_2 = \frac{\left\{ n_2 \sum_{i=n_1+1}^{n_1+n_2} x_{i2} y_{i2} - \left(\sum_{i=n_1+1}^{n_1+n_2} x_{i2} \right) \left(\sum_{i=n_1+1}^{n_1+n_2} y_{i2} \right) \right\}}{\left\{ n_2 \sum_{i=n_1+1}^{n_1+n_2} x_{i2}^2 - \left(\sum_{i=n_1+1}^{n_1+n_2} x_{i2} \right)^2 \right\}} \tag{6}$$

197

Looking now at the estimator $\tilde{b}_1$, as opposed to the point estimate formulated above, and bearing in mind the model assumed in (1), it is not difficult to show that

$$\tilde{b}_1 = \beta_1 + \frac{\{n_1 \Sigma x_{i1} \epsilon_i - (\Sigma x_{i1})(\Sigma \epsilon_i)\}}{\{n_1 \Sigma x_{i1}^2 - (\Sigma x_{i1})^2\}}$$

A little algebra now reveals that:

$$E(\tilde{b}_1) = \beta_1$$

and

$$\text{Var}(\tilde{b}_1) = \sigma^2 / \{n_1 \Sigma x_{i1}^2 - (\Sigma x_{i1})^2\}$$

Since $\tilde{b}_1$ is a linear combination of normally distributed random variables, ϵ_i, it is itself normal, with the mean and variance given above. Clearly similar results concern $\tilde{b}_2$. Furthermore, $\tilde{b}_1$ and $\tilde{b}_2$ are independent — since the ϵ_i are independent for all $i = 1, \ldots, n_1 + n_2$ — and we conclude that

$$\tilde{b}_2 - \tilde{b}_1 \sim N \left\{ \beta_2 - \beta_1 , \ \sigma^2 \left[\frac{1}{\Sigma x_{i1}^2 - (\Sigma x_{i1})^2 / n_1} + \frac{1}{\Sigma x_{i2}^2 - (\Sigma x_{i2})^2 / n_2} \right] \right.$$

In an analogous manner, it can also be shown after some tedious but elementary algebra that

$$\tilde{\alpha}_1 - \tilde{\alpha}_2 \sim N \left\{ \alpha_1 - \alpha_2 , \ \sigma^2 \left[\frac{\Sigma x_{i1}^2 / n_1}{\Sigma x_{i1}^2 - (\Sigma x_{i1})^2 / n_1} + \frac{\Sigma x_{i2}^2 / n_2}{\Sigma x_{i2}^2 - (\Sigma x_{i2})^2 / n_2} \right. \right.$$

and

$$\text{cov} \left\{ (\tilde{\beta}_2 - \tilde{\beta}_1), \ (\tilde{\alpha}_1 - \tilde{\alpha}_2) \right\} =$$

$$\sigma^2 \left[\frac{\Sigma x_{i1} / n_1}{\Sigma x_{i1}^2 - (\Sigma x_{i1})^2 / n_1} + \frac{\Sigma x_{i2} / n_2}{\Sigma x_{i2}^2 - (\Sigma x_{i2})^2 / n_2} \right]$$

Accordingly, our estimator of the level of production at point P, i.e., $(\tilde{\alpha}_1 - \tilde{\alpha}_2)/(\tilde{\beta}_2 - \tilde{\beta}_1)$ is the ratio of two correlated and normal random variables.

The implication of the preceding analysis — which has led to a ratio of the same nature as that considered in the second section of this article — is that the estimate of the critical production level at P is subject to a systematic bias. Armed with this knowledge, however, the bias can be allowed for, and an estimate of the sampling variance can be calculated. The following example illustrates the previous theoretical considerations.

Numerical example

The data for the example are given in Table 6.3. Note that $x_{i1} = x_{i2}$, i.e., the total costs for each case are given at the same levels of production. This is no way invalidates the argument, but has the advantage of simplifying the computation.

Table 6.3
Cost data for two products/processes

x_{i1}	y_{i1}	x_{i2}	y_{i2}
1	41	1	21
2	50	2	38
3	58	3	53
4	58	4	63
5	76	5	73
6	98	6	98
7	105	7	108
8	110	8	134
9	136	9	134
10	120	10	135
11	133	11	135
12	156	12	166
13	174	13	163
14	167	14	196
15	203	15	191

Thus

$$
\begin{aligned}
n_1 = n_2 &= 15 \\
\Sigma x_{i1} = \Sigma x_{i2} &= 120 \\
\Sigma x_{i1} y_{i1} &= 16534 \\
\Sigma x_{i2} y_{i2} &= 17050 \\
\Sigma y_{i1} &= 1685 \\
\Sigma y_{i2} &= 1708 \\
\Sigma y_{i1}^2 &= 223709 \\
\Sigma y_{i2}^2 &= 236644
\end{aligned}
$$

Substitution of these figures into (3) – (6) yields:

$$a_1 = 25 \cdot 08$$
$$a_2 = 17 \cdot 15$$
$$b_1 = 10 \cdot 91$$
$$b_2 = 12 \cdot 09$$

Thus, $(a_1 - a_2)/(b_2 - b_1) = 7 \cdot 93/1 \cdot 18 = 6 \cdot 72$.

Unfortunately, in practice we do not have an exact value for σ^2. However an estimate, s^2, can be obtained from the data, and in the present example we have thirty points on which to base this estimate. Since four regression parameters have been estimated from the data, the appropriate number of degrees of freedom is $30 - 4 = 26$, giving:

$$s^2 = \frac{\sum \{y_{i1} - (a_1 + b_1 x_{i1})\}^2 + \sum \{y_{i2} - (a_2 + b_2 x_{i2})\}^2}{26}$$

$$= 89 \cdot 62 .$$

Thus, approximately:

$$\tilde{a}_1 - \tilde{a}_2 \ \sim \ N\left\{(\alpha_1 - \alpha_2), \ 89 \cdot 62 \left(\frac{1240}{15 \times 280} + \frac{1240}{15 \times 280}\right)\right\}$$

$$= \ N\left\{(\alpha_1 - \alpha_2), \ 52 \cdot 92\right\}$$

$$\tilde{b}_2 - \tilde{b}_1 \ \sim \ N\left\{(\beta_2 - \beta_1), \ 89 \cdot 62 \left(\frac{1}{280} + \frac{1}{280}\right)\right\}$$

$$= \ N\left\{(\beta_2 - \beta_1), \ 0 \cdot 6401\right\}$$

$$\operatorname{cov}\left\{(\tilde{a}_1 - \tilde{a}_2), (\tilde{b}_2 - \tilde{b}_1)\right\} = 89 \cdot 62 \left(\frac{120}{15 \times 280} + \frac{120}{15 \times 280}\right)$$

$$= 5 \cdot 121 .$$

Using (1), the estimated average percentage bias in the estimate of the critical production level is seen to be:

$$100 \left\{\frac{0 \cdot 6401}{(1 \cdot 18)^2} - \frac{5 \cdot 121}{(7 \cdot 93)(1 \cdot 18)}\right\} = -8 \cdot 8 \text{ per cent.}$$

Additionally, the variance of the estimate is approximated by (2) as:

$$\text{var} \left\{ \frac{(\bar{a}_1 - \bar{a}_2)}{(\bar{b}_2 - \bar{b}_1)} \right\} = \left(\frac{7 \cdot 93}{1 \cdot 18} \right)^2 \left\{ \frac{52 \cdot 92}{(7 \cdot 93)^2} - \frac{2 (5 \cdot 121)}{(7 \cdot 93)(1 \cdot 18)} + \frac{0 \cdot 6401}{(1 \cdot 18)^2} \right\}$$

That the point estimate of the critical value of production level is very unreliable scarcely needs underlining further.

Conclusion

The object of the preceding discussion has been to show that the application of statistical methods, without a full realisation of the implications of the analysis, can lead to conclusions and statements which may be grossly in error. Unfortunately, there are too few accountants who have the necessary level of statistical knowledge to be aware of the type of trap into which they may be led, and too few statisticians who know sufficient of the accountants' work to help when necessary. The message — that greater cross-fertilisation of ideas between the two professions is essential — is abundantly clear.

References

1   Dickinson, J.P., *Bias in the Estimation of Portfolio Weights*, to be published, 1974.
2   Fieller, E.C., 'The distribution of the index in a normal bivariate population' *Biometrika* 24, 1932, pp. 428–40.
3   Geary, R.C., 'The frequency distribution of the quotient of two normal variates' *Journal of the Royal Statistical Society B* 93, 1930, pp. 442–6.
4   Geary, R.C., 'A note on biased and inconsistent estimation' *European Economic Review*, 1972, pp. 441–9.
5   Hinkley, D.V., 'On the ratio of two correlated normal random variables' *Biometrika* 56, 1969, pp. 635–9.
6   Merrill, A.S., 'The frequency distribution of an index when both the components follow the normal law' *Biometrika* 20, 1928, pp. 53–63.
7   Moonitz, M., 'Changing Prices and Financial Reporting,' Occasional Paper no. 3, International Centre for Research in Accounting, University of Lancaster, 1973, pp. 75–6.
8   Quenouille, M., 'Notes on bias in estimation' *Biometrika* 43, 1956, pp. 353–60.

Business Failure

Although the first article in this section is concerned to some extent with capital investment, and therefore could have been included in Section 5, its central theme is that of ruin, and it is more appropriately placed alongside the paper of Bierman and Thomas. The authors make the point that normally investment theory has resolved risk into two components — that of ruin and that involved in forecasting future cash flows. They then proceed to explore the previously somewhat neglected characteristics of business failure and formulate an analytical method enabling uncertain cash flows to be adjusted specifically for the risk of ruin.

The second article, whilst still centred on business failure, examines — from the viewpoint of the shareholder rather than of the company — the relationship between the risk of ruin and the issuance of debt.

A Quantitative Measure of the Risk Factor in Investment Decisions[1]

Problem setting

The period since World War II has been generally prosperous for the American economy, but this prosperity has been accompanied by an increase in the rate of business failures. In absolute numbers, the failures among wholesalers and retailers increased 315·9 per cent, while the rate (number per 10,000 firms) of failure for all business increased 242·7 per cent from 1947 − 67 [15].

Several analyses of structure change in American industry have suggested that rapid adoption of new technology has been an important force behind structural development [8], [9], [10]. Changing patterns of technology have been accompanied by high attrition rates due to obsolescence, even though the business community has prospered as a whole. Structural change in American industry seems certain to become a permanent fixture of corporate life. New technological methods coupled with the rapidly changing character of consumer products will cause obsolescence and attrition to become even more commomplace in the future than it has been thus far. In addition, plant or functional attrition seems destined to become relatively more important than corporate attrition. Already conglomerate growth points in this direction.

Against this backdrop of change and uncertainty, the businessman is faced with making investment decisions. These decisions commonly entail comparing investment opportunities involving differing degrees of risk and the choice of plant size to satisfy the investment selected. The analysis is generally carried out through present value calculations by adding a risk premium to the discount factor. The premium enlarges as risk increases.[2] This procedure effects a reduction in the present value of the cash flow generated by the investment. The difficulty with this kind of analysis is that the risk premium is subjective; the cash flow may be reduced by a greater or lesser amount than the risk conditions actually warrant. The method is directionally correct but lacks the precision necessary for an adequate quantitative analysis. Of all the problems in investment apprais-al, the handling of uncertainty has most stubbornly resisted rigorous treat-ment.

Quantifying the risk premium

The basic stochastic model used in this analysis was presented by Adelman [1]. The model involves a Markov Chain process with transition matrices expressing the probability of moving from size category i to size category j within one time period. The size categories characterise firms within the industry and include the possibility of entry and exit. The probability matrix, representing firm growth in a given time period, can be used to extrapolate structural development from the type of growth observable within an industry.[3] Several studies of this kind are available [3], [6], [11]. The studies characterise the net effect of entry and exit of firms within the industry and within the size categories, but they do not produce data illustrating the likelihood of business failure within a particular size cate-gory. Since the transition matrix includes the probability of moving from one particular size category to any other including exit, all necessary information for an attrition function is at hand.[4]

Consider the following model:

$$
[P] =
\begin{bmatrix}
p_{1,1} & p_{1,2} & \cdots & p_{1,N-1} & p_{1,N} \\
p_{2,1} & p_{2,2} & \cdots & p_{2,N-1} & p_{2,N} \\
\vdots & \vdots & & \vdots & \vdots \\
p_{N-1,1} & p_{N-1,2} & \cdots & p_{N-1,N-1} & p_{N-1,N} \\
\hline
p_{N,1} & p_{N,2} & \cdots & p_{N,N-1} & p_{N,N}
\end{bmatrix}
=
\begin{bmatrix}
P^L & D \\
\hline
B & C
\end{bmatrix}
\tag{1}
$$

where

P is $N \times N$ matrix of transition probabilities,

$p_{i,j}$ is probability of moving from state i to state j in one time period,

P^L is first $N-1$ rows and $N-1$ columns of P,

= transition probabilities excluding entry and exit vectors,

D is first $N-1$ elements of the Nth (exit) column of P,

B, C is entry vector, not relevant to the attrition function.

All elements of P are non-negative and sum to one row—wise. It may be

208

noted that D is the likelihood of attrition for each size category in one time period. From this it may be seen that $P^L \cdot D$ yields the vector of attrition probabilities during the second time period. The probability of attrition from each category in the kth period may be represented by $(P^L)^{k-1} D$. The cumulative attrition probabilities (A) from each size category for the first K periods may be expressed as follows:

$$[A_k] = \begin{bmatrix} \alpha_{1k} \\ \cdot \\ \cdot \\ \cdot \\ \alpha_{ik} \\ \cdot \\ \cdot \\ \cdot \\ \alpha_{N-1,k} \end{bmatrix} = \sum_{k=0}^{K} (P^L)^k D \ . \tag{2}$$

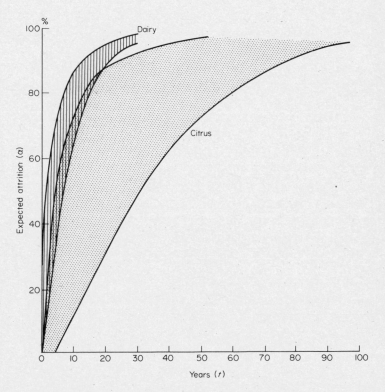

Fig. 7.1   Expected attrition rates in the dairy production and citrus packing industries

Data presented in this analysis have been drawn from several research efforts [4], [5], [10], [14]. Figure 7.1 shows the cumulative attrition rates of eight different size categories of dairy farms, and eight different size categories of fresh citrus packing plants. Figure 7.2 shows the cumulative attrition rates of seven different size categories of poultry processing firms and four different size categories of retail food chains.[5] These figures are generated by applying (2) to each industry in turn.

A separate attrition line is calculated for each size category (α_i), but only the extremes are plotted, thereby simplifying the picture. The shaded zone for each industry indicates the differential in expected attrition between the smallest (upper bound) and largest (lower bound) classifications of firms. In each case the attrition was appreciably higher in the smaller categories and lower among the larger size categories.

Each graph provides a visualisation of attrition rates for several investment classes. The task remaining is to find a family of equations that will

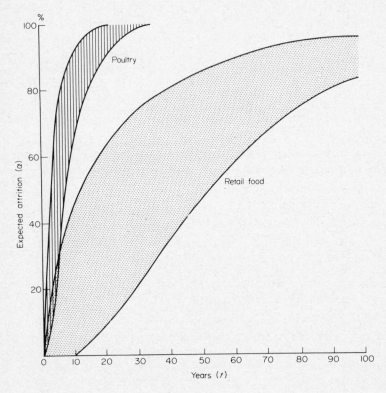

Fig. 7.2   Expected attrition rates in the poultry processing and retail food chain industries

210

parametise attrition with sufficient precision to allow construction of a present value function. The development of such a family of equations follows.

The exponential distribution function $(1-e^{-ct})$ was fitted to the expected attrition for each size category. The parameter c was estimated with a simple linear regression on the data generated by the Markov process. The conversion to linear form follows:

$$\alpha_{it} = 1 - e^{-c_i t} \qquad i = 1, \ldots, N - 1 \tag{3}$$

$$1 - \alpha_{it} = e^{-c_i t} \tag{4}$$

taking natural logarithms of both sides,

$$Ln\,(1 - \alpha_{it}) = -c_i t \tag{5}$$

The distribution function parameters and their corresponding size classifications are listed in Table 7.1.

Using the data from Table 7.1, the present value discounting function for a given plant size may be represented as follows.[6]

$$EPV = \int_0^T (\text{annual cash flow})\,(e^{-rt})(e^{-ct})\,dt \quad, \tag{6}$$

where

EPV is expected present value of the plant investment,
T is planning horizon in years,
r is interest rate used for time discounting,
c is parameter characterising the size classification under consideration,
cash flow is estimated annuity generated by the plant,
e^{-rt} is continuous discount factor,[7]
e^{-ct} is probability that the firm will be in existence, during year t,
    $= 1 - $ probability of attrition by year t,
    $= 1 - (1 - e^{-ct})$.

The annual cash flow may be treated as a constant and taken outside the integral leaving only the discount factor to be solved for. Cash flows that are not constant may be first reduced to present value, using r as the discount rate, then spread over the planning horizon as an annuity, again using r as the interest rate. The remaining terms of (6) solve as follows:

$$\int_0^T e^{-(c+r)t}\,dt \tag{7}$$

$$= 1/(c + r)[1 - e^{-(c+r)T}] \tag{8}$$

211

Table 7.1   Distribution parameters for selected industries

Industry	Class limit		Estimate of c	Standard error	Coefficient of determination
Poultry processing	Smallest to largest by percentage of output				
	96 –	100	·188	·0018	·966
	91 –	95	·177	·0011	·999
	81 –	90	·162	·0027	·991
	71 –	80	·138	·0035	·981
	51 –	70	·132	·0038	·975
	31 –	50	·121	·0041	·967
	0 –	30	·102	·0042	·954
Dairy farming	lbs. of milk per month				
	000 –	2,499	·169	·0037	·937
	2,500 –	4,499	·149	·0018	·984
	4,500 –	6,499	·137	·0009	·996
	6,500 –	9,499	·128	·0003	·999
	9,500 –	13,499	·119	·0003	·999
	13,500 –	19,499	·111	·0007	·997
	19,500 –	29,499	·106	·0009	·995
	over	29,500	·104	·0008	·996
Fresh citrus packing	1,000 boxes per season				
	0 –	10	·055	·0021	·455
	10 –	49	·041	·0010	·835
	50 –	99	·034	·0004	·970
	100 –	199	·029	·0001	·999
	200 –	299	·025	·0002	·990
	300 –	399	·027	·0001	·999
	400 –	699	·026	·0001	·999
	over	700	·024	·0003	·985
Retail food chains	Smallest to largest by percentage of output				
	35 –	40	·023	·0003	·943
	30 –	35	·022	·0002	·962
	20 –	30	·015	·0001	·993
	0 –	20	·012	·0002	·940

Source: [4], [5], [10], [14].

212

As the planning horizon lengthens, (8) approaches

$$\lim_{T \to \infty} 1/(c + r)[1 - e^{-(c+r)T}] \to 1/(c + r) \ . \tag{9}$$

The solution of (6) becomes

$$EPV \ = \ (\text{annual cash flow}) \left[\frac{1}{c + r} \right] \ . \tag{10}$$

This represents the plant investment discounted both for the time value of money and for the risk of business failure. In addition, the simplification of (9) makes the calculation of present value relatively simple once the industry parameters are known.

When plant construction is under consideration, the planning horizon will normally be long enough to justify the simplification in (9). Using $1/c + r$ as the base, the percentage error resulting from this assumption becomes:

$$\frac{\dfrac{1}{c + r} - \left[\dfrac{1}{c + r}\left[1 - e^{-(c+r)T}\right] \right]}{1/(c + r)} = e^{-(c+r)T} \tag{11}$$

To maintain this error below 10 per cent, $(c + r) \, T$ should be equal to or larger than 2.3.

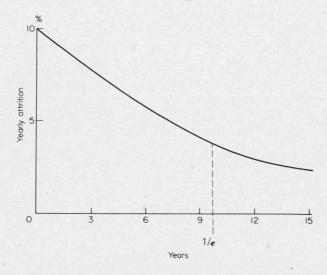

Fig. 7.3   Expected yearly attrition of large dairy farms

213

The interpretation of the risk parameter (c) is not difficult when it is related to firm life. This is done by differentiating the cumulative attrition function,

$$\frac{d}{dt} (1 - e^{-ct}) = ce^{-ct} \tag{12}$$

Figure 7.3 depicts this density function for the largest size classification of dairy farms.

The mean of (12) may be obtained as follows.[8]

$$c \int_0^\infty te^{-ct} \, dt \tag{13}$$

$$= c \left[\frac{e^{-ct}}{c^2} (1 + ct) \, \Big|_0^\infty \right] \tag{14}$$

$$= 1/c \, . \tag{15}$$

Clearly, the mean of the attrition density function is the mean life of the firm size grouping which c parametises. Since logarithms are without dimensions, it may be seen from (5) that the units of c must be $(years)^{-1}$ and the units of mean life, the reciprocal of c, must be years.

The quantity $1/(c + r)$ represents the discounted value of $\$1.00$ per year cash flow from the proposed plant. As the firm's mean life approaches infinity, the parameter c approaches zero and

$$\lim_{c \to 0} \frac{1}{c + r} \to \frac{1}{r} \tag{16}$$

The quantity $1/r$ is the standard discount factor for an annuity in perpetuity received with certainty.[9] As the risk of failure increases, the mean life of the firm decreases, c increases, and the present value of the cash flow is reduced. Table 7.2 illustrates the results of (9) and of (15) for each industry studied.

Present value found through the use of (10) and the discount factors of Table 7.2 represents a mathematical expectation. This should be thought of as the *a priori* best estimate which may be made and which would be realised from an average of repeated investments. Although experience on any one trial may differ from the mean, (10) provides a benchmark useful for making valid comparisons between investment alternatives.

Table 7.2 may be used for comparison of investment alternatives in different industries and for plant size selection within each industry. However, a decision cannot be reached on the basis of Table 7.2 alone. A high cash flow may offset a low present value factor and, of course, the reverse

214

Table 7.2

Investment data for selected industries

Industry	Class limit	Mean life $1/c$ (years)	Present value* of $1\cdot00$/year $1/(c+r)$	95 per cent confidence interval
Poultry	Smallest to largest by percentage of output			
	96 – 100	5·33	$ 4·04	$ 3·68 – 4·39
	91 – 95	5·65	4·22	3·85 – 4·57
	81 – 90	6·16	4·50	4·15 – 4·87
	71 – 80	7·23	5·05	4·62 – 5·44
	51 – 70	7·58	5·21	4·78 – 5·61
	31 – 50	8·26	5·52	5·08 – 5·93
	0 – 30	9·80	6·17	5·71 – 6·62
Dairy farming	lbs. of milk per month			
	000 – 2,499	5·91	$ 4·36	$ 4·21 – 4·50
	2,500 – 4,499	6·70	4·78	4·63 – 4·93
	4,500 – 6,499	7·28	5·07	4·91 – 5·22
	6,500 – 9,499	7·80	5·31	5·16 – 5·47
	9,500 – 13,499	8·38	5·57	5·42 – 5·73
	13,500 – 19,499	8·97	5·83	5·67 – 5·99
	19,500 – 29,499	9·47	6·04	5·87 – 6·20
	over 29,500	9·56	6·11	5·91 – 6·24
Fresh citrus packing	1,000 boxes per season			
	0 – 10	18·13	$ 8·68	$ 8·06 – 9·17
	10 – 49	24·16	9·86	9·32 – 10·33
	50 – 99	29·39	10·64	10·11 – 11·09
	100 – 199	34·47	11·24	10·73 – 11·66
	200 – 299	39·94	11·76	11·29 – 12·15
	300 – 399	37·62	11·55	11·06 – 11·96
	400 – 699	37·97	11·59	11·10 – 11·99
	over 700	41·99	11·93	11·47 – 12·32
Retail food chains	Smallest to largest by percentage of output			
	35 – 40	44·16	$12·11	$11·21 – 12·74
	30 – 35	45·87	12·22	11·35 – 12·85
	20 – 30	65·38	13·29	12·55 – 13·79
	0 – 20	86·86	13·99	13·37 – 14·41
An annuity in perpetuity received with certainty			$16·67	

* $r = \cdot06$ for all calculations.
Source: [4], [5], [10], [14].

is also true. The analysis presented solves the problem of comparing plant investments involving differing degrees of life expectancy risk; it does not remove the jeopardy of forecasting cash flows. See [7] for a discussion of this problem.

Appropriate discount rate

The cost of capital is the most popular choice for the discount rate (r). This is a weighted average of the estimated cost of each source of capital used by the corporation. The weighting factor is a ratio of the market value of corporate securities from the specific source of capital to the market value of all securities issued by the corporation.

The cost of capital to the firm includes the investors' valuation of the average level of risk encountered by the company. Funds are not loaned to an unstable corporation at the rate granted a corporation dealing in low-risk operations. Consequently, it would be an error to use the cost of capital as r in (10). Risk of bankruptcy is handled explicitly by the c parameter and should not be reflected in the r value.

To circumvent the double inclusion of risk, a default-free interest rate should be used. The interest rate on government debt is probably the best choice for r; 6 per cent was used throughout this article. Since this rate will normally be under 10 per cent, any error resulting from the use of continuous discounting will be small.

Salvage value

As attrition due to obsolescence gains in importance, the value of salvage declines. The emphasis shifts toward viable productive assets and away from recovery of capital which is no longer useful. This is simply a cost of keeping pace with advancing technology. Nevertheless, salvage values are likely to remain significant enough to warrant consideration. A present value function may be calculated for salvage as follows:

$$PVS = \sum_{t=1}^{T} (\text{salvage value in year } t)(ce^{-(c+r)t}) , \qquad (17)$$

where

PVS is expected present value of plant salvage,
T is planning horizon in years,

216

c is parameter characterising the size classification under consideration,

r is interest rate used for time discounting,

$ce^{-(c+r)t}$ is (time discount factor)(probability of failure in year t)

         $= (e^{-rt})(ce^{-ct})$.

This tends to be a rather laborious calculation. As an alternative, salvage may be handled by adding the present value of the estimated salvage at the end of the investment mean life to the cash flow. This method produces satisfactory results and simplifies the computation considerably. Adjustment for both start-up cost and salvage must be made after, not before, applying the risk discount factor to the cash flow.

It must be remembered that present value alone does not provide a direct comparison for investments having unequal life spans. For example, a positive present value generated over twenty years is certainly superior to an equivalent present value generated over a thirty year period. To achieve comparability, the risk discounted present value of each investment should be spread over its expected life as an annuity, then carried to a common terminal date using $r + c$ as the discount factor.

Applicability of model

Of the twenty-seven size classifications studied, all have high coefficients of determination except the smallest fresh citrus packing firms ($\cdot455$). Though the exponential distribution function fits most groups extremely well, the behaviour of this one class appears to diverge appreciably from the model. This sampling of industries indicates that the hypothesised family of equations has widespread but not universal applicability. Care should be taken to ascertain whether the coefficient of determination is acceptable before an analysis is carried out.

The corporation wishing to proceed without an industry analysis may still obtain useful results if sufficient intraorganisational data are available. The reciprocal of the mean life of similar previous ventures may be substituted for the parameter c. Extreme care must be taken to assure that the previous investments adequately represent the situation at hand.

The Markov model projects industry growth to be expected assuming the trends of the base period continue. Therefore, the c parameters for an industry are not stable indefinitely and should be updated whenever new data become available. The most important step in this analysis is selecting a base period. Every effort should be made to obtain an adequate representation of the future period spanning the life of the proposed plant. If

217

desired, models other than the Markov process may be employed to generate the expected attrition rates used as data for fitting the exponential distribution function.

The two leading errors in investment decisions are exclusion of relevant but not easily quantifiable variables (such as economic life, salvage value, and future obsolescence) and casual or imprecise handling of those variables included [16]. This article is intended to be a direct attack on these two sources of error and to foster a more rigorous approach to investment appraisal.

Notes

[1] Reprinted by kind permission from *Journal of the American Statistical Association* vol. 65, no. 330, June 1970, pp. 602–12.

[2] Only present value methods are considered. For a discussion of the superiority of this technique as an investment criterion, see [2].

[3] The applicability of Markov Chain processes, as well as other stochastic processes, for modelling industry development is discussed in [12].

[4] This is an elaboration of a model first presented in [5].

[5] Base periods and sample sizes are: 2,100 dairy farms, 1946–61; 246 fresh citrus packing plants, 1948–49 to 1952–53; 286 poultry processing firms, 1960–64; and 77 retail food chains, 1960–62. For purposes of this study, retail food chains are defined as those operations comprising the top 40 per cent of industry output. Note: The smallest size classification of citrus packing plants has been omitted from the graph to reduce overlap.

[6] Start-up costs and salvage values are treated below.

[7] Continuous discounting (e^{-rt}) has been used throughout this article. Discrete discounting $(1 + r)^{-t}$ assumes that cash flows accrue in lump sums at the beginning and ending of yearly periods. Since business transactions actually occur throughout the year, continuous discounting is more representative of the capital flow. In addition, much computational simplicity is gained.

[8] The variance of equation (12) is needed for confidence interval estimation. This is most readily found through use of the moment generating function,

$$\psi(t) = (1 - t/c)^{-1}, \; \psi'(0) = 1/c, \; \psi''(0) = 2/c^2 \; .$$

The variance becomes:

$$2/c^2 - (1/c)^2 = 1/c^2 \; .$$

[9] All discount factors are from [13].

References

1   Adelman, I.G., 'A stochastic analysis of the size distribution of firms' *Journal of the American Statistical Association* vol. 53, 1958, pp. 893–904.

2   Bierman, H., and Smidt, S., *The Capital Budgeting Decision*, The Macmillan Company, New York 1966, pp. 18–49, 293–4.

3   Collins, N.R., and Preston, L.E., 'The size structure of the large industrial firms, 1909–1958' *The American Economic Review* December 1961, pp. 986–1011.

4   Courtney, R., 'Structural Change and Economic Behaviour of Ohio Dairy Producers' unpublished M.S. thesis, Ohio State University, 1964.

5   Farris, P.L., and Padberg, D.I., 'Measures of market structure change in the Florida citrus packing industry' *Agricultural Economics Research*, 16, US Department of Agriculture, October 1964.

6   Hart, P.E., 'The size and growth of firms' *Review of Economic Studies*, 1962, pp. 29–39.

7   Hirschleifer, J., 'Investment decision under uncertainty: choice – theoretic approaches' *Quarterly Journal of Economics*, November 1965, pp. 509–36.

8   Moore, J.R., and Walsh, R.G., *Market Structure of the Agricultural Industries*, Iowa State University Press, Ames 1966.

9   National Commission on Food Marketing, *Organisation and Competition in the Milling and Baking Industries*, Technical Study no. 5, June 1966, Chapter 1.

10 National Commission on Food Marketing, *Organisation and Competition in the Poultry and Egg Industries*, Technical Study no. 2, June 1966, Chapter 2.

11 Padberg, D.I., 'The use of Markov processes measuring changes in marketing structure' *Journal of Farm Economics*, February 1962, pp. 189–99.

12 Quandt, R.E., 'On the size distribution of firms' *American Economic Review*, June 1966, pp. 416–32.

13 *Standard Mathematical Tables*, 12th ed., Chemical Rubber Publishing Company, pp. 451, 467.

14 'Supermarket News Annual Reports', 'Supermarket Merchandising Reports' and 'Federal Trade Commission Reports' furnished raw data for these calculations.

15 US Department of Commerce, *The Handbook of Basic Economic Statistics*, vol. XXIII, no. 4, 15 April 1968, p. 150.

16 Walker, R.G., 'The judgement factor in investment decisions' *Harvard Business Review*, March–April 1961; reprinted in Wolf, H.A., and Richardson, L., (eds), *Readings in Finance*, Meredith, New York.

Ruin Considerations and Debt Issuance[1]

Introduction

The current literature of business finance states that debt is a cheaper source of capital than stock (tending to reduce the firm's cost of capital), because interest is deductible for income tax purposes while the return to common stockholders is subject to tax[2]. It is even possible to issue debt without increasing the risk to the owners (the debt is issued to stockholders in proportion to the ownership of stock, or equivalently investors buy a mixture of stocks and bonds on the market). However, it is argued in this paper that if we assume that the present stockholders have no further resources available for investment in the firm, but the enterprise needs additional resources, then the present stockholders have to make a basic decision about whether to issue stock or debt to raise the additional needed capital. The issuance of debt in this situation increases risk,and the issuance of stock dilutes ownership. Even when stockholders require a much lower contractual return than the expected annual return of stockholders, the issuance of more stock may be preferred to the issuance of debt.

This paper will attempt to incorporate an aspect of risk associated with the issuance of debt that has been somewhat neglected, the risk of ruin.[3] Introducing the possibility of ruin means that the initial owners may not realise the profits that they know exist if they continue the 'game'.

This paper focuses on the well-being of the stockholders, not on that of the firm. We will assume the objective of the stock or debt-issue decision is to maximise the risk-adjusted expected value of the initial stockholders' investment where value is measured in terms of present value of future dividends, decreased by a risk adjustment. It is assumed that the stockholders are risk averters. As new stockholders are added to the firm, their interests will be considered identical to those of the initial stockholders. We will study two situations that are somewhat simplified and restricted but that contain sufficient elements of reality so the importance of incorporating ruin considerations in the analysis can be seen. In both situations the market value of the stock is assumed to reflect accurately the expected profitability of the firm.

Situation one

In this first situation we shall assume that the initial stockholders have no further funds to invest and that the firm cannot grow beyond its proposed size (i.e., no growth after the initial security issue). In addition, the dividend policy is to pay out funds earned rather than retire long-term debt or increase the size of the firm in excess of its proposed size. Let V be the amount of resources desired and needed by the firm, but the actual resources provided may temporarily be less than V. Assume the firm is to be financed initially by D_o dollars of debt and S_o dollars of stock where D_o and S_o are to be detemined so as to maximise the present value of the initial investors' position and where $S_o + D_o = V$. The market yield of debt is r_b and the annual expected return required by stockholders is r_s. Unless the firm is ruined, the incomes for each year are independent and identically distributed random variables with the possibility of zero operating income, but the expected value of the distribution is positive. (After ruin the income is zero.) After the initial year, the firm either cannot or will not raise more common stock capital. This holds if the firm is profitable, since it pays all earnings as a dividend (there are no growth possibilities) unless $S + D < V$, in which case the firm will retain earnings to bring S up to the size necessary for S plus D to be equal to V.[4]

If the firm has a net loss, it cannot raise more capital in the following year since we assume investors have a strong aversion to committing new funds to a firm with a deteriorating financial position. The absolute magnitudes of S and D are not important. However, the amount of buffer between the present stockholders' position and a critical level that leads to bankruptcy is important. Also, the amount that the sum of the present S plus D is below V (the actual resources are less than the resources needed by the firm) is important. We will act as if S and D are both measurable for purposes of the models of this paper, but the exact way they are measured is not crucial to the logic of the model. The change in S and its relationship to a situation where liabilities can no longer be paid is important.

We will initially assume that we do not have to discount the results of operations for time (the time value of money is zero). This assumption is made in order to observe what happends in this extreme case, and then this unrealistic assumption will be changed.

The maximum amount of resources available to the organising stockholders is S_{max}, where S_{max} is less than V, the desired size of the firm. Should the stockholders issue debt or more common stock to outsiders? The optimum decision hinges on:

(a) the cost of debt and the cost of stock,

(b) the probability of ruin (investor risk preferences will not be considered),

(c) the rate of discount used to transform future results back to the present (initially assumed to be zero).

If $S \leqslant 0$, we declare the firm is ruined, and the stockholders lose their entire financial interest in the firm.[5]

Despite the fact that operating incomes cannot be negative, the stockholders' required annual expected return r_s is defined to be higher than the rate of interest required by bondholders. The stockholders have more risk since the bondholders have to receive their interest before the stockholders can receive dividends, thus it is possible for bondholders to receive interest and stockholders to receive no dividends. However r_b is the market yield of the debt, and this is higher than the expected return required by bondholders where there is some probability of default on interest or principal. Thus we cannot predict with certainty the relationship of r_s and r_b since r_s is a desired expected return and r_b is a market return. We will assume $r_s > r_b$. Since the probability of debt payment is normally high, this is a reasonable assumption.

The nature of r_s and r_b and their relationship to each other are somewhat confusing. Define r_s to be the annual expected return that is required in order to attract stockholder investment. For example, if there are two possible equally likely outcomes for next year of $0 and $480,000 (the expected value is $240,000) and if the stockholders will pay a maximum of $200,000 for this investment, we would say r_s is ·20. To explain r_b, assume that a $1,000 bond issued at par promises an interest payment of $200 after one year and repayment of principal; thus r_b is ·20. However, assume the market thinks there is less than a probability of one for payment, thus the expected yield, $E(y)$, from the point of view of the investor is less than r_b. While with risk aversion the annual expected return of stockholders, r_s, must logically be greater than the expected yield of the debt, $E(y)$, it may be less than the market yield of the debt, r_b. The stockholder return, r_s, is only used to determine the percentage of ownership to be given the new stockholders.

Example 1

The initial stockholders want to maximise the expected present value of their position. They have $200,000 to invest.

Assume:

V = \$1,000,000,
S_{max} = 200,000,
r_b = ·10 (the required market interest rate for \$800,000 of debt),
r_s = ·20 (the required expected one-year return if new stockholders invest \$800,000; if debt is issued, the required return will be higher).

The distribution of income outcomes for each year that the firm operates (is not bankrupt) is:

Probability	Outcome (operating income)
·6	\$ 0
·4	\$590,000

The expected operating income and expected dividend of each year with 100 per cent stock financing is:

$$E(P) = \cdot 6\,(0) + \cdot 4\,(590,000) = \$236,000 .$$

This is a ·236 expected one-year return (yield) on investment, and this is a desirable investment from the point of view of stockholders wanting a ·20 expected one-year return. The organisers can finance with 100 per cent stock and can earn an expected return of ·236 on their \$200,000 investment, if all stockholders pay the same price per share. However, the question of optimum financing remains.

Baxter [2] also has an example where there is a positive probability of ruin only where there is debt outstanding, but in his example some debt can be outstanding without there being a positive probability of ruin. His analysis leads to the conclusion that 'when leverage is very low, an increase in the reliance on debt is not likely to exert a significant effect on the probability of bankruptcy'.[6] In the above example a probability of ruin is introduced with the first dollar of debt. The requirement that contractual interest payments be made means there is a possibility of bankruptcy.

The cost of stock and the cost of debt are defined for two particular capital structures. Since the market interest yield for \$800,000 of debt is one-half the required expected one-year return of additional common stock, one might assume that the average cost of capital can be decreased and the value of the initial stockholders' position can be improved by adding more debt. However, the addition of debt increases the risk to the initial stockholders; thus we cannot conclude that either the cost of capital is decreased or the value of their holdings is increased as the proportion of debt is increased.

We will show that the optimum solution for the above situation is to sell stock to outsiders. If this is done, the value of the initial stockholders' position will be maximised despite the indicated 'lower cost' of debt. However, as assumptions are changed, the solution will change.

For an $800,000 investment, the new stockholders will want $160,000 of expected return per year. This is approximately 68 per cent of the expected earnings, We will now assume the new investors will receive 68 per cent of the shares for $800,000, and the initial investors will receive 32 per cent for $200,000 of cash and their organisational efforts. The initial investors will expect to receive 32 per cent of $236,000, or $76,000, per year on their $200,000 investment, and the secondary investors will expect to receive $160,000 on an investment of $800,000.

If $800,000 of debt were raised at a contractual cost of ·10, the expected earnings available to the initial stockholders, assuming the interest is guaranteed by the stockholders, would be:

$$\begin{array}{ll} \text{Operating income} & \$236,000 \\ \text{Less interest} & \underline{\quad 80,000} \\ & \$156,000 \ . \end{array}$$

This $156,000 per year is larger than $76,000 per year; thus debt seems to be more desirable than additional stock. However, consider the fact that with zero debt there is zero probability of a loss, and the present value of the $76,000 per year is infinite (the discount factor for time is initially assumed to be one, and the discount rate, zero). With any amount of debt introduced with fixed claims, there is a probability of negative earnings to stockholders, and the probability of ruin is no longer zero for the initial stockholders. With the restrictions of the assumptions (no retention of earnings and no growth), the expected present value of the stockholders' position with a debt-financed firm is finite.[7&8]

For example, in the present situation at time zero with $800,000 of debt, there is ·218 probability that the firm will have three loss years in a row and be ruined. There is also the probability that the firm will have one or more profitable years and then be ruined. In fact, with the situation as described and with any amount of debt issued, assuming an infinite horizon, the probability is that the firm will be ruined at some time in the future (but the probability of it being ruined in any finite time period may be very small if the probability of a loss is small and/or if the loss is small).

Let us define $F(S)$ as the expected value of the stockholders' investment with S dollars of common stock investment. Thus if the firm is initially financed with \$200,000 of stock and \$800,000 of debt, we would use $F(200,000)$ to represent the expected value of the investment of the stockholders. If the firm has had a net loss of \$80,000, the expected value of the stockholders' investment after the loss is $F(120,000)$. Even though we can have operating income of \$590,000 and interest of \$80,000, $F(710,000)$ is not possible since we have initially assumed that all excess earnings will be paid as dividends.

The basic model employed uses a recursive relationship. For simplicity we will assume there are two possible operating results (e_1 and e_2):

Event	Probability	Income	
e_1	p	L_1	$(L_1 < 0)$
e_2	$1 - p$	L_2	$(L_2 > 0)$.

The basic equation we will use is:

$$F(S_o) = (1-p) L_2 + pF(S_o + L_1) + (1-p) F(S_o), \text{ or}$$

$$F(S) = (1 - p)(L_2 - \Delta S) + pF(S + L_1) + (1 - p) F(S + \Delta S), \text{ for } S < S_o,$$

where
$$\Delta S = \min(S_o - S, L_2).$$

If the stock level is at its initial (highest) value, we pay out all of a positive return (L_2), and in the next period we will have either S_o or S_o minus a loss (L_1). If $S < S_o$, we use positive returns to get back to S_o (pay trade creditors) before paying dividends. We either pay the entire amount of the short-term debt ($S_o - S$) or use all positive returns (L_2) to pay as much as possible. Thus $\Delta S = \min(S_o - S, L_2)$, and the future stock level is either $S + L_2$ or $S + \Delta S$. In the above equation:

$F(S)$ = the expected value of the stockholders' investment with current stock value equal to S. There is one expected value (and equation) for each possible S value; since $F(S \leqslant 0) = 0$, the system of equations can be solved for $F(S_o)$. (Since the transition probabilities to new S-values depend only on the current S-value, the system is a Markov Chain with rewards. See [4].)

$(1 - p) L_2$ and $(1 - p)(L_2 - \Delta S)$ = the expected dividend if $S = S_o$ and $S \neq S_o$ respectively.

$pF(S + L_1)$ = the probability of a loss times the value of the stockholders' new position after the loss.

$(1 - p) F(S_o)$ or $(1 - p) F(S + \Delta S)$ = the probability of a gain times the expected value of the stockholders' new position after the gain and any short-term debt payment, ΔS.

226

In the example being considered with \$800,000 of debt and \$200,000 of stock, we would have:[9]

$$F(200,000) = 204,000 + \cdot 6\,F(120,000) + \cdot 4\,F(200,000)$$
$$F(120,000) = 172,000 + \cdot 6\,F(\ 40,000) + \cdot 4\,F(200,000)$$
$$F(\ 40,000) = 140,000 + \cdot 6\,F(0) \qquad + \cdot 4\,F(200,000)\ .$$

There are three unknowns and three equations ($F(0)$ is equal to zero). Solving for $F(200,000)$, we obtain $F(200,000) = \$1,653,000$. The expected value to the initial investors of a firm financed with \$800,000 of debt is \$1,653,000 compared to an infinite value if it is financed completely with stock.

Since there is more risk with debt outstanding, we would assume that the stockholders' risk adjustment (a deduction from the expected present value) is greater with the debt situation than with 100 per cent stock financing and that the addition of risk aversion would move the decision even further towards using 100 per cent stock.

We will now remove the assumption of zero time value of money and will use a default-free interest rate to adjust for the time value of money. Risk aversion will again be taken into consideration by the deduction of a risk adjustment from the expected value. It is assumed that one payment is received immediately (for example with a $\cdot 01$ time value of money we have $76,000 + 76,000/\cdot 01$). The method of solution is analogous to that shown above except that the results of the next period are multiplied by $(1+r)^{-1}$ where r is the time value factor. For different interest rates we get the following results.

Expected present value of initial investor's equity

Amount debt	Time value of money					
	$\cdot 00$	$\cdot 01$	$\cdot 05$	$\cdot 10$	$\cdot 20$	$\cdot 50$
Zero debt	∞	7,676,000	1,596,000	836,000	456,000	228,000
\$800,000 debt	1,653,000	1,555,000	1,256,000	1,080,000	780,000	505,000

The preference for an issuance of stock changes to a preference for debt with a time value of money for the stockholders between $\cdot 05$ and $\cdot 10$. As the time value of money increases, the quick high returns from debt leverage overcome the risk of ruin.[10] If we deducted risk adjustments from the expected values with debt, this would increase the break-even time value of money.

The debt option can be made more attractive by having the new stockholders buy in at the same price as the present stockholders. For example, assume that for an $800,000 investment, the new stockholders want 80 per cent of the income, or $188,800 of expected return per year. The initial stockholders would receive $47,200 per year (compared to $76,000). If the firm issues 1,000,000 shares of common stock in total, the new investors will now receive 800,000 shares for $800,000 (a cost of $1 per share), and the initial investors will receive 200,000 shares for $200,000 (again a cost of $1 per share). Now with an interest rate of ·05 the value of the initial stockholders' position is ·2 of $4,956,000 or $991,000 instead of $1,596,000 (that is ·32 of $4,956,000) as with the initial assumption of stock issue price.

We have shown that with the assumptions as given, the initial stockholders are better off issuing the additional stock rather than the low cost debt if their time value of money is low. The issuance of the stock insures that the firm will not be ruined.[11]

Now we will change the distribution of outcomes so that there is a positive probability of ruin even with zero debt.

Probability	Outcomes
·6	$-200,000
·4	890,000

The expected profit for a year of operations is again $236,000, but now there is a probability of ruin without debt.

$$E(P) = ·6(-200,000) + ·4(890,000) = -120,000 + 356,000 = 236,000$$

If the loss of $200,000 occurs, there is no dividend. If the $890,000 of profit occurs, the stock equity is increased in blocks of $200,000 to the desired level of stock, and the remainder is paid as a dividend. Debt can be issued at a market yield of 10 per cent.

Assume the new stockholders pay $800,000 for 80 per cent ownership (they require a ·236 expected one-period return). With zero debt and $1,000,000 of stock, the return to the firm for different S values can be found as follows:

$$F(1,000,000) = ·4 \times 890,000 + ·4 F(1,000,000) + ·6 F(800,000)$$
$$F(800,000) = ·4 \times 690,000 + ·4 F(1,000,000) + ·6 F(600,000)$$
$$F(600,000) = ·4 \times 490,000 + ·4 F(1,000,000), + ·6 F(400,000)$$
$$F(400,000) = ·4 \times 290,000 + ·4 F(1,000,000) + ·6 F(200,000)$$
$$F(200,000) = ·4 \times 90,000 + ·4 F(1,000,000) + ·6 F(0) .$$

$F(0)$ is zero, so we can solve for $F(1,000,000)$:

$$F(1,000,000) = \$7,997,000 .$$

Assuming the initial investors own 20 per cent of the stock, the expected value of their ownership is $1,599,000. With $800,000 of debt and $80,000 of interest:

$$F(200,000) = 324,000 + \cdot4\, F(200,000) + \cdot6\, F(0)$$

where 324,000 is equal to $\cdot4\,(890,000 - 80,000)$. $F(0)$ is zero again, and:

$$F(200,000) = 540,000\ .$$

The expected value is $1,599,000 to the investors of the initial $200,000 of stock if they obtain the remainder of the financing from stock, compared to an expected value of $540,000 if they obtain the $800,000 of financing from debt. Thus despite an apparently lower cost of the debt, the optimum decision from the point of view of maximising the expected present value of the initial stockholders' position is to issue common stock. It is better to dilute the claim against future incomes than to risk the possibility of not obtaining them.

Even if the cost of debt were zero, the expected value to the initial stockholders would be only $593,000. [12] In this example, the debt decision is relatively insensitive to the interest cost of the debt. Other factors (such as the probability of loss and the size of the buffer) are more important.

Now we will assume the firm has a time value of money of $\cdot20$ (the time value factor for one period is $1\cdot20^{-1}$). This time value is excessively high compared to the cost of debt and is used only for illustrative purposes.

Example 2 with time discounting

$$F(200,000) = 324,000 + \cdot4\,(1\cdot20)^{-1}\, F(200,000) + \cdot6\,(1\cdot20)^{-1}\, F(0)$$

Thus $\qquad\qquad \cdot67\, F(200,000) = 324,000 \qquad\qquad$ and

$F(200,000) = 484,000$ (compared to $540,000 with no time discounting).

With zero debt, the expected value of the stockholders' investment is:

$$F(1,000,000) = 356,000 + \cdot4\,(1\cdot20)^{-1}\, F(1,000,000)$$
$$+ \cdot6\,(1\cdot20)^{-1}\, F(800,000).\ \text{(Other equations are similar}$$
$$\text{to the zero time value example.)}$$

Solving for $F(1,000,000)$ we obtain:

$$F(1,000,000) = \$1,580,000$$

(compared to $7,997,000 with a zero discount rate).

The equity of the initial investors is $\cdot2$ of $1,580,000 or $ 316,000.

Unless there is a large aversion to risk, the inclusion of a high discount factor has reversed the decision between no debt and 80 per cent debt. With a discount rate of ·20, the future benefits decrease in terms of present value very rapidly; thus, with zero debt the total present value of the initial stockholders' position is decreased by the inclusion of the discount factor from $1,599,000 to $316,000. The $316,000 is less than the $484,000 expected benefits if $800,000 of debt is issued.

We have tested two amounts of debt ($0 and $800,000). Other amounts should also be tested. For the example we can conclude that, without time discounting of the benefits, there is an incentive to use stock in order to avoid the ruin situation. With time discounting, the debt decision depends on the rate of discount, the cost of debt, the probability of loss, and the extent of risk aversion.

We are now ready to change an important assumption. Given the assumptions of situation one, only an initial decision is made. With situation two, there is a series of dividend-debt retirement decisions.

Situation two

In situation two the holders of stock are not forced to pay out all profits as dividends, but they can use retained earnings to retire debt, up to the total amount of debt. Thus the initial stockholders are faced with two different decisions: (1) how to raise the cash needed initially, and (2) how much of the outstanding debt to retire in each period. If the first decision is to add new stockholders, once stock is issued the two groups have identical goals, maximisation of the stockholders' total expected discounted profit. Again the size of the firm is kept equal to or below a maximum level (no growth is allowed).

The second set of decisions (debt retirement in each period) will depend on the risk of ruin and the discount rate we place on our earnings stream, as in the initial decision. The combination of risk of ruin and discount rate will determine the desirability of foregoing dividends so that cash may be used to retire debt. If debt is retired, the lower debt amount (and therefore higher stock amount) implies less likelihood of ruin and therefore greater future expected profits, but his safety is purchased at a cost measured in current dollars.

We assume that debt retirement can be made only from positive net earnings, and ruin occurs, as before, when the value of S is equal to or less than zero. The retiring of debt implies an equal increase in S. To simplify the discussion we will assume the initial stockholders' wish to maximise

230

their total expected discounted return, with no deduction from expected monetary value for risk aversion; the ruin state is to be avoided because it will result in a zero income stream.

The firm is still limited in size to some value V, with $S + D \leq V$. Losses causing $S + D < V$ are temporarily made up by no cost borrowing (this assumption is not crucial to the method of analysis). We assume that temporary loans can be obtained from trade creditors at a negligible cost to cover operating costs that cannot be paid immediately. The operating returns earned are assumed to be independent of the actual size of $S + D$ as long as $S > 0$.

To formulate the problem we separate the two decisions so that, once the initial stock issue is made, the second decision is faced. The decisions are made by comparing the initial shareholders' returns for each possible stock issue, combined with optimal debt retirement for that situation. The formulation of the problem is given below.[13] We do not discuss the method of solution here since it is covered extensively in Howard [4].

$$\overline{F}(S, D) = \sum_{r_i = R}^{\infty} \max_{D_i} [(r_i - aD - D_i - S_d) + \alpha \overline{F}(s + D_i, D - D_i)] \phi(r_i)$$

$$+ \alpha \sum_{r_i = -\infty}^{R-1} \overline{F}(S + r_i - aD, D) \phi(r_i)$$

where:

$R = aD + S_d$

$D_i \leq \min\left\{r_i - aD - S_d, D\right\}$ when $r_i > aD + S_d$

$D_i = 0$ when $r_i \leq aD + S_d$.

Also, $\overline{F}(S, D)$ = the total discounted expected value of future dividends to all stockholders, given that the firm is currently in state (S, D), and assuming that optimal decisions are made in the future. State (S, D) denotes a situation with S stock value and D debt level.

In the next period the state is

$$(S + S_d + D_i, D - D_i) \qquad \text{if} \quad r_i \geq aD + S_d$$

and

$$(S + r_i - aD, D) \qquad \text{if} \quad r_i < aD + S_d .$$

If $r_i < aD + S_d$, no dividend is paid and no debt is retired. In the former case we can retire debt and/or pay dividends.

r_i = the operating income, a random variable;

D_i = the decision variable — the amount of debt retired, where there is one D_i for each r_i that is realised;

231

α = the discount factor, $0 < \alpha \leqslant 1$, with $\alpha = \dfrac{1}{1 + \rho}$ where ρ = the time value of money;

$\phi(r_i)$ = the probability mass function of possible values of r_i;

S = the current value of stock (equal to the amount of difference between the present asset position and the position where bankruptcy takes place);

S_d = the amount that the stock equity has been reduced by losses and that has to be retained before a dividend can be paid. $S_d = V - S - D$. One explanation is that trade creditors must be repaid as soon as possible.

D = the amount of outstanding debt, and $S + D \leqslant V$, the value of the firm $(S + D)$ may become less than V due to losses temporarily financed.

a = the interest rate on outstanding long-term debt.

Equation (1) when solved for all state values, gives the optimal debt retirement decision in any situation. We only need state values such that $S + D = V$ for the initial decision of debt and stock issue size. (Other values are necessary to give the optimal debt retirement after losses.) Given $\bar{F}(S,D)$ for $S + D = V$ and an assumption as to how much ownership is retained by the original owners, the original owners can maximise their return by maximising the product of $\bar{F}(S,D)$ and the fraction of ownership still held by them. Thus the general method is:

1   Solve (1) for all feasible state values (S,D) using Howard's Iteration in the Policy Space method [4].
2   Using the price at which the stock can be issued to raise the necessary capital, determine the initial stockholders' percentage of ownership and the corresponding portion of $\bar{F}(S,D)$ for all values with $S + D = V$ and $S \geqslant S\,\widehat{\max}$ and choose S and D to maximise their return.
3   Optimal debt retirement is given by the solution in step 1 for any state value.

Before proceeding to a numerical example, some discussion of computational efficiency is needed. It would be very helpful to show that there is a single critical value of S, say S^*, the stock value state variable, and that we should want to reach S^* as quickly as possible. That is, if $S < S^*$, the revenues are all used to retire debt until S is set equal to S^*. [14]

In a real situation, a reasonable approximation is to assume that a value of S^* and a simple policy exist. Since stock and debt issues are made in blocks, the state space can be given by a fairly coarse grid. The advantage of these two statements is that Howard's complete method need not be used, but we can try different S^* values and only use the Value Determination Operation (Markov Chains with rewards).

We will use $F(S,D)$ without a bar to indicate the total expected discounted profit of any particular set of decisions. They will not be subscripted for each decision set since the meaning will be clear from context.

The optimal initial policy is found by choosing the best initial value of $F(S,D)$ for the S^* values tried. Since this method is much more efficient, it is used for the numerical examples; the general method can always be used to give the solution, and it can also handle additional complications as discussed later in this section.

Example

The possible outcomes are:

Probability	Outcomes
0·6	−200,000
0·4	890,000

The expected return of each period is $236,000. The ruin level is $S \leqslant 0$ with $F(S < 0, D) = 0$. $D + S \leqslant V = 1,000,000$; the total size of the firm is bounded.

$$S_{max} = 200,000.\text{ (The initial stockholders cannot invest more than \$200,000.)}$$
$$r_b = \cdot10.$$

For ease of computation we assume stock and debt is issued only in units of $200,000 and that debt can be retired in blocks of $200,000. The assumptions enable us to indicate the type of solutions that can be obtained. The discount factor, α, equal to the reciprocal of one plus the discount rate, is varied from $1\cdot0$ to $1/1\cdot2$. We continue the assumption that if $S + D < V$, operations are financed by short-term loans at negligible cost in comparison to other costs.

The $\alpha = 1\cdot0$ case is shown below to demonstrate the method.

Example 1. No discounting; $\alpha = 1\cdot0$.

We will intuit that the optimal policy in this case will be eventually to have no debt. Thus $S^* = 10^6$ is tried first. Assume that S_o (the initial stock investment) and S^* (the level of stock value to which debt is retired with $S^* + D = V = 10^6$) are both equal to 10^6. If $S_o = S^* = 10^6$, the value of $F(1,000,000; 0)$ can be obtained as follows:

$$F(1,000,000; 0) = \cdot 4 \times 890,000 + \cdot 4\, F(1,000,000; 0) + \cdot 6\, F(800,000; 0)$$
$$F(800,000; 0) = \cdot 4 \times 690,000 + \cdot 4\, F(1,000,000; 0) + \cdot 6\, F(600,000; 0)$$
$$F(600,000; 0) = \cdot 4 \times 490,000 + \cdot 4\, F(1,000,000; 0) + \cdot 6\, F(400,000; 0)$$
$$F(400,000; 0) = \cdot 4 \times 290,000 + \cdot 4\, F(1,000,000; 0) + \cdot 6\, F(200,000; 0)$$
$$F(200,000; 0) = \cdot 4 \times 90,000 + \cdot 4\, F(1,000,000; 0) + \cdot 6\, F(0; 0)$$

Since $F(0; D) \equiv 0$, the set of equations can be solved. The solution is:

$$
\begin{aligned}
F(1,000,000; 0) &= \$7,997,000 \\
F(800,000; 0) &= 7,404,000 \\
F(600,000; 0) &= 6,548,000 \\
F(400,000; 0) &= 5,256,000 \\
F(200,000; 0) &= 3,235,000 \\
F(0; 0) &= 0 \ .
\end{aligned}
$$

Thus with $S_o = 1,000,000$ the stockholders' equity has a value of $7,997,000 (the original owners' return is given later). Next, suppose $S_o = 600,000$ and S^* remains $1,000,000. There are now debt payments, and we can write: [15]

$$F(600,000; 400,000) = 180,000 + \cdot 4\, F(1,000,000; 0)$$
$$+ \cdot 6\, F(360,000; 400,000)$$
$$F(360,000; 400,000) = 84,000 + \cdot 4\, F(1,000,000; 0)$$
$$+ \cdot 6\, F(120,000; 400,000)$$
$$F(120,000; 400,000) = 0 + \cdot 4\, F(1,000,000; 0)$$
$$+ \cdot 6\, F(0; 400,000).$$

$F(1,000,000; 0)$ has been found above to be $7,997,000, and $F(0; 400,000) \equiv 0$.

The solution is:

$$
\begin{aligned}
F(600,000; 400,000) &= \$6,500,000 \\
F(360,000; 400,000) &= \$5,202,000 \\
F(120,000; 400,000) &= \$3,199,000
\end{aligned}
$$

Similarly we can have other S_o values (S^* still equals $1,000,000) and solve the resulting set of equations.

S_o	$F(S_o, D)$
800,000	7,379,000
400,000	5,210,000
200,000	3,203,000

Step 2 of the method requires the computation of the initial stockholders' ownership. First assume the ownership of the stockholders is proportional to their cash contribution.

S_O: Common stock	Initial investors	Proportion	Total expected return	Return accruing to initial investors
1,000,000	200,000	$\frac{2}{10}$	7,997,000	1,599,000
800,000	200,000	$\frac{1}{4}$	7,379,000	1,845,000
600,000	200,000	$\frac{1}{3}$	6,500,000	2,167,000
400,000	200,000	$\frac{1}{2}$	5,210,000	2,605,000
200,000	200,000	1	3,203,000	3,203,000

The optimum strategy (assuming $S^* = 10^6$ is optimal) is to initially borrow \$800,000 and have \$200,000 of common stock (all owned by the initial investors) and retire the entire debt.

If the new investor in common stock can be attracted under more (from the point of view of initial investors) advantageous conditions than an equal price for all stock, then the solution changes. Assume we can issue stock based on an expected return of 20 per cent for the first period. Thus we can obtain the ownership by multiplying 0·20 by (S_o − 200,000), subtracting that from \$236,000 (the total one-period expected return) and dividing the result by \$236,000. [16]

At $S_o = 1,000,000$, e.g., the initial owners retain:

$$\frac{236,000 - (800,000)(0\cdot2)}{236,000} = 32\cdot2 \text{ per cent.}$$

The following table contains the information needed for the decision in the $\alpha = 1\cdot0$ case with all debt that is issued initially retired as rapidly as is feasible.

S_o	Total return to all stockholders	Percentage of stock held by initial owners	Return to initial owners
1,000,000	7,997,000	32·2	\$2,575,000
800,000	7,379,000	49·2	3,630,000
600,000	6,500,000	66·1	4,297,000
400,000	5,210,000	83·0	4,324,000
200,000	3,203,000	100·0	3,203,000

The values in the far right hand column indicate that neither extreme is optimal. A larger amount of debt is not chosen because of the ruin possibility, and the zero debt is not chosen because of dilution of ownership. $S_o = \$400,000$ (still with $S^* = 1,000,000$) is optimal for this stock price with $S_o = \$600,000$ close.

If we wanted to check other debt retirement levels, the method of analysis would be the same. To show one possibility, consider $S_o = \$400,000$, $S^* = \$400,000$. We have the following set of equations:

$$F(400,000; 600,000) = 332,000 + \cdot 4\, F(400,000; 600,000)$$
$$+ \cdot 6\, F(140,000; 600,000)$$
$$F(140,000; 600,000) = 228,000 + \cdot 4\, F(400,000; 600,000)$$
$$+ \cdot 6\, F(\qquad 0; 600,000)$$

These yield the solution: $F(400,000; 600,000) = \$1,307,000$, which is less than the value with total retirement ($\$5,210,000$), bearing out the conjecture that we would optimally retire debt with the assumptions as given (the assumption $\alpha = 1\cdot0$ is particularly important).

Let us now check how a change in α affects the value of decisions of $S_o = \$400,000$ and $S^* = \$400,000$. Assume the time value of money is $\cdot20$ ($\alpha = \dfrac{1}{1\cdot20}$). We have now:

$$F(400,000; 600,000) = 332,000 + \frac{\cdot4}{1\cdot20}\, F(400,000; 600,000)$$

$$+ \frac{\cdot6}{1\cdot20}\, F(140,000; 600,000)$$

$$F(140,000; 600,000) = 228,000 + \frac{\cdot4}{1\cdot20}\, F(400,000; 600,000) + 0.$$

Solving for $F(400,000; 600,000)$ we have:

$$F(400,000; 600,000) = 892,000 \ .$$

With $\alpha = 1/1\cdot2$, $S_o = \$400,000$, and $S^* = \$1,000,000$ we only obtain $\$882,000$, indicating that total debt retirement is not optimal (we just solved for a value of $\$892,000$ with $S^* = 400,000$).

Conclusions and areas for further study

The optimal capital structure (including initial structure and debt repayment policy) is a function of probabilities of various returns (especially negative returns that cause ruin), the cost of debt, the terms of stock issue, and the time value of money for the stockholders. The examples show that the optimum policy may be sensitive to the time value of money.

A modification of the model that would enrich it would include making stock issue price an explicit function of the debt/equity ratio. Another modification would be to make returns a function of the current size of the firm, $S + D$. This implies that, as the firm has less capital available, the returns it can obtain are decreased. Another possibility is to allow short-term borrowing. At the cost of enlarging the state space of the formulation (1), we can define a history variable, H, that contains information about previous years and thus gives information about the distribution of returns. One example of H would be: last year had a positive return: $H = 1$; last year had a negative return: $H = 0$.

Other problems that need to be investigated are the situations where a 'buffer stock' of assets (and capital) can be maintained and the situation where the firm may grow larger than V. How large a stock of assets should the firm hold in short-term securities to cover possible financial embarrassment? A different definition of ruin may be necessary for this case. Secondly, if there is growth, what are reasonable assumptions about the form of the probability mass function of the returns as the firm grows? The larger firm is likely to be less subject to ruin than the smaller firm, but there are complexities that require study.

There is no question that ruin considerations must be brought systematically into the analysis if the stockholders of the firm want to maximise the expected value of their financial position. This paper has shown that there can be circumstances where it is better for the firm to issue 'high cost' stock than 'low cost' debt. Also, we have shown that a policy of issuing debt and retiring some or all of it may be reasonable.

Notes

1 Reprinted by kind permission from *Journal of Financial and Quantitative Analysis* vol. 7, January 1972, pp. 1361–78.

[2] See E. Solomon [6, p. 117] and Baumol and Malkiel [1, pp. 561–562].

[3] See N.D. Baxter [2] for a discussion of leverage, risk of ruin, and the cost of capital. Our efforts differ from those of Baxter since we focus on how the value of the initial stockholders' investment is affected by the debt–stock decision, rather than how the firm is affected. Also we will attempt to quantify the effect of the leverage decision on this investment and will consider a wider range of risk situations. However, our conclusions are consistent with the conclusions reached by Baxter.

[4] For temporary declines in the size of the firm (D and S), we will assume that trade creditors will carry the debt necessary to finance the normal level of operations at a negligible cost. We could also allow bank borrowing of a short-term nature but have not done so. The trade credi-

tors must be repaid before any dividends are paid, thus forcing the firm to move toward $S + D = V$ in so far as they are able.

⁵ We can define ruin for a situation where S is less than some amount R, but here we will assume $R = 0$. The general conclusions do not depend on the value of R. Also, ruin could be defined in terms of working capital instead of s.

⁶ Baxter [2, p. 402]. Baumol and Malkiel [1, p. 562] also state, 'When borrowing reaches a point where insolvency becomes a real possibility, the self-interest of management as well as the interests of the stockholders may restrain the firm from going further in this direction', Also see Solomon [6, p. 117].

⁷ If some of the earnings were to be retained, it is not obvious that the value of the stockholders' position will still be finite.

⁸ Baxter [2] considers ruin from the point of view of the firm; thus he focuses attention more on the costs of disruption and transactions than on the loss of the investment of the stockholders.

⁹ The values of $F(S \leqslant 0)$ are defined to be zero. The $204,000 is the expected dividend and is equal to $\cdot 4 (590,000 - 80,000)$. If a loss occurs, there is no dividend.

¹⁰ The higher interest rates are for illustrative purposes only. The time value factors must be lower than r_b and r_s.

¹¹ The strategy of 'no debt' is similar to the strategy of placing small bets in a game that is favourable to you. Both strategies tend to increase your ability to play the game long enough for the favourable probabilities to take effect. See Feller [3, pp. 313–16].

¹² Assuming the firm is ruined if $S \leqslant 0$:

$$F (200,000) = 356,000 + \cdot 4 \, F (200,000),$$
$$F (200,000) = \$593,000.$$

¹³ The debt retirement problem and formulation are similar to a game of economic survival. A simplified game of economic survival is studied by Shubik and Thompson [5]. Their ruin level is also defined by some value, R, but their return function is simplified.

¹⁴ This policy is optimal if $\bar{F} (S.D)$ is convex in S. If that were true, reduction of debt would be worthwhile up to a point and would never be worthwhile thereafter. Since the horizon is infinite, the value S^* would be the same in all periods. However, since $\bar{F}(S<0,D) = \bar{F}(0,D) \equiv 0$, the function is not convex. It can be shown to be monotonic non-decreasing, but that is not sufficient to imply the optimality of the type of policy we seek. Arguments can be given to justify the S^* type policy as a reasonable

policy, but since the policy is reasonable in the real context, the arguments are omitted.

[15] The $180,000 of the first equation is equal to: $\cdot4(890,000 - 440,000)$. The $84,000 of the second equation is equal to: $\cdot4(890,000 - 640,000 - 40,000)$. There are no dividends with $S = 120,000$. We assume the stock equity with a favourable event is $1,000,000. It would actually be $970,000. We have rounded for computational purposes.

[16] We realise that the assumption that stockholders demand the same expected return for the first period regardless of the leverage of the firm does not hold, but it is used for simplicity. Other assumptions about the issue price can be included in the method with no difficulty. We would expect the average return required by the stockholders to be larger than the borrowing cost and default-free rate because of risk aversion.

References

1 Baumol, W.J., and Malkiel, B.G., 'The firm's optimal debt-equity combination and the cost of capital' *The Quarterly Journal of Economics*, November 1967, pp. 547–78.
2 Baxter, N.D., 'Leverage, risk of ruin and the cost of capital' *The Journal of Finance*, September 1967, pp. 395–403.
3 Feller, W., *An Introduction to Probability Theory and Its Application*, J. Wiley and Sons, Inc., New York 1957.
4 Howard, R.A., *Dynamic Programming and Markov Processes*, J. Wiley and Sons, Inc., New York 1960.
5 Shubik, M., and Thompson, G., 'Games of economic survival' *Naval Research Logistics Quarterly*, June 1959, pp. 111–23.
6 Solomon, E., *The Theory of Financial Management*, Columbia University Press, New York 1963.